CW00538081

THE INSIDER'S GUIDE TO

AUSTRALIA

THE INSIDER'S GUIDES

AUSTRALIA • BALI • CALIFORNIA • CHINA • EASTERN CANADA • FLORIDA • HAWAII •
HONG KONG • INDIA • INDONESIA • JAPAN • KENYA • KOREA • NEPAL • NEW ENGLAND • NEW
ZEALAND • MALAYSIA AND SINGAPORE • MEDITERRANEAN FRANCE • MEXICO • PORTUGAL •
RUSSIA • SPAIN • THAILAND • TURKEY • VIETNAM, LAOS AND CAMBODIA • WESTERN CANADA

The Insider's Guide to Australia
(Second Edition)

© 1995 Kümmerly + Frey AG

Moorland Publishing Co Ltd
Moor Farm Road, Airfield Estate, Ashbourne, DE61HD, England

First published 1987
Second Edition published 1995
published by arrangement with Kümmerly + Frey AG, Berne, Switzerland

ISBN: 0 86190 520 2

Created, edited and produced by Allan Amsel Publishing
53 rue Beaudouin, 27700 Les Andelys, France
Telefax: (33) 32 54 54 50
Editor in Chief: Allan Amsel
Design: Hon Bing-wah/Kinggraphic

Printed by Samhwa Printing Co Ltd, Seoul, Korea

THE INSIDER'S GUIDE TO

AUSTRALIA

by Harry Blutstein

MPC

Contents

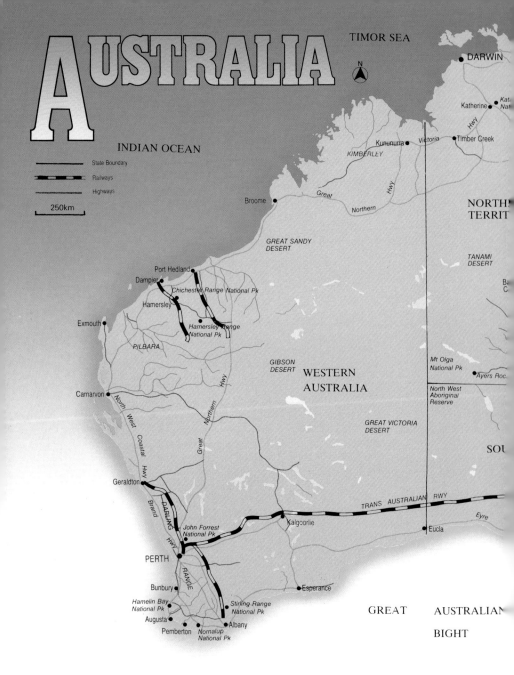

The Land Down Under

A SUNBURNT COUNTRY

Let me introduce you to a typical Australian: me, myself, and I have a few admissions to make.

I was twenty-two before I saw my first kangaroo in the wild, at dawn in the small town of Blackwood which lies 110 km (66 miles) from Melbourne. A troop of them was breakfasting on the front lawn of the house I rented: they looked up briefly when I appeared at the door, but a human being in the wild was less novelty to them than they were to me.

When I was about seven, my first kookaburra appeared on the back verandah of the country guesthouse to which my parents took me each year for the summer holidays. Having been thrown some bacon rind by the cook, it swooped down, grabbed it in its powerful beak in the belief that it had snared a dozy snake, and thrashed it on the ground to "kill" its breakfast before swallowing the whole thing.

Sightings of koala bears in the wild are rare; three years ago on a drive to Daylesford in Victoria I saw my first one. Two other cars had stopped by the side of the road and a small crowd had gathered to watch (and photograph) the startled creature. After a while the koala regained its composure, ignored his audience and continued to munch the gum leaf in his paw.

I don't recall seeing a Tasmanian Devil, although a dark hunched shape glimpsed one wet night at the Cradle Mountain National Park could have been one. And platypuses outside nature sanctuaries have so far eluded me.

And finally for the darkest admission of all. Unlike Mike Dundee, I have never wrestled a crocodile; that film *Crocodile Dundee* has a lot to answer for.

These revelations should not be taken to suggest that the country is not teeming with native wildlife recognized around the world as uniquely Australian. It is more a consequence of the fact that, like most Australians until recently, I seldom emerge from the comfort of suburbia and then only for a brief holiday or Sunday drive in the country.

I became aware of the vast size of Australia when I made my first trip out of the country, flying diagonally across from the south-east to north-west, which took about six hours. I was making the almost compulsory pilgrimage to England: there names like The Strand and Mayfair were more familiar to me from playing endless games of Monopoly than the places over which I flew, such as Coober Pedy, Alice Springs or the Kimberley Ranges. The great irony of this trip to the "old country" was that my parents were from Europe, coming to Aus-

tralia in the great post-war migrant flood; I have neither Anglo-Saxon nor Celtic blood in me.

It is only over the last nine years that I have begun to travel around Australia in preference to trips overseas. This was prompted, at first, by the drop in the value of the Australian dollar and increased cost of traveling overseas. This taste for the beauty, variety and exotic nature of the Australian landscape has made me "a true believer." It was like discovering a new country on my doorstep, and writing this book allows me to share this enthusiasm with others.

To understand Australians it is necessary to appreciate that they have an unrealized yearning for "the bush." The affection for the Australian countryside is encapsulated in Dorothea Mackellar's ditty which starts:

OPPOSITE: A road train on the dusty Bourke Cobar highway TOP and symmetry in sandstone BOTTOM at Western Australia's Bungle Bungle range.
ABOVE: Arnhem Land Aborigine.

I love a sunburnt country
A land of sweeping plains
Of ragged mountain ranges
Of drought and flooding plains
I love the far horizons
I love her jewel-sea
Her beauty and her terror
The wide brown land for me!

I learnt to recite this poem at primary school, looking out over streets of endless rows of houses in suburban Glen Iris, eight kilometers from the central Melbourne area and thousands of kilometers from the land Mackellar was describing. With the clear vision and imagination of eight year olds my class-mates and I recited it on Speech Night in front of our proud parents, sure that we were at one with this great land which few of us had ever seen or would for many years, if at all.

There is a second Australia to be discovered. It is found in the cities and major provincial towns where approximately 90 per cent of the population live. Nevertheless the Outback, even unvisited, has shaped the Australian psyche. The idea that we are a nation of "urban bushmen" is widespread. There is a famous poem by "Banjo" Patterson, called *Clancy of the Overflow* where a clerk sits in his city office dreaming of droving sheep in the Outback. There are many Clancys in the cities of Australia.

We Australians may imagine ourselves as outdoors types, but this seldom goes further than sitting in a sidewalk cafe in Melbourne's Lygon Street watching the football, or surfing at Bondi Beach in Sydney. This identification with the great outdoors can be seen in the number of four-wheel drive vehicles on the streets in our major cities, which are seldom used for anything other than picking up the kids from school or going shopping.

As Australia has become a major tourist destination the idea that this country could have worth-while attractions is beginning to dawn on the locals. It is not unusual to see Australians eschewing the pleasures of Rome or Singapore for a trip to the Top End or the Great Barrier Reef; indeed, it has become the norm.

So traveling in Australia is a choice between seeing sprawling cities with their cosmopolitan lifestyle, or touring the Outback — with its space dotted with small towns full of fascinating characters. Given sufficient time, all these different Australias can be explored.

I have tried to provide a balance in this book between the two realities. It is worth lingering in the cities as a country cannot be appreciated unless its inhabitants are understood; fortunately Australians are forthright and ever ready to let the tourist share their lifestyle. The wonders of nature, such as Ayers Rock, the Great Barrier Reef and Kakadu National Park are also described. Foreign tourists to the southern continent are short-changing themselves if they choose to view one without the other, because together they make up Australia.

THE GREAT SOUTHERN TREASURE HUNT

The immediate constraint I have in writing this book is that of space. In a country the size of Europe, or just a shade smaller than the United States, with so much to see and do how can one book suffice? Like Aladdin, I was faced with a cave full of treasure. He could only carry out an armful, while I have the unenviable task of condensing a country overflowing with scenic gems, exotic locations and culturally unique experiences into pitifully few pages.

In Europe tourists can look in awe at 1,000-year-old cathedrals with their rose windows, soaring arches and formidable facades. Australia too has its cathedrals, but they are millions of years old and not fashioned by medieval architects, but rather by the majestic forces of nature. There are rain forests with giant eucalypts that would dwarf Notre Dame, and waterfalls that plunge down the Arnhem Land escarpment which will leave you breathless.

Australia has 665 national parks occupying nearly 410,000 sq km (160,000 sq miles), eight of which have been classified as World Heritage areas. In addition, there are more than 220 off-shore areas protected by legislation because of their unique ecology, or historic importance, such as being the site of a shipwreck. These national parks also contain a wide variety of native animals not seen anywhere else in the world. For example, there are 48 species of kangaroo, from the Great Red that lives on the plains, growing to about two meters (six to seven feet), to the tree kangaroos, whose habitat is the forests of Cape York in northern Queensland.

Each choice of place was a source of great angst — not which to include in the *Insider's Guide*, but which to omit.

The easy way out would have been to provide an exhaustive list of places to see.

prices are given for double or twin share rooms, which have been divided into luxury (over $110), moderately priced ($60 to $110) and inexpensive (under $60). I have taken prices from the high season, so tourists may find that out-of-season prices are lower.

The greatest burden a tourist has to bear is not how many suitcases he or she is willing to cart around (and is a hair drier really essential?) but how to spend a short time in a country that offers so much. I have tried to relieve some of this burden. However, for travelers with time on their hands I have

This would have avoided letting some gem slip through, but travel by catalogue is unsatisfying. Rather than establish objective rules I have relied on my own reactions to places to guide my choices.

I have not confined myself to the traditional modes of seeing a place. Floating across the landscape on a balloon, a leisurely cycle through the countryside, exploring desert landscapes on a camel, or roaring down an empty road in the Outback on a Harley Davidson are some ways to make a visit more memorable. If you can't take a risk on a holiday, then it never will happen. Go on, indulge yourself occasionally!

At a more practical level, I recognize that tourists come with different budgets. Hotel

provided a section at the end of the *Guide* of recommended reading about additional attractions.

See as much of the country as you can, photograph its mountains and national parks, but also pause to speak to the locals about what Australia means to them. The Aboriginal writer and University lecturer Eric Willmot said, of Australia, that "only those who can be possessed by her can know what secret beauty she holds." Come and find out.

Tourists gaze at the wondrous sandstone monoliths called "The Hidden City of Nathan" in Northern Territory's Nathan River property.

An
Ancient
Continent

DREAMTIME AND AFTER

When I was at school my history books started with the discovery of Australia by Europeans, the exploration of the eastern coastline by Captain Cook in 1770 and the establishment of a penal colony at Botany Bay in New South Wales.

Little thought was given to the original inhabitants, who have occupied Australia for between 40,000 and 50,000 years. The Aborigines were relegated to a footnote in Australian history.

Aboriginal history does exist: it spans many more years and is richer than European exploration and the settlement of Australia. Academic historians have not given due weight to it because of the absence of written records; they have difficulty with a history that is told around the fire and passed on from one generation to the next.

THE DREAMTIME

Aboriginal history is the story of the Dreamtime; it recounts the origins of the land and the people who inhabited it for hundreds of generations, how every river, mountain and gorge came into existence, fashioned by ancestral mythical beings. These creators also made birds, animals, plants, and all other living creatures, including man, and the legends established inter-relationships between the Aborigines and every element of their environment. The creators of the Aboriginal world have since left, but they can be resurrected through ritual and dance.

Archaeological evidence indicates that the Aborigines migrated south either across a land bridge linking Southeast Asia to Australia or using boats to cover the relatively short distance between the islands scattered between the two land masses: it is believed by some that they originated in Sri Lanka. Once on the Australian continent, Aborigines adapted to conditions and spread into every corner of the vast land.

It is a fallacy to believe that they lived in harmony with the soil, maintaining it as they found it. They did learn to master it and controlled burning of the bush was used to encourage re-growth, which in turn attracted animals that could be hunted. Aborigines modified their habitat in other ways to increase food supplies. Sophisticated weapons such as the boomerang were developed to hunt kangaroos and other wildlife, some to extinction. In Victoria, an area rich in wildlife and fish all year round, Aborigines established permanent stone settlements, and in coastal areas they built intricate structures to trap fish.

Before the arrival of the First Fleet, Aborigines had reached an equilibrium with the land. This balance was based on a profound

knowledge of the seasons and how to survive in a country that appeared to outsiders to be poor in natural resources.

EUROPEANS ARRIVE

Captain James Cook, on his voyage of discovery, wrote in his journal that the Aborigines "appear to be the most wretched people upon the Earth, but in reality they are far happier than we Europeans." Despite Cook's insight, it did not stop him basing his claim on the Eastern seaboard of Australia

OPPOSITE: Beautifully textured Aboriginal paintings at Obiri Rock in Arnhem Land, Northern Territories. ABOVE: An Aboriginal as portrayed by an early Western observer.

An Ancient Continent

on the legal fiction that he had discovered a *terra nullius* — a land without people.

At the time of Cook's visit the Aboriginal population was probably between 500,000 and a million people. The subsequent interaction between white settlers and Aborigines almost turned Cook's legal fiction into fact. Disease, high child mortality rates and persecution of the local inhabitants dramatically reduced their numbers during the eighteenth and nineteenth centuries. At the beginning of the twentieth century the Aboriginal population was reduced to 50,000. Today it is estimated that there are about 230,000 people of Aboriginal descent in Australia.

Aborigines were displaced, often by force, by early white settlers who were spreading out from their first settlements to secure grazing land for sheep. In Tasmania dispossession turned to genocide, its Aborigines almost entirely wiped out; only a few survived on off-shore islands.

The fight between the Aborigines and the white invaders was unequal, as Stone Age weapons were pitted against firearms. To suppose, however, that the Aborigines just gave up their land without a fight is untrue.

The expansion of the colony, however, was not greatly hindered by Aboriginal resistance, much weakened by the diseases brought by Europeans. The introduction of alcohol further debilitated their society.

Ironically it was the government in Britain who tried to curb the excesses of the colonists but these efforts were largely ignored by the colonial administration.

During the nineteenth and first half of the twentieth centuries the Aborigines provided cheap labor that helped build wealthy grazing properties, but they were not really relevant as a factor in Australian economic development.

They first obtained the recognition and admiration of white Australia for their prowess in sport: in 1868 the first cricket team to go to England was an Aboriginal side. They acquitted themselves well, winning 14, losing 14 and drawing 19 matches during the tour. That did not mean that there was no racism in Australia at the time: in 1897 the Queensland Home Secretary sought to bar Aborigines from foot races because they always won!

In 1905, the government adopted a policy of "protecting" the Aborigines by segregating them from the bad influences of white society which formalized and accelerated a movement initiated in the 1870s of putting the Aborigines on missions and reserves. While the intention behind this policy purported good, Aborigines were removed from traditional lands, different tribes were moved onto the same reserve without regard to kinship or relationships, and, most tragically, many Aboriginal children were removed from their parents and put into the foster care of white families to promote assimilation.

In 1967, a referendum was held to give Aborigines and Torres Strait Islanders citizenship. This marked the end of institutionalised racism.

Today Aborigines have established themselves in many aspects of Australian life. Sir Doug Nicholls became the Governor of South Australia in 1976 and Neville Bonner took his seat in the federal Senate in 1971 as the first Aboriginal parliamentarian. Prominent Aboriginal artists' and writers' contributions have enriched Australia's cultural heritage.

There is a saying among Aborigines that he who loses his dreaming is lost. In the Outback and urban Aboriginal communities, elders are making every effort to ensure that their children are told the secrets of the Dreamtime so that they do not loose touch with their culture, with its rich religious and spiritual values.

A festering sore remains Aboriginals' claims to their traditional lands. A recent High Court decision overturned the legal concept that Australia was occupied as *terra nullius* and has opened the way for Aboriginal land rights.

The reconciliation between the Aboriginal people and the rest of the country has only just begun, and the government has said that it wants a formal treaty. There is a tentative optimism among Aborigines, but one tempered by two hundred years of accumulated disappointments.

There are other changes heralding a period of reconciliation: school books now include sections on Aboriginal history, contemporary Aboriginal art is shown in the

best galleries and the relationship traditional Aborigines have with their land is starting to be appreciated by a world that has shown itself incapable of reaching a balance with nature.

WHITE SETTLEMENT

DISCOVERY OF AUSTRALIA

There is evidence that the first visitor to Australia after the original migration of Aboriginal people was the Chinese admiral Cheng Ho, who explored waters south of the Indian Ocean between 1405 and 1432. A Chinese statuette and sandstone carving were discovered near Darwin, confirming other evidence of visits by northern fishermen.

Subsequent visits were by European sailors — Dutch, English and French — blown off course on their way to the Spice Islands. Other explorers went in search of *Terra Australis*, the land to the south, which might offer similar riches to those discovered in the nearby East Indies. Early reports of sightings of the west coast, which the Dutch named New Holland, were not promising. Dutch commander Jan Carstens wrote "This land is a barren and arid plain, where no fruit trees grow, nor is there any growth fit for man." In 1696 another, explorer Willem de Vlamingh was happy when his ships turned away from the "miserable South Land." Botanist Joseph Banks, who accompanied Captain Cook on his voyage along the east coast in 1770 also noted the barren soil which might not support cultivation.

With all these adverse reports, it is not surprising that the only justification to settle this newly discovered land was to establish a penal colony on its shores. In 1787, King George III instructed Captain Phillip to found a colony at Botany Bay.

THE FIRST SETTLEMENT

On 26 January 1788 Captain Arthur Phillip established the penal colony at Port Jackson on what he described as "one of the finest harbors in the world," finding Botany Bay unsuitable.

The First Fleet consisted of 443 seamen, 568 male and 191 female convicts, 160 marines and 51 officers. The expedition cost the government £84,000, which they judged less expensive and less troublesome than keeping convicts locked in hulks moored on the River Thames.

While it may be that Australians suffer a stigma from having convict forebears, today tracing one's family tree back to the First or Second Fleet is cause for pride. Convicts sent to Australia were often nothing more than petty criminals, victims of an ethic which harshly punished all attacks on society. On the other hand troops sent to guard the convicts were far from an elite. In the early days of the colony it was the authorities who were responsible for much of the corruption and violence, as the bemused criminals observed in their impotence.

By the 1790s the New South Wales Corps, established to maintain law and order, developed instead a lucrative trade in spirits

Sandhurst (Bendigo) as it appeared in 1857, the goldrush period. Illustration by S.T Gill from *Victoria Illustrated*, first published in in 1857.

and rum. The government proved powerless to stop this destructive trade. In 1799 alone 36,000 gallons (100,000 liters) of spirits and 22,000 gallons (165,000 liters) of wine were landed to supply Sydney's 5,000 inhabitants. In 1808, Governor William Bligh, who had already faced one mutiny on the *Bounty*, now faced another from the New South Wales Corps. The Corps resisted his efforts to ban its trade, and in defying the governor started what became known as the Rum Rebellion. Bligh returned to England and the rebels were left virtually untouched, only a few of them spending short periods in exile or jail.

The fight over whether the trade in rum should continue was irrelevant to the convicts who were put to work building roads and constructing the first settlement. The work was back-breaking and the discipline harsh. In Sydney, the Reverend Samuel Marsden, in his role as magistrate, was known to sentence a prisoner on Saturday, admonish him on Sunday in Church and carry out the punishment on Monday. Marsden, not surprisingly, was known as the "flogging parson."

New penal colonies were established for re-offenders in godforsaken places like Port Arthur in 1830, Norfolk Island in 1824 and Moreton Bay in 1824 as well, where the treatment of convicts was inhuman. On Norfolk Island prisoners were known to draw lots to decide who would kill whom, because murder meant a trial in Sydney and some hope of escape.

It is little wonder that many of the tourist attractions relating to Australia's early history are prisons and barracks for the troops who guarded them.

The standard of government and public morals improved when Governor Lachlan Macquarie took over after the Rum Rebellion.

He undertook a major building program using convict architect Francis Greenway, whose classically inspired buildings established the face of early nineteenth century Sydney. Greenway also planned satellite settlements like Pitt Town, Castlereagh, Richmond and Liverpool — each with a church, jail and guard house. Many of his fine buildings still stand and are popular tourist attractions.

Convicts who served out their time quietly were rewarded with land, and many went on to become valuable pioneers and respected citizens. For example Simon Lord, who was sentenced to seven years transportation for stealing cloth, became a prominent merchant and went on to found the Bank of New South Wales.

Transportation of convicts ended in 1864. It is estimated that over 160,000 convicts were sent to Australia, and their presence touched every colony except South Australia, which was founded by free settlers.

Cheap labor provided by the convicts allowed the colonies to develop more quickly against the natural disadvantages of remoteness and the hostility of the land to European ways.

An Ancient Continent

As the colonists came to terms with the new country, they began to appreciate that they were better off than had they stayed in England. The first generation of Australian-born citizens established an indigenous culture based on cooperation to overcome the hostile environments, and a distaste for authority. They were called "currency" lads and lasses. The name was originally coined as a put-down, in that a pound in local currency was not worth as much as a pound Sterling. For the locals the name was worn as a badge of pride.

The colonial economy was agrarian and explorers, who found good pastoral land beyond the Great Dividing Range, were quickly followed by farmers and graziers in droves. Land was cheap, and fortunes were quickly made in sheep farming on allotments the size of English counties. In the first half of the nineteenth century settlements were established along the eastern seaboard and in Perth. As these settlements grew they eventually agitated for and obtained status as colonies.

THE GOLD RUSHES

The colonies obtained a major boost to their economies when gold was found in New South Wales in 1851 and then in prodigious quantities in Victoria. The gold

Dust rises as cattle are gathered on the dry expanse of a Northern Territories ranch.

rush that followed affected the economy as men left the land and crews jumped ship to seek riches on the goldfields. Fortune-seekers came from all corners of the globe, arriving in overcrowded ships. At its peak in 1852, over 86,000 people arrive in Australia from the British Isles.

The goldfields were roisterous. Untamed shanty towns were peopled by men who worked hard during the day and dreamed of having great wealth at night, as they sat around the camp-fire or in a pub to discuss their day with the other diggers. It was on

the goldfields that the Australian notion of mateship developed.

The upheaval of the gold rushes was most marked in Victoria where one strike followed another, and old hands and newcomers alike chased the latest rumor of gold to the newest field. By the middle of October 1851 there were 10,000 men at the Ballarat goldfields and an estimated £10,000 of gold a day was extracted from this area alone. In three years the gold-fevered population increased fourfold. As the gold ran out many towns were deserted, but some continued to prosper. For example, the fine Victorian cities of Ballarat and Bendigo survived the the the collapse of the gold rush.

Ballarat is also famous because it is the site of the only armed insurrection against authority in Australia, to use such grand language. To discourage laborers leaving the land for the goldfields the government set a license fee for each claim: diggers without licenses were harassed by troopers. On 29 November 1854 they had had enough, and a blue flag with the Southern Cross

constellation was raised in defiance of the authorities. Licenses were publicly burnt and the police attacked what has become known as the Eureka Stockade, swiftly putting down the rebellion by killing 22 and arresting 114 diggers. The action by the government was not popular and most of the men of the Eureka Stockade were eventually freed; their leader, Peter Lalor, later became a member of the Victorian Parliament.

The Eureka Stockade caught the public's imagination because Australians admire anyone willing to defy authority, so it is little wonder that bush-rangers were among the first "heroes" of colonial Australia. The term was coined in 1805 to describe escaped convicts who had turned to robbery to survive in the bush. Many poor farmers and laborers also tried their hand at bush-ranging, some with colorful names like "Yankee" Jack Ellis, Captain Moonlight and "Mad Dog" Morgan became household names, while songs celebrating their exploits became popular. Governor George Gipps forbade a ballad that praised "Bold" Jack Donohoe because he was worried that others would follow "Bold" Jack's example.

The best known bush-ranger was Ned Kelly who, after his mother was wrongfully arrested, ambushed and killed three troopers. Outlawed in 1878, he and his gang held up banks and successfully evaded the police for two years. Ned Kelly was finally trapped in Glenrowan in June 1880 where he defied the police, protecting himself with home-made armor. Realizing that they could not penetrate his plough-share mask they shot his feet which were unprotected. He was sentenced to death and hanged in Melbourne on 11 November 1880. His last words were "Such is life." Ned Kelly's last stand quickly entered the realms of folklore, and after his death the legend spread by way of ballads, poems, books, paintings and films.

AN AUSTRALIAN IDENTITY

The prosperity that gold brought to Australia allowed the country's development to accelerate, with roads and railway lines linking the colonies creating a new-found confidence around the nation, and people began talking about an Australian identity that incorporated the sense of mateship developed on the goldfields. It entailed a feeling that Australia, rather than Britain, was now home.

After the gold rushes Australia went through several cycles of boom and bust. During the second half of the 1890s it entered a severe depression which saw businesses bankrupted, farmers losing their land and workers having their conditions and wages reduced.

Shearers, dock workers and miners, united by mateship, resisted attacks on their working conditions. During the 1890s newly formed unions engaged employers in pitched battles and strikes. The government took the side of the employers and the failure of the strikes led working men to conclude that to create a more equal society they would need their own representatives in parliament. The Labor Party was formed out of this industrial ferment and, in the early years of the twentieth century, was the most successful social democratic party in the world.

Many men without permanent jobs took to the road to survive. Known as "swagmen," their swag being the small sack in which they kept all their worldly goods, they had a healthy disregard for authority and their exploits were celebrated in folk songs, the most famous being *Waltzing Matilda*.

Australians at the turn of the century were called "Cornstalks," just as John Bull represented Great Britain and Uncle Sam the United States. The Cornstalk was typically 2 m (6 ft) tall, wearing corded pants, red shirt, wide blue sash and a cabbage tree hat, high boots and a stock whip wrapped around his arm. His character was described by a contemporary source as "slow, easy, indolent in the ordinary way, proud of his country and himself and capable of holding his own in anything in which he is interested." This popularly accepted view of Australians as outdoors types was at odds with the trend towards urbanization, and by the turn of the century nearly half the population lived in the six capital cities.

FEDERATION

In the colonial parliaments, visionaries promoted federation of the six independent colonies, to create one country.

The task of the "Fathers of Federation" was made difficult by inter-colonial jealousies and rivalries. Each colony had its own priorities and objections. New South Wales felt that its free trade policy would be threatened; Queensland resisted because its Pacific native labor in the cane fields was at odds

with the federalist White Australia Policy; thinly-populated Western Australia, Tasmania and South Australia were concerned that the federation would be dominated by the more populous states; and Victoria was concerned that its policy of protecting local industry would be phased out.

Despite the arguments put forward by self-seeking politicians, it was quite clear that the fractured colonial system of government could not give undivided support and protection to a nation with a population of just three and half million people.

Australia comprises five states, represented by a star on the flag, ABOVE and two territories (Northern Territory and Australian Capital Territory). OPPOSITE: State Parliament building, New South Wales.

An Ancient Continent

The obstructions put in the way of federation by squabbling politicians were finally swept away when referenda gave the federalists a resounding victory. In 1901 the colonies came together to form the Commonwealth of Australia and on the first day of the New Year, to celebrate the event a procession snaked its way through Sydney to the wild cheering of 150,000 onlookers. After the Queen's proclamation was read in Centennial Park a 21-gun salute was fired and a new nation was born.

Despite its new status, Australia remained

loyal to the British Empire, and imperial foreign policy was slavishly followed.

COMING OF AGE

In 1901 the birth of the new nation was marked with parades and fireworks. Children, dressed in white, danced about maypoles, but Australia's coming of age happened fourteen years later on the battlefields of the First World War, and a very bloody right of passage it was.

When Britain declared war on Germany Australia did the same, "to our last man and our last shilling" according to Prime Minister, Andrew Fisher. Australians in all states

flocked to the flag, and the country united in a sense of purpose to defeat "the Hun." It was also an opportunity for adventure, as many Australians had not traveled beyond the borders of their own State. They were dubbed the "six-bob-a-day tourists" because they were paid six shillings to fight at the front line.

The first major encounter involving Australian troops was when they were thrown against a strong Turkish force at Gallipoli. Australia suffered 8,000 dead but, in spite of their impossible position, there were displays of great heroism. Australian soldiers, who were known as "diggers," went on to acquit themselves with honor on the battlefields of France.

By the end of the war Australia had lost 59,000 men, a high proportion of casualties.

Gallipoli is remembered on Anzac day, when soldiers from all wars march proudly through the streets of every capital city and major town.

Along with many other countries, Australia's fortunes slumped after the Great War under the burden of debt and low export prices for its farm produce. In 1930 the depression set in and scarred a generation of Australians: many men took to the countryside in search of work, with their swag on their backs, and urban Australians renewed their links with the bush.

The declaration of war in 1939 helped end the depression: when Japan entered the war in 1941, Australia was thrown into a panic because its territory was threatened. Japan conducted bombing raids against Australia's northern coastline between March 1942 and November 1943, and with Britain fighting for its very survival and unable to help, the entry of the United States into the Pacific theater of war was welcomed by Australia. Within weeks of Pearl Harbor 4,600 American troops arrived in Australia. On 17 March 1942 General Douglas MacArthur arrived to establish his headquarters in Brisbane, and over the next few years hundreds of thousands of American troops passed through with a reputation for being free-spenders; the Australians, especially the troops, resented the success the Americans had with the local women. GIs were criticized as being "over sexed, over paid and over here," but despite some tension a lasting bond and mutual respect developed between the fighting men of Australia and the United States.

In the aftermath of the war, debate on Australia's future turned to its pitifully small population. To overcome this weakness the catch-cry was coined "populate or perish." And so the great post-war immigration began.

Australia became a popular destination for thousand of Britons who had seen their homes demolished during the Blitz, and for the displaced people and refugees of Europe who desperately wanted an opportunity to build a new future for themselves and their children.

Australians were also urged to do their bit so that the country did not "perish," and there was a sharp rise in the post-war birth rate, giving rise to a generation dubbed the "baby boomers."

It is to this influx of immigrants that Australia owes its post-war economic boom, which lasted through the 1950s and 1960s. More than two and half million New Australians entered the country between the end of the war and 1970 when boatload after boatload arrived, speaking many languages and coming from a multitude of backgrounds. Almost half were from the British Isles, lured by cheap passages, promises of good wages and tempted by posters showing sunshine and golden beaches. Large numbers came from Mediterranean countries and from northern and central Europe where refugees freed from concentration camps sought a better life in Australia. Almost 21 percent of the current population was born overseas.

Australians were unused to non-English speakers: the initial cultural shock gave way to a liberalization and an acceptance that Australia was a multicultural society.

THE INFLUENCE OF IMMIGRANTS

Every aspect of contemporary Australian life has been influenced by the immigrant influx.

At first they found their way into laboring jobs, and the construction of the Snowy Mountain Scheme, Australia's greatest engineering project, is evidence of their hard work. Others found their way into retailing, and the local fruit shop owned by an Italian, or the

fish and chip shop by a Greek became commonplace. Slowly change came, albeit in very small ways. Eggplants were on sale next to tomatoes and potatoes, and instead of fish and chips we kids would occasionally try *souvlaki*.

Immigrants established restaurants that allowed them to enjoy foods from their homelands. For a few years they had these to themselves, But in the late 1960s students would hunt out some Balkan or Greek restaurant, which was not only exotic but amazingly cheap.

As ethnic communities gathered around different suburbs, the character of neighborhoods began to change. For example, walking through Cabramatta in Sydney is like visiting an Asian city, while Johnston Street in Melbourne with its Tapas bars is like a little bit of transplanted Spain. In a number of capitals Chinatown is a major tourist attraction, and its restaurants employ the best chefs from Hong Kong, Shanghai and Singapore. Whereas once Australians might venture to the local Chinese restaurant for some chow mien, today you are more likely to find diners arguing the relative merits of

OPPOSITE: Army cadets marching on Anzac Day, April 25, the day when Australia honors its war dead.
ABOVE: Opal miners in Coober Pedy.

An Ancient Continent

Cantonese regional cooking and the more spicy Sichuan cuisine.

But the stamp of immigrants goes deeper than the pleasures of the table. Newcomers have widened Australian perspectives of the world and as the continent itself is over a tectonic plate sluggishly moving a few millimeters a year towards Asia, so are Australia's attitudes and policies towards Asia.

For years, under the shame of what was called the "White Australia Policy," the continent might well have been geographically linked to Europe. This policy prevented non-white immigrants from moving to this country until the early '70s when the perfume of Asian prosperity became too much for greedy local officialdom to endure. Since then Australia has uneasily moved closer to Asia.

The Vietnam War brought home to Australia that it was geographically part of Asia, and Australia's involvement there provided the first local in-depth reporting of that part of the world. It was the Whitlam government of the early 1970s, not surprisingly, which turned the country's foreign policy towards its neighbors. The slow continental drift is now being overtaken by a cultural shift as for better or worse, Australia is accepting more immigrants from South East Asia.

Although they compose just five percent of the population, industrious East Asians are the fastest growing immigrant group. The debate on immigration is no longer how well newcomers will assimilate into Australian society. With high levels of unemployment, the issue is now whether the country's population matches its resources.

Australia remains a monarchy, and Queen Elizabeth II of Great Britain is also the Queen of Australia, but over the last few years the notion that Australia should become a republic has been voiced in the newspapers, and fanned by politicians.

The strong economic ties that Australia once had with Britain were broken when Britain joined the European Economic Community, and further weakened as Japanese and American investment replaced British investment in Australia.

The traditional view is that, as the country was founded by Britain it would be denying its roots to become a republic. Needless to say the Aboriginal minority has not been impressed by this argument. Another view is that as Australia is forging new ties with Asia it needs to break its links with Europe, a non sequitur if ever there was one.

A few changes have occurred: in 1974 British honors were replaced by Australian ones, causing a great outcry among traditionalists. In 1984 *Advance Australia Fair* replaced *God Save the Queen* as the national anthem but the Union Jack still occupies a corner of the national flag.

The debate on whether Australia becomes a republic continues with passion, and occasionally with a grain of sense.

THE LUCKY COUNTRY

Slowly the cultural traditions of the migrants permeated Australia's lifestyle, while immigrants took enthusiastically to the Australian outdoors and sport. Today the game of Australian Rules Football includes the sons of these immigrants, such as Daicos, Silvangni and Jakovich.

Australia's post war prosperity derived from mineral exports. Quantities of iron ore were discovered in the Pilbara, oil found in the Bass Strait, diamonds at Argyle and nickel at Mt. Newman.

As the standard of living rose, giving Australia the second highest in the world in the 1960s the population became increasingly complacent. There was a belief that Australia was the *Lucky Country*, when, however, a credit squeeze in the early 1970s, followed by a period of inflation and high unemployment, made clear how vulnerable Australia's economy was, particularly as it was based on primary products like wheat, wool and minerals, while industry and labor were highly protected and inefficient.

The 1980s and 1990s have become a period of painful adjustment, as protection in both industry and labor reduces and Australia works towards becoming internationally competitive. The country is placing greater emphasis on its innovative scientists and engineers to try and enter new markets in Asia, where at last Australia rightly sees its future.

OPPOSITE: Wave-worn columns at sunset off the Victorian Coast.

A Nation
of
Hedonists

FOR AUSTRALIANS, there is little in their country's short history to generate the sort of patriotism taken for granted in most other countries. Solitary flags fly outside some public buildings but in general Australians are seldom moved by such symbols. On Australia Day, celebrating the founding of European settlement, or Anzac Day in rememberance of those soldiers who died in the wars, a few more flags fly.

Britain, a nation some 16,000 km (10,000 miles) away, chose Australia as the site of its penal colony because of its remoteness. No wonder that the Founding Fathers are not revered, or that the early history of the colony is no source of inspiration.

As settlers became acclimatized to the land an indigenous culture arose, influenced in no small part by the large number of Irish who were either transported for crimes or immigrated to Australia to escape poverty at home. From them many Australians have inherited the two characteristics of a disregard for authority and a taste for strong drink.

Australians take every advantage of their temperate climate to spend as much time as possible out-of-doors. Friday evening is a time for joining friends in an after-work drink, or heading off to the beach in summer or the snow fields in winter. Saturday afternoon is usually dedicated to sport, and every town and suburb has an oval where ball games are under way. A dinner party with friends, either at home or at a restaurant is a favorite way to pass Saturday evening when the etiquette, if invited for dinner at someone's home, is to bring a bottle of wine or flowers for the host.

Sunday is a day for relaxing, drives in the country or just watching TV.

Festivals are now run throughout the year in all capital cities and in many towns. They include parades, concerts, food stalls and sporting events. Art and film festivals are annual events in all capital cities and are a good time to sample the best of the country's culture. There are also some bizarre events, like the Henley-on-Todd in Alice Springs where teams race bottomless boats down a dry river bed. A list of festivals is included at the end of each State chapter.

BATTLERS FROM THE BUSH

If you leave the cities and enter the Outback, there is more than a change of scenery; there is a shift in perspective and lifestyle. The wit can be as dry as the red dust in the street outside the pub.

Social life in the bush revolves around the pub. It's the information office you go to if you want to know where someone is, the bank if you want to borrow a couple of dollars and the committee room when

a local political problem needs to be solved.

On walking into a country pub the locals will cautiously look you over, and then go about their business. A remark about the weather or crops is all that is usually necessary to strike up a conversation: country folk like nothing better than a yarn with a stranger and soon the ice will be broken. By the end of the evening it will be difficult to get away. Don't forget that when you join a group, they will "shout" you drinks and it is polite to keep up the same rate of consumption as the locals. When it comes

OPPOSITE: Hang gliding TOP and hire boats BOTTOM near Sydney. ABOVE: Aborigine station hand in the outback.

to your turn, don't forget to buy a round of drinks because there can be no greater social blunder than missing your "shout."

Farmers from outlying areas enjoy coming to town for an outing, and local dances provide such an opportunity. These are not as popular as they once were but if a country dance is on don't miss it. Usually held in the local hall, it starts with a progressive dance, a little like a slow square dance where men and women stand opposite one another in a large circle, and after a few steps move onto the

next person. There is no better way of being introduced to everyone in town.

The social highlight of the year is the local agricultural show; farmers travel hundreds of kilometers for the big event where they have a chance to meet neighbors, buy new stock and chew the fat.

The show ring is a non-stop procession of cattle and sheep being judged. An event I always enjoy watching is sheep dogs in competition. The owners instruct them with coded whistles, and in no time at all these highly intelligent beasts have even the most uncooperative sheep penned.

For women there are competitions for the best jams, cakes and pickles. After some shows the entries are for sale.

For all the talk of the remote Outback, life there does have its basic creature comforts: air-conditioning is generally available and TV is beamed from satellites.

A number of families in the Outback offer farm holidays which allow city folk to see at first hand how country people live.

THE DEITY OF SPORT

Enter into a conversation with an Australian on the achievements of a great statesman, scientist or writer and you can be sure that the praise will be mute. Mention a sporting hero or even a successful horse and reverence and adoration will enter his voice.

Australia has produced more than its fair share of sporting heroes: in tennis there are Wimbledon champions Lew Hoad, Evonne Goolagong and Pat Cash; in golf there is Greg Norman; Dawn Fraser won the 100 m freestyle in three successive Olympic Games between 1956 and 1964.

Fortunately Australia's climate is ideal for all-year-round outdoor activities. Every weekend Australians are hitting or kicking balls around an oval, speeding around the court after a judiciously lobbed tennis ball or enjoying eighteen holes of golf.

As well as taking to the field or swimming pool Australians are great spectators, devoting their weekends to watching football in winter, cricket and tennis in summer and horse racing in Spring.

FOOTBALL

Perhaps the greatest passion is reserved for football. There are two major codes in Australia, a source of serious division among Australians. Rugby, played mainly in New South Wales and Queensland, is referred to disparagingly in places where it is less popular as "wrestling on the run." For its followers the climax of the season is the State-of-Origin series when New South Wales and Queensland battle it out for State pride.

Australian Rules is a unique code of football born in the inner suburbs of Melbourne and now common in other States except New South Wales, where its antics are disparagingly referred to as "aerial ballet."

In the *Melbourne Times* the section on football is titled "Religion," and so it is for many Australians.

Australian Rules grew out of Gaelic football brought to Melbourne in the mid-nineteenth century. It has developed into a distinct game that hardly resembles the original, a fast-running sport in which mostly large, mobile men launch themselves above the pack to pluck the ball out of the air, or kick it over 60 meters on the run with ease. It is also a game in which its combatants engage in bone-crushing physical encounters, all without padding. During winter league games are played in most capital cities. There is no more awesome sight than the Australian Football League Grand Final, in which over 100,000 fanatical fans cram into the Melbourne Cricket Ground for the climax of the year.

Australians received cricket from England, and the first game was played in Sydney on Phillip's Common (now part of Hyde Park) in 1803. Before long colonial teams were traveling to England to show off their prowess, and by the late nineteenth century Australia was able to defeat the Mother Country. This so shocked England that the following notice was placed in the *Sporting Times* of London: "In affectionate memory of English Cricket which died at The Oval, 29th August, 1882. Deeply lamented by a large circle of sorrowing friends and acquaintances.

Soccer, while not as popular as other variations of football is gaining in popularity. The national competition takes place in summer and autumn.

CRICKET

To the uninitiated, cricket must seem painfully slow. Test matches are played over five or six days, and even one-day matches can take eight hours. But to a true cricket follower a Test can be an occasion of high drama, of poetry, of delicate skills, of fine shades and nuances, all woven into a fascinating encounter which may later be analyzed (over an ale) with the detailed attention given to a chess match between Grand Masters.

R.I.P.
N.B. The body will be cremated and the ashes taken to Australia."

The cricket stumps were subsequently burnt and put in an urn, which became a trophy known simply as "the Ashes," over which Australia and England have fiercely fought for more than a hundred years.

Each summer teams from cricketing countries like New Zealand, the West Indies, India and Pakistan come to Australia for a series of games. The greatest enthusiasm of cricket followers is reserved for when an English side comes out to fight for "the Ashes."

OPPOSITE: A night match at Melbourne Cricket Ground. ABOVE: A close finish at Sydney's Rosehill course.

Horse Racing

If Australia had a hall of sporting fame, the race horse Phar Lap would hold pride of place. During the Depression this giant red gelding won 37 out of 51 starts, including the prestigious Melbourne Cup in 1930. Phar Lap's heart was removed after his death and found to be twice the normal size. There is no higher praise to be told that you have "a heart as big as Phar Lap." His body was stuffed and is on display in the Melbourne Museum.

Today the passion for horse racing continues unabated, and Victoria must be the only place in the world that has a public holiday for a horse race — Melbourne Cup Day. Over $30 million is wagered on just this one race, the fame of which goes beyond Melbourne, being the one day of the year that most Australians have their ears glued to the radio: at precisely 3:20 pm on the first Tuesday in November. Even the Federal Parliament has been known to adjourn for the race. Horse racing combines, for Australians, the twin attractions of sport and some honest betting on the outcome.

Gambling

Australians combine their love of sport with another passion — gambling. Money is wagered on anything, from the outcome of the federal elections to a cockroach race.

For many years governments tried to ban it but with little success. Just a few years after the colony of New South Wales was established the First Judge Advocate, David Collins, condemned uncontrolled betting among the settlers that had resulted in them loosing "the very clothes on their wretched backs ... [and left them standing] as naked and as indifferent about it as the unconscious natives of the country."

Eventually the government decided that it simply could not curb the appetite for gambling, so they legalized it. Taxation raised from this vice is one of the largest sources of government income.

From the earliest days of the colony a local game called two up became popular, and was played using two pennies. The

game is controlled by "the spinner" who throws the coins into the air using a stick called a "kip," and bets are made with "the boxer" on two heads or two tails. One of each is a "no-throw" and all bets are held to the next throw. As the game was illegal, the players would post sentries called "cockatoos" to keep watch. Today a small number of two-up schools have been licensed, and the game is played in casinos. Otherwise it remains illegal.

Surfing

Any beach in Australia with good surf will quickly become crowded with youngsters, hair bleached by the sun, looking to catch a wave. Dressed in colorful shorts or

wet-suits, they can be seen tramping down to the beach at dawn or after school if "the surf is up."

Theirs is a serious, dedicated society, whose members regularly spend many hours a few hundred meters off-shore, ever-vigilant for the next good wave.

They think nothing about taking off for the weekend to a new beach hundreds of kilometers away if it promises good waves.

The first international surfing competitions were held at Manly in New South Wales in 1964. With the help of sponsors, the most accomplished exponents of the sport can now make a living touring the international circuit, including Hawaii, California and Australia.

A Nation of Hedonists

FOOD AND DRINK

What claim can Australia have to its own cuisine when one of its national dishes is made of yeast slops left over from brewing? Yet every Australian child happily spreads this black paste called Vegemite onto his toast, and savors the unique taste almost invariably loathed by the uninitiated foreigner.

When it comes to national dishes, Australia has few, and the reason is not difficult to discover. With good quality meat, seafood and vegetables, little needs disguising with

Surfer demonstrates acrobatic skills on a wave crest. A good surf attracts aficionados from hundreds of miles around.

condiments and spices. So say those who use spices for disguise!

The traditional Australian meal, until recently, was roasted or grilled meat, mashed potatoes and vegetables.

During summer people like nothing more than eating outside around a barbecue where sausages and steaks are cooked over an open fire, and even the occasional "shrimp is thrown on the barbie." The meat is usually accompanied by green salad and bread, and washed down with beer or wine.(Coin-operated gas and wood barbecues are available in many national parks, caravan parks and even in roadside rest areas.)

Today the Australian diet is more varied, and rather than just having a steak or "shrimp" on the barbecue, it is more likely to be a satay or even a lamb on the spit.

AUSTRALIAN CUISINE

If Australia can lay claim to having created any new dishes, they are desserts.

The pavlova is a cake with a meringue shell filled with cream and topped with passion-fruit pulp. The pavlova was created by Perth chef Bert Sachse to honor the visit of the ballerina that gave the cake its name. Anna Pavlova had a delicate figure, and it is doubtful whether she would have risked more than a mouthful of this rich confection.

Lamingtons were also conceived in Australia, and are made from sponge cake cubes coated in chocolate and then sprinkled with coconut; they were named after Lord Lamington, Governor of Queensland from 1895 to 1901. The apocryphal story of their origin tells of a grazier's wife from the same part of Scotland as the Governor, who covered a sponge cake in chocolate to prevent it becoming stale. She served it to her husband's shearers as "Lamington's cake."

FAST FOODS

A traditional fast food for Australians is fish and chips. Be warned — if the fish is called flake then it is shark. Fish and chips are best when eaten out of the paper wrapping, and the chips liberally sprinkled with salt and lashings of vinegar.

After the gold rushes, Chinese migrants set up restaurants that served both Australian and Chinese food. They also sold takeaway food like fried or steamed dumplings, called *dim sum*, and chiko rolls, large fried spring rolls. These snacks were more the Australian idea of Chinese food than the genuine article. Today you can still buy *chiko* rolls and *dim sum* from fast food outlets, but Chinese restaurants now cater for a more educated Australian palate and the food is no different from that served in Hong Kong or Singapore.

Meat pies are unavoidable at any sports venue. Served hot and covered in tomato sauce (ketchup), they are guaranteed to keep the cold out on the chilliest winter day.

The final item of popular Australian fast foods is the real hamburger. Take a bun (sesame seed free), toast it and then add a mince meat patty, cooked onions, a fried egg and slice of pineapple. Unfortunately, most people today prefer mass produced hamburgers. The genuine Australian specimen, however, can still be obtained from some take away shops, particularly in small country towns that McDonalds have never heard of.

BUSH TUCKER

Tucker is the Australian word for food, and there is new interest in indigenous edibles that grow naturally in the bush.

The Aboriginal diet was composed of an estimated 10,000 plants and animals grown locally, yet Australians rarely eat foods different from those of their European or Asiatic forebears.

A series on TV called *The Bush Tucker Man* made viewers aware of the rich food sources that exist around them. The only place I know that sells bush tucker in Melbourne is **Robin's Food Store** at 424 Toorak Road, Toorak, ✆ (03) 827-9201, and in Sydney **The Wattleseed Deli** at 37 Ultimo Road, Ultimo, ✆ (02) 281-9532. These shops sell such oddities as banya-banya nuts, wattleseeds, Illawarra plums and bush tomatoes. Qantas has included bush tucker on its menu for international flights, where first and business class passengers are tempted with bread rolls baked with wattle seeds, bush tomato chutney and lemon aspen curd tartlets. In Sydney **Riberries** at 411 Bourke Street, Darlinghurst, ((02) 361-4929, is a restaurant renowned for its innovative use of bush ingredients.

With most of the population living around the coastline, it is to be expected that local seafoods are popular. Sydney's rock oysters are among the best in the world, while Adelaide has superlative whiting, and Queensland its mud crabs and Moreton Bay Bugs. Every child who has lived on a farm would know the delights of fishing for yabbies, freshwater crayfish the size of a shrimp, and then cooking these delicacies in a can of boiling water. All are usually available at better fishmongers. Meat from kangaroos is edible, but there is resistance to eating the country's national symbol; still, the meat is lean and low in saturated fats but the taste gamey and usually needful of a light sauce, like red currant, to disguise its smell.

CUISINES OF THE WORLD

The start of the post-war immigration was the death-knell for bland Anglo-Saxon food, and over the years Australians have experimented with such unfamiliar flavors as garlic, yoghurt and curry. Today these ingredients are used without thought.

Cosmopolitan Australians are now adventurous with their food, and scores of ethnic restaurants have proliferated to meet this demand. Establishments serve food from Burma, Thailand, Macedonia, Turkey, Japan, Malta, Argentina and Egypt; they are but a few examples of the influence of immigrants on the eating habits of Australians.

Many of these started out by catering for the specific ethnic community which sought its customary taste in cooking. This tradition continues today, and the best regional food is usually found where the people in question live, and is generally unpretentiously presented and inexpensive.

BEER OR WINE?

Australians have a reputation for being monumental beer drinkers. With an average annual consumption at 113 liters (200 pints)

per person, the heavy-drinking Australians are among the top ten beer-drinking nations in the world. Many are switching to "light" low-alcohol varieties, an encouraging sign.

Despite long-overdue changes in drinking habits many men still sport great beer-bellies, and the further north one travels into the Outback, the higher the consumption.

The revival of the Australian wine industry started in the 1970s. Many locals now enjoy a glass of wine with dinner but seem not to have taken to their beverage with the same gusto as beer drinkers; the average consumption of wine is just 18 liters (32 pints) per person. A reasonable bottle of wine costs between $7 and $15.

DRINKING ETIQUETTE

"It's your shout mate" is a phrase that any visitor who intends to soak up the local pub culture needs to learn fast.

The origin of this phrase comes from the days when shearers after picking up their pay would head for the nearest pub. The place would be packed with thirsty men, and there was no time to take individual orders. Drinkers in each group would take it in turns to "shout" above the din for another round. Even today, from the roughest Outback boozer to the trendiest city pub, the tradition of the "shout" continues.

While no one may say anything if you either miss your "shout," or even worse, leave before your turn comes around, following your exit a mutter will go around that "he wouldn't shout if a shark bit him," characteristically the most damning of all Australian insults.

THE "YARTZ"

Australia has produced world class artists: writers, painters, dancers and singers. Unfortunately, local recognition only comes after the artist is dead or has succeeded overseas. The satirist Barry Humphries dubbed Australia the "Koala Triangle, a mysterious zone in the Southern Hemisphere where talent disappears without trace." This jaundiced view was no doubt influenced by his own experience. A highly gifted humorist, he had to succeed in London's West End theaters before being accepted at home; as a sweet revenge on his countrymen, Humphries invented the vulgar Sir Les Patterson, Australian Cultural Attache in Britain who was there to promote "the yartz" — Strine for "the arts." Sad to relate, not all Australians can laugh at themselves!

LITERATURE

Australian identity was created in the bush during the 1880s, combining a disregard for authority, struggle against adversity in the harsh natural environment of the country, and a laconic humor. Above all, the bush ethic promoted "mateship" as the highest of human attributes. These qualities were celebrated in poems and prose published in such workmen's magazines as the Sydney *Bulletin*. Founded in 1880, the *Bulletin* became known as "the bushman's Bible," although it was just as popular in the cities. For the first time Australian voices were heard, the countryside lovingly described and the vernacular used in popular literature. Henry Lawson was one of the most typical of the bush poets, and his verse expressed the usual contempt for authority. For example, in *Freedom on the Wallaby* he wrote:

But Freedom's on the Wallaby.
She'll knock the tyrants silly,
She's going to light another fire
And boil another billy.
We'll make the tyrants feel the sting
Of those that they would throttle;
They needn't say the fault is ours
If blood should stain the wattle.

Another writer for the *Bulletin*, "Banjo" Paterson, is said to have written the well-known national song, *Waltzing Matilda*.

This popularity was short-lived, and the *Bulletin* declined in the early years of the twentieth century.

Over the next fifty years only a few Australian authors succeeded. Xavier Herbert gave voice to the plight of Aborigines in his novel *Capricornia*, while poet Alex Hope questioned the values of his generation. Several writers like George Johnson and Christina Stead left for Europe and the U.S., where they believed that they would be more readily accepted. However, when Pa-

trick White won the Nobel Prize for literature in 1973 Australian literature gained widespread recognition. The theme in Patrick White's novels like *Voss*, *The Tree of Man* and *The Eye of the Storm*, dealt with the struggle of the human spirit against a hostile environment.

Today, the works of a new generation of authors including Peter Carey, Elizabeth Jolley and Tim Winton have received universal acclaim and are widely read.

THEATER

As late as the 1960s the major theater companies in Melbourne and Sydney would ration themselves to one Australian play a year. For the rest of the year theatergoers were fed a diet of Bernard Shaw, Shakespeare and Oscar Wilde.

The birth of Australian theater happened at La Mama in Melbourne and the Nimrod theater in Sydney, where the twang of the Australian accent and slang were heard in local plays, which had exuberance and energy. Some, like Jack Hibbert's *Stretch of the Imagination* and David Williamson's *The Removalist*, have become modern classics.

The cultural cringe, in which everything Australian is devalued, has in some measure been replaced by a jingoistic, not-very-mature defensiveness. Today, many of the plays put on twenty years ago are part of the repertoire of major companies.

In Melbourne La Mama is still going strong, and has been joined by the Courthouse and Anthill, while Sydney's Nimrod has competition from the New Theater and Stables Theater where the latest plays are showing.

MUSIC

There are various streams to Australian music, and to concentrate exclusively on high culture would ignore the wide range of music available.

The earliest musical tradition in Australia was the ballad: the cruelty of the penal settlements inspired songwriters in a way

The arts in Australia are performed in some magnificent auditoria, such as His Majesty's Theatre, Perth OPPOSITE with its pleasantly styled dome.

that, sadly, the genocide of the Aborigines did not. For example, the song *Moreton Bay* denounced the harsh conditions established by Captain Logan at Brisbane's penal settlement. It goes:

> For three long years I was beastly treated,
> And heavy irons on my legs I wore,
> My back with flogging was lacerated,
> And oft-times painted with my crimson gore.
> And many a man from down-right starvation
> Lies mouldering now underneath the clay:
> And Captain Logan he had us mangled
> All on the triangles of Moreton Bay

This tradition continues today. Eric Bogle's anti-war song *And the Band Played Waltzing Matilda* re-tells the Anzac story from the point of view of a soldier who returns from World War II without any legs. At the end of the song he laments that he can no longer "go Waltzing Matilda" with his comrades. Mercifully, folk music is no longer strong in Australia, but clubs in each city keep the tradition alive, and songwriters persist in composing new offerings.

Many great opera singers were born in Australia, none as adored as Dame Nellie Melba. Born Helen Porter Mitchell in 1861, she changed her name to Melba in honor of her home town. Her talent was quickly recognized and she stayed at the pinnacle of international fame for nearly forty years. Melba returned to Australia in 1926 for her farewell performance: so successful was this recital that Dame Nellie continued to give farewell performances until 1930, leading to the saying "more farewells than Melba" for anyone who overstays his welcome.

Dame Nellie was followed by other great Divas, such as Joan Hammond and Joan Sutherland. State and national companies in capital cities continue to foster opera and tickets are always sold out well before the season commences.

A survey of Australian music would not be complete without looking at what is happening on the rock and roll scene.

During the 1960s in my teenage years we listened to overseas groups like the Beatles, Rolling Stones and the Monkees. There was very little indigenous pop music but in the 1970s the situation changed, as the BeeGees and The Seekers successfully launched themselves onto the international pop circuit. By today's standards their music was quite wholesome and while these groups undoubtedly had talent, they also needed luck to compensate for the naivete of the local industry in its infancy.

Today there is a revolution afoot in pubs in the capital cities, particularly Sydney and Melbourne, where local groups are given a chance to play before an audience, launching a new generation of Australian pop stars like Midnight Oil, InXs and Mental As Anything into international fame

PAINTING

Australia's early painters saw the landscape as exotic, but few succeeded in capturing its essence. Looking at these canvases today it is evident that something of the European light and conventions in these works remains. Perhaps the first painter who came to terms with it was Hans Heysen, who painted massive gums with a vividness and nobility in stark contrast to the unsympathetic interpretations made by early colonial painters.

In the 1880s the Heidelberg School came into being on the outskirts of Melbourne. Painters like Tom Roberts and Arthur Streeton took their easels outdoors and represented the different light, space and color of the Australian bush in a way that hadn't been done before.

Traditional Aboriginal art on stone and bark were not appreciated by European Australia until quite recently. The first Aboriginal artist to gain national attention, the tragic Albert Namatjira, painted his vision of the landscape, and in the 1930s and 1940s his works became much sought after.

The current generation of Aboriginal painters has moved away from the European tradition of landscape painting and represents their spiritual world in abstract work based on tribal motifs and patterns.

The visions of the painters of our time range from the luscious and sensual lines of

Brett Whiteley to the dark threatening works of Peter Booth.

National art galleries show Australian paintings, but usually only those of established painters. Nonetheless there is a plethora of commercial and independent galleries offering contemporary works for sale. Visiting them is the best way to see how artists of today perceive and interpret the country and the world. The *Art Almanac* provides a listing of private galleries in all States, and can be purchased for $2 from major bookshops, galleries and newsstands.

CINEMA

The first feature film ever produced was made in Australia. Called *Soldiers of the Cross*, it was made in 1900 by the Salvation Army. The scene with lions mauling the Christian — filmed in someone's backyard — caused women in the audience to faint. The next major landmark was *The Story of the Kelly Gang* in 1906.

Australia led the world in the production of silent movies, when Hollywood was merely a dusty country town, but by the 1930s the local industry was virtually dead.

In 1966 *They're a Weird Mob*, followed by *The Adventures of Barry McKenzie* in 1972, showed that Australians could make feature films again and that the public was willing to support them at the box office.

Over the next few years splendid productions like *Caddie*, *Breaker Morant* and *Picnic at Hanging Rock* gained critical acclaim. Many Australian directors from this first flowering emigrated to Hollywood.

Crocodile Dundee was an immense commercial success although it lacked the artistic greatness of earlier films, and grossed $US440 million. Many Australian films have also won international prizes, and, in 1993, Jane Campion's *The Piano* won the highest award at Cannes.

RELIGION

In the last census, 73 percent of Australians said they were Christian. Observance, however, is low as most Australians prefer to be outdoors on Sunday than to be in Church.

This was not always the case. Irish Catholics, who formed a high proportion of convicts and early migrants, were divided from the well-heeled Protestant middle class by religion. In towns around the country Catholics and Anglicans vied to secure the highest point to erect their churches. Religion also influenced political allegiances: for many years the Australian Labor Party was supported by Irish Catholics because it claimed to stand for the (white) under-dog. Such divisions are no longer strong, and Australians are generally apathetic about religion; still, the Catholics are in a fizz because it appears that the Vatican may soon canonize Mary McKillop, making her Australia's first saint.

At the last census the Catholics were slightly ahead of the Anglicans, with the non-conformist denominations and Eastern Orthodox church making up the remainder.

While most religions have declined, the reverse is true for the Orthodox Church. Its emphasis on family and community life and pride in ethnic traditions are strong influences in Greek and Orthodox Slavic communities.

During Orthodox Easter the streets of Melbourne and Sydney are lit up by the candles of thousands of people in procession, participating in the most important celebration of their calendar.

Non-Christian denominations have established themselves as well: the oldest of these is Judaism. Several Jews were on the First Fleet and in 1844 the first synagogue was built in Sydney; their numbers were significantly bolstered by post-war immigrants and strong communities thrive in all States.

The Moslem population consists largely of Turkish, Lebanese and Indonesian immigrants who built mosques in the bigger cities, their number bolstered by more recently-arrived adherents.

Small communities of Sikhs, Buddhists and Hindus flourish in Australia as well.

GEOGRAPHY AND CLIMATE

Australia is the largest island in the world, covering 7,682,300 sq km (2,975,000 sq miles), which makes it a little smaller than the United States excluding Alaska, or rather smaller than Europe. Over the last 100 to 200 million years the continent has slowly eroded, leaving most of the landscape flat and the soil relatively poor.

One of the features of the continent is the Great Dividing Range. By world standards

system. Increasing salinity has reduced the potential of the river for irrigation, and in South Australia water taken from the Murray for drinking is of poor quality.

The furthest point north is latitude 10°41' south of the Equator, which puts it well within tropical climes, while the southern tip of Tasmania has a latitude of 43°39' south, the same as Rome in Italy or Toronto in Canada are north.

Being in the southern hemisphere, seasons are the opposite of those in the northern hemisphere and January and February are

this is not high, but it does serve as a catchment for most of the rain. Very little falls on the rest of the continent, other than the Top End which is watered by the monsoons. Most of the center of the country is desert: one-and-a-half million square kilometers of sand, scrub and boulders. Lakes Torrens, Eyre and Frome, marked on maps of northern South Australia, can be salt pans for years on end.

Despite being in a dry continent the Murray-Darling River system is enormous, with a catchment covering Queensland, New South Wales and Victoria. The past agricultural practice of indiscriminate clearing of the land has raised the water tables and caused severe salting of this important river

high summer. The climate is generally temperate in most State capital cities, and in winter it never gets cold enough to snow at sea level except occasionally in Hobart and Canberra.

The mean maximum temperature in Sydney varies between 15.9° and 25.8°C (55° to 78°F), and the best time to visit Sydney is between September and November when the temperature is mild and the rainfall lowest. Summer can be quite humid.

Mean temperatures in Melbourne vary between 13.3° and 25.8°C (60° to 78°F). Spring is the wettest season and the most stable weather occurs in autumn, which is also quite dry. During a heatwave in summer the temperature can plummet in half an hour by 10°C (20°F) as a cool south wind blows, and it has been said that Melbourne can have four seasons in a day. North of the Great Dividing Range the weather is more stable; the nights in places like Ballarat can be very cold.

Tasmania is the coldest State but still mild because it is an island. The average temperatures vary between 12.5° and 21.5°C (54° to 70°F). Nights can be cool throughout the year. In winter the prevailing winds are from the north-west. When the wind occasionally turns southerly, an icy blast straight from

(68°F), and in summer 29.4°C (84°F). Summer can be particularly wet and humid.

Canberra is the furthest inland of all Australian capital cities, and therefore its climate is not moderated by the ocean. Maximum temperatures range between 11.1° and 27.7°C (51° to 81°F), while in winter the average minimum temperature is -0.3°C (32°F). Early mornings in Canberra can be very frosty.

Darwin has two seasons: a wet season from November to April and a dry season for the remainder of the year. It is

Antarctica cuts to the bone. In the Highlands care should be taken as the weather can deteriorate suddenly.

Adelaide has the lowest total rainfall of all state capitals. The average temperatures vary between 15° and 22°C (59° to 71°F) and winter is the wettest season.

Summer in Perth can consist of days on end of temperatures between 30° and 40°C (85° to 105°F), and the only relief is an afternoon breeze from the west, called the Fremantle Doctor. Fortunately the heat is dry and easier to bear. The rest of the year is mild but winter can be wet.

Brisbane has a sub-tropical climate and temperatures throughout the year are warm. In winter the average temperature is 20.4°C

generally hot all year round and even in the coolest months, June and July, the daily temperatures are between 19° and 30°C (65° to 85°F)

Towards the center of the continent it can be extremely hot, the highest temperature ever recorded being 53.1°C (127°F) at Cloncurry in 1889.

Tasmania's Cradle Mountain and Dove Lake OPPOSITE, and Uluru National Park ABOVE, Australia's "Red Centre," dramatize the country's climatic contrasts.

New South Wales

The Premier State

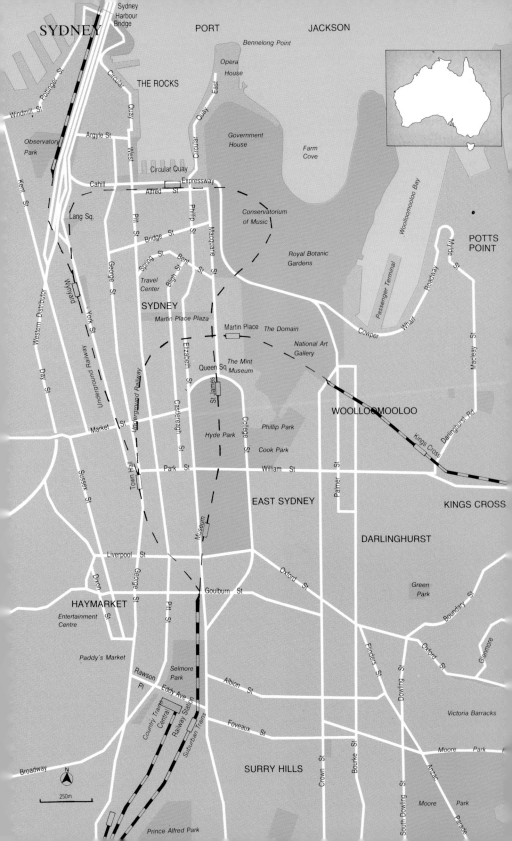

SYDNEY: A NATURAL WONDER

Sydney's reputation is based on its natural beauty. Built on one of the most magnificent harbors in the world, framed by the Harbour Bridge (known irreverently by the locals as the coat-hanger) and the sails of the Opera House, Sydney is one of the world's truly great cities.

It also has history and atmosphere, whether it be the "Rocks" early colonial streetscape, with its sandstone and bluestone buildings, or cosmopolitan Bondi Beach.

Rather than take their breathtaking setting for granted, Sydneysiders would almost kill for a glimpse of water from where they live, even if it's a sliver of blue only visible from the top floor bathroom by standing tiptoe on a chair. The real estate market feeds off this mania and apartments or houses with a view of the water fetch astronomical prices.

Fortunately Sydney harbor contains numerous inlets and estuaries, maximizing the opportunities to acquire real estate with a view of the water. There are 300 km (188 miles) of foreshore and 56 km (35 miles) of city beaches for locals to fight for.

The harbor is always packed with pleasure cruisers, yachts, commuter ferries and motor boats, as Sydneysiders take advantage of the temperate climate that allows outdoor activities to be pursued in all seasons by the intrepid.

At night the streets of suburbs like Manly, Paddington and Bondi are packed with people taking the air. Sydney is made for promenading.

The *nouveaux riches* feel more comfortable in Sydney, revel in brashness and unashamedly admire success.

BACKGROUND

Governor Phillip ignored his original orders to establish a penal colony in Botany Bay. Instead he landed at Sydney Cove, a few kilometers to the north, which he judged a better site.

He raised the Union Jack where the ferry terminal now stands and the 736 convicts, 211 guards and handful of officials set about erecting tents and crude shelters.

The first settlers were ill-prepared and the colony almost foundered. Food was scarce, they did not know how to farm the new land and the indigenous population was hostile.

As this sad rabble overcame its early privations and the population grew, it sought to venture across the natural barrier of the Blue Mountains west of Sydney. Once this hurdle was surmounted, the local Aborigines subdued and the rich pastoral land be-

yond the mountains made available for exploitation their future was assured.

The Victorian era brought prosperity to Sydney and endowed it with scores of handsome buildings. Many survive to this day, nestling amongst modern office blocks.

The twentieth century and two World Wars established its industrial base and today it is the premier city in the country.

GENERAL INFORMATION

The **New South Wales Government Travel Centre**, at 19 Castlereagh Street, ℂ (02) 231-

---

Martin Place ABOVE in downtown Sydney forms part of a traffic free plaza stretching five blocks.

4444 is open weekdays during office hours. It gives excellent access to all tourist information.

Maps with major attractions marked on them can be obtained free from the Rock's **Visitors Centre** at 104 George Street, ((02) 247- 4972.

There are information booths at Manly, ((02) 977-1088 and Kings Cross, ((02) 357-3883.

For information on public transport phone:

Ferries ((02) 256-4670 or 13-13-15

Buses (13-13-15
City rail (13-15-00
Water taxis ((02) 955-3222

WHAT TO SEE AND DO

The Harbor

Sydney's biggest lure is its magnificent harbor. Governor Phillip described it as "the finest harbor in the world, in which a thousand sails of the line may ride in the most perfect security." While Phillip was probably thinking of the English fleet, today his prediction has come true as thousands of pleasure craft, yachts and commuter ferries enjoy the safe waters of Sydney harbor and its stunning beauty.

Sydneysiders are energetic water-lovers and appreciate their waterways to the full. In summer the numerous beaches and shoreline of the harbor are dotted with people enjoying their attractive environment.

The best way to see the harbor is from the water, and there are a number of organized cruises available. **Captain Cook's Harbour Explorer,** ((02) 251-5007, does a circuit of the harbor, stopping at major attractions, such as The Rocks, Sydney Opera House and Toronga Zoo. Ferries leave every two hours, between 9:30 am and 3:30 pm from Jetty Number 6 at **Circular Quay**. It is possible to hop off at any stop and then catch the next ferry to continue the tour.

The other way to see Sydney harbor is how locals see it — from a commuter ferry. Timetables and information on routes can be obtained from the **Sydney Ferry Information Centre** opposite Wharf 14 at Circular Quay, ((02) 256-4670. The best time to take a ferry is at sunset when the colors of the sky tinge the harbor with yellows and pinks. Regular services across the harbor take between 30 and 90 minutes.

The Old Quarter

The historic precinct called **The Rocks** is close to the Harbour Bridge, on the south shore. The Rocks is Sydney's oldest section, where Governor Phillip established the first settlement, built around winding streets connected by flights of narrow stone steps, giving it a distinctive character.

The history of The Rocks is an unhappy one. In the nineteenth century it became an iniquitous den of vice; as Sydney grew, so the nasty streets of The Rocks became nastier, terrorized by gangs, thugs and bandits. With colorful names like "The Forty Thieves," "Cabbage-tree Boys" and the "Golden Dragons," various gangs engaged in pitched battles around **Argyle Place**, which at that time was the village green.

As the neighborhood became increasingly run-down it surprised nobody when in 1900 there was an outbreak of bubonic plague, which prompted the city fathers to react by demolishing parts of the area.

After degenerating into a slum the original face of The Rocks was whittled away by successive developments. When the Sydney

Harbour Bridge was built further destruction of historic houses occurred, but the last assault which was almost the fatal and final one in the 1960s was when speculators in league with the government tried to redevelop the entire quarter and tear down its historic buildings. Thankfully local residents resisted, and restoration of the buildings in the 1970s and 1980s has revitalized The Rocks, making it a worthy destination for tourists.

At 110 George Street is Sydney's oldest surviving dwelling, **Cadman's Cottage,**

Adjacent to The Rocks is **Circular Quay,** the main commuter terminal for harbor ferries. On its west side is the **Museum of Contemporary Art,** ((02) 252-4033, an imposing six storey Art Deco building. It exhibits modern art from a collection of 4,500 paintings, sculptures and works on paper, and from visiting international collections. The museum is open daily for an admission fee. On the terrace outside is **MCA Cafe,** which has a good view of the bustle of Circular Quay and the harbor beyond.

On Saturday and Sunday George Street, just under the Bridge, becomes a crowded

built in 1816. When John Cadman was alive his house was on the shoreline and boats would moor at his front door. Now open to the public it is an information center for the NSW National Parks and Wildlife Service.

Convict houses have been transformed into arcades housing taverns, boutiques and craft shops, such as with the **Argyle Arts Centre** at 16–20 Argyle Street.

There is even an authentic village green, surrounded by nineteenth century cottages and the pseudo-Gothic **Garrison Church,** built between 1840 and 1843. The inside of the church is adorned with the dusty flags of the British regiments of the line who once worshipped here.

market with crafts, antiques and jewelry sold from its many stalls.

The Opera House

At Bennelong Point on the opposite side of Sydney Cove from The Rocks, fly the white sails of the Opera House.

The design was selected from submissions to a competition in 1956, won by a 37 year old Danish architect, Joern Utzon. The original budget of $7.5 million began escalating and politicians, public servants and the architectural Establishment began

ABOVE: Syndey's most famous landmarks, the billowing sails of the Opera House and the Harbour Bridge. OPPOSITE: The convict built Argyle Centre, once a warehouse now houses shops and taverns.

to express reservations as to whether Utzon could realize his bold design. Ten years after he started the project Utzon fled the country under an assumed name to escape the hostility of officialdom and Press harassment. When finally the Opera House opened in 1973 the cost had ballooned to over $100 million: while costs were escalating, one wit suggested that it would have been cheaper to build it overseas and sail it to Australia! Ballet companies have complained that the stages are too small and opera singers grumble about the acoustics. Still, the Opera House is truly a spectacular sight, although functionally flawed. In 1978 Utzon won the Queen's Gold Medal for Architecture, citing him as "the greatest architect of the twentieth century." Hmmm....

It is worth taking a tour of the building to gain an appreciation of its architecture. Guided tours leave from the Lower Concourse Arcade daily between 9 am and 4 pm. There are numerous performances on at the Opera House, and attending one provides another chance for you to make up your own mind about the building.

Darling Harbour

Darling Harbour, just south-west of Circular Quay, can be reached by foot from The Rocks or by Monorail from the city.

Once a derelict area of rotting wharves and decrepit warehouses, Darling Harbour has undergone a major transformation. Today it has been redeveloped as a leisure area with restaurants, museums, shops and an exhibition center. Over weekends the place is crowded, and its management seems determined to find any excuse for a fireworks display over the harbor.

Sydney Aquarium, ℂ (02) 251-4211, provides an opportunity to see fish, sharks and stingrays swimming around you as you walk inside a plexiglas tube running through the Aquarium. This experience greatly appeals to children.

The **Powerhouse Museum** at the corner of Macarthur and Harris Streets in Ultimo, ℂ (02) 217-0111, is a sympathetically converted power station which once supplied the electricity for Sydney's trams. Exhibitions are changed regularly, the themes being everyday life, social history, science and

technology. Its high roof allows the curator to develop imaginative displays utilizing the space to its best advantage.

City Walks

The haphazard layout of roads in Sydney and its inner suburbs owes its pattern to convenient paths created by the meanderings of the bullock carts which moved goods between the business district and Sydney Cove.

Today most are flanked by high rise buildings, making them appear even narrower. Streets to the south of the city are more orderly, with **Pitt**, **George** and **Castlereagh Streets** forming the heart of the shopping district.

Macquarie Street leads from the Opera House, skirting the eastern boundary of the

city, and ends at Hyde Park. This road passes several neoclassical buildings associated with the early history of the colony. The **State Library**, fronted by an imposing Doric colonnade, contains the Mitchell Wing housing the finest collection of early Australian books and manuscripts. Almost next door is **Parliament House**, the oldest section of which was built between 1811 and 1816 as a hospital and then donated in return for the concession for the importing of rum. Just before reaching the park, on your left you will see **Hyde Park Barracks** and on your right **St. James' Church**. Both were built by Francis Greenway, the colony's best known architect.

To the east of the city, a pleasant stroll through the Domain, is the **Art Gallery of New South Wales** which has an extensive collection of late nineteenth and twentieth century Australian art. Continuing past the gallery you will come to the **Royal Botanic Gardens**, a favorite spot for Sydneysiders to picnic. From **Mrs Macquarie's Chair** there is a fine view of the Opera House and **Farm Cove**.

West of Macquarie Street, catch the Monorail at the corner of Market and Pitt Streets and weave your way between buildings in a loop of 3.6 km (2.2 miles), linking Darling Harbour to the city center. While it may be an eye-sore, the Monorail provides an admirably convenient form of transport around the center of Sydney.

Darling Harbour, a once derelict part of town imaginatively rejuvenated to house museums, restaurants and shops, is especially lively at weekends.

For a bird's eye view of the city take the lift in **Sydney Tower** at 100 Market Street to the Observation Level. Both night and day this vantage point, 305 m (1,000 ft) above street level provides panoramic views of Sydney and the Harbour. There is an admission fee to the Observation Level, open from 9:30 am to 9:30 pm Sunday to Friday and 9 am to 11:30 pm on Saturday.

Sydney also has the liveliest **Chinatown** in Australia. Located just beyond the southern end of the main city shopping area in **Haymarket** with its wonderful perfumes haunt for Sydney's homosexual community, reputedly second only to San Francisco in number.

It starts at Hyde Park in the city and runs south-east to form the border between **Darlinghurst** and **Surry Hills**.

There are various inexpensive restaurants, bookshops and interesting emporia selling a plethora of goods as well as a number of good galleries just off Oxford Street. **Lime Gallery** at 271 Goulburn Street Darlinghurst exhibits paintings and photographs by contemporary artists and the

which would not be out of place in Singapore or Hong Kong, it contains some of the best Chinese restaurants in the country, centered around Dixon Street where there are also Chinese cinemas and grocers.

Oxford Street

The liveliest street in Sydney is **Oxford Street**. Snaking through the inner suburbs, lined by working men's cottages and pubs (with one on almost every corner), Oxford Street is always bustling with people walking to work, to the local pub for a drink, or simply on the prowl; most are promenaders just out for a stroll and hankering for a cappuccino, shopping or casting an eye over the passing parade. The street is a popular

eclectic **Jeremy Gallery** is at 362 Riley Street, Surry Hills. Just north of Oxford Street off William Street lies the infamous **Kings Cross**, a red light district peppered with strip joints and porn shops where aggressive hawkers importune likely customers.

O innocent Travelers, lock up your wives and daughters! And at night, avoid dark streets.

Back on Oxford Street, the next suburb is **Paddington** (or "Paddo" to the locals) where the shops are more upmarket and call themselves "boutiques." It is worth taking a detour off the main drag — so to speak — at Elizabeth Street to see restored double-storey Victorian terraced houses. If you are tired of walking then this may be a good moment to drop into the **New Editions Bookshop** at 328 Oxford Street. You can take your purchase into the adjacent tearoom, part of the bookshop, and browse through the English newspapers while having coffee or a light meal.

To garrison British troops **Victoria Barracks** was built in 1848, replacing the original quarters on George Street, and housed British army regiments until 1870. Hidden behind high sandstone walls the architecture of the Barracks is symmetrical and orderly, reflecting the profession of its de-

Beyond Centennial Park, Oxford Street is residential until it meets **Bondi Junction**.

Bondi Beach

With good surf beaches so close to Sydney, it is no surprise that a warm summer's day will see teenagers heading down to catch a wave. Just seven kilometers (five miles) from the city, Bondi Beach has become synonymous with sun-bronzed Australians. The country's first lifesaving club was established there in 1906.

During any summer weekend a carnival

signer, Colonel George Barney. On Wednesday at 10:30 am witness the changing of the Guard and afterwards visit the Army Museum located in the former jail-house and which is reputed to be haunted.

It is then only a short distance to **Centennial Park** at the junction of Oxford Street and Lang, Darley and York Roads, which was built in 1888 to commemorate Sydney's first hundred years. The 220 hectare (550 acre) complex of sporting fields, rose gardens and ornamental lakes is a soothing oasis of peace after the bustle of Oxford Street. The best way to see the Park is on wheels, and conveniently **Centennial Park Cycles**, ((02) 398-5027, hire out bicycles and roller blades.

celebrating sea and surf is bound to be held on at least one of Sydney's surf beaches. The most exciting events are the boat races in which teams of five men work hard to maneuver their boats through waves and breakers.

Bondi has been through several transformations, from fashionable seaside suburb to home for successive generations of immigrants. When I first visited it in 1969 the foreshore was a seedy, depressing place. In the intervening years the area has transformed itself and today Bondi is a lively mixture of good cafes, excellent ethnic res-

OPPOSITE: Sydney's harbour and beaches are its summer playground. ABOVE: The best known beach of them all, Bondi.

New South Wales

taurants and a foreshore crowded with people. And, of course, there is the surf. Swimming has become rather more agreeable since the government stopped the discharge of raw sewage into the sea, but regrettably the local council has authorized several large, ugly construction developments, spoiling parts of the foreshore.

The North Shore

People who live on the **North Shore** are quick to identify themselves as a race apart from the unfortunates on the other side of

the Sydney Harbour Bridge. The general image conveyed by the North Shore is of affluence; there mansions line the streets and the chatter of yuppies brings life to the cafes of Neutral Bay and Mosman.

Manly can be reached by the Harbour Bridge or Harbour Tunnel but the best way across is by the Manly Ferry, a leisurely 45 minute journey. Alternatively, take the Hydrofoil and whiz across in 20 minutes.

A hundred years ago Manly was a fashionable seaside resort; today it remains a popular place for Sydneysiders to go for a meal or a stroll along its bustling streets. The main pedestrian mall, the **Corso**, is opposite the surf beach and overflows with cafes, shops and people enjoying the sea air. Free walking-maps of Manly and its environs are available at the information booth, open from 10 am to 4 pm daily. If you have three or four hours to spare, pick up a map of the **Manly Scenic Walkway**, which follows the

OPPOSITE: Elegant Victorian era iron lace curtains a Sydney terrace. ABOVE: Secluded moorings on Sydney's North Shore.

edge of the harbor through quiet inlets and bushland reserves to **Spit Bridge**; it crosses over to **Balmoral Beach** at **Mosman**, which being in the harbor has no surf and so is preferred by windsurfers and families with small children.

SYDNEY BY NIGHT

Sydney at night can be loud and wild or quiet and cultured, but never dull.

Lovers of music and traditional performing arts can enjoy the **Opera House** where there are fine performances of opera and ballet, and where good plays and concerts are always on the program at one of its various halls. While the interior of the Opera House has its detractors, its location is unsurpassed and the views at night are bewitchingly lovely.

Numerous playhouses are in the suburbs. The **Stables Theatre** at 10 Nimrod Street, Kings Cross and the **Belvoir St. Theatre** at 24 Belvoir Street in Surry Hills show good plays in season. The **New Comedy Store** at 450 Parramatta Road in Leichhardt show-cases Australia's best humorists, and Tuesday night is when new talent is let loose on the audience.

Half price tickets for some plays are available on the day of performance from the **Halftix** booth in Martin Place which is open from noon to 5 pm daily.

On warm evenings the streets come alive as Sydneysiders promenade along the mall at Manly or Oxford Street's busy pavements, settling themselves into an outdoor restaurant for a convivial meal.

Sydney after dark can be a naughty place, as the profusion of strip joints and prostitutes in Kings Cross attest. Its streets are alive with neon and noise as passers-by are accosted by hustlers touting for trade. Prostitutes (clad in alarmingly little attire) stand on street corners ready to negotiate with anyone interested. Lively shows and restaurants in the Cross abound but there are better places to eat around town.

As you would expect in a city this size there is no shortage of choice; one can dine and dance in a sedate ambience or gyrate to ear-bruising disco-music. For cabaret try the **Sydney Show Club** in Darling Harbour.

Sydney has long been a stronghold of jazz and many well-established clubs are situated near The Rocks. **Soup Plus** at 383 George Street and **The Basement** at 29 Reiby Place are a brace of venues which dish out supper with hot music. A number of pubs have live music at night: try **Mercantile Hotel** in The Rocks and the **Cock 'n Bull** in the Grand Hotel at 89 Ebley Street, Bondi Junction. Depending on the band some pubs charge admission. **The Bridge** at 135 Victoria Road, Rozelle, known for its rock music, appeals to younger people. At the **Rhino Club** in The Orient at The Rocks you can disco to live music until 3 am.

Unique to Sydney, there is a wide range of entertainment at 1,500 licensed clubs which offer relatively inexpensive shows and meals to entice patrons to gamble on their poker machines. Run by sporting bodies and returned servicemen's associations, the larger ones stage shows at which international stars perform.

George Street, near the Town Hall, is movieland and Sydney's other main entertainment center. Two theater complexes screen more than a dozen movies at once, at least one of which is usually the premiere of an Australian film.

Information on what's on in Sydney can be found in the entertainment section of the *Sydney Morning Herald*, called *Metro*.

WHERE TO SHOP

In the city Pitt, George and Castlereagh Streets are the heart of the shopping district. Multi-storey centers and arcades offer a plethora of shops while major department stores, such as Myer, David Jones and Grace Brothers straddle several blocks joined by elevated walkways. Four floors at the base of **Centrepoint Tower**, at the corner of Pitt and Market Streets, contain 170 retail businesses. In nearby Castlereagh Street is the **MLC Centre**, that has several levels of shopping floors. Each one, with its own theme, is built around a glass-domed hall. Gift shops are on the lower level and above them, elegant fashion boutiques. The complex also houses the **Theatre Royal**, one of the city's most respected, as well as several open-air cafes.

A world away from the ambience of modern shopping centers is the nineteenth century **Strand Arcade** in George Street. Its galleries gleam with wrought iron and polished wooden balconies, while shop signs are restricted to discreet shingles. In **Strand Hatters** on the ground floor of the Strand Arcade, famous Australian Akubra hats can be purchased. Also on George Street is the magnificently restored **Queen Victoria Building**, built in 1898, endowed with a choice of nearly 200 shops, cafes and restaurants. The center modestly advertises itself as "the world's most beautiful shopping center." Nine awards for excellence, including the Australian Heritage Award, uphold this characteristically self-effacing claim.

Access to the central city shopping district is easy from all stations on the subway loop, other than Circular Quay.

For the up-market shopper, Double Bay, approximately 15 minutes from the city, provides an opportunity to browse through designer clothes, jewelry and shoes in the company of the well-heeled of Sydney's North Shore.

Ken Done's bold paintings and designs of Sydney with their views of the Harbour, Opera House and the Bridge are popular with visitors. Recalling the warmth and vivid colors of the city and its setting, his work can be bought from the more fashionable shops or from his two galleries at 123-125 George Street, the Rocks, and Shop G42 in the Queen Victoria Building.

Amongst the excellent galleries in Paddington where good local art can be purchased are **Sherman Galleries** at 1 Hargrave Street and **Hogarth Galleries** at 7 Walker Lane, opposite Liverpool Street, which exhibit contemporary Aboriginal art. **Australian Galleries** at 15 Roylston Street largely confine themselves to mainstream artists like Brett Whiteley and Arthur Boyd, while younger aspirants have their works shown at the **Michael Nagy Fine Art Gallery** at 159 Victoria Street.

On weekends a number of flea markets offer all manner of wares. Modest examples are **Paddy's Market** in Garden Street, Red-

The Strand Arcade OPPOSITE houses some of Sydney's most elegant shops.

fern, just a short walk from the city, while in the grounds of the Eastside Parish Church on Oxford Street is the **Paddington Bazaar** where 250 stalls sell jewelry, crafts and bric-a-brac.

SPORT

Sydney offers the choice of three football codes during winter — Rugby League, Rugby Union and Australian Rules. Football is played between March and September and information on venues for games can be obtained from Friday's newspaper. Rugby League is by far the most popular sport in NSW. Its Grand Final takes place at the Sydney Football Stadium at Moore Park and tickets can be obtained through BASS Booking Agency, ((02) 266-4800.

When the football season is over, cricket commences. Details of where games are can be obtained from the NSW Cricket Association, ((02) 299-1299. The best games to see are international sides against Australia, guaranteed to attract a monstrous crowd.

There are 69 golf courses in Sydney open to the public; the NSW Golf Association, ((02) 264-8433, should be contacted for details.

Top-class tennis can be seen at **White City** at 30 Alma Street, Paddington, ((02) 331-4144, and at the **Sydney Entertainment Centre** at Darling Harbour, ((02) 211-2222. Booking tickets well ahead for major tournaments is a good idea.

WHERE TO STAY

Luxury
Within The Rocks there are small, top class hotels with an intimate atmosphere not found in larger establishments. **The Observatory Hotel** at 113 Kent Street, ((02) 256-2222, (008) 806-245 or fax: (02) 256-2233 is comfortably furnished and the management has tried the create the atmosphere of an English country house. For views of Campbell's Cove stay at the **Park Hyatt** at 7 Hickson Road, ((02) 256-1690, (008) 089-819 or fax: (02) 256-1996, which has an unassuming lobby and friendly staff. Not all the rooms have good views so when booking it is advisable to express a preference.

The **Russell Hotel** at 143A George Street, ((02) 241-3543 or fax: (02) 252-1652, has combined its nineteenth century charm with twentieth century comfort.

The **Ramada Grand Hotel** at the corner of Campbell Parade and Beach Road, Bondi Beach, ((02) 365-5666, (008) 222-431 or fax: (02) 365-5330, dominates the foreshore and the views from the balconies on the sea side of the hotel are magnificent.

Several good "boutique" hotels — those smaller hotels which combine luxury with intimacy — provide a more personal kind of

service than the larger luxury hotels do.

In North Sydney **The McLaren Hotel** at 25 McLaren Street, ((02) 954-4622, fax: (02) 922-1868, is located in a beautiful old house built at the turn of the century; with just 25 rooms, guests are assured of personal service. In a quiet tree lined street in Newtown you will find **The Pensione** at 27 Georgina Street, ((02) 550-1700 or fax: (02) 550-1021 in an old terrace house, built in 1882.

Moderate
Staying close to the city center is generally expensive and moderately priced hotels are thin on the ground.

In the style of a guesthouse of the nineteenth century, **Periwinkle** at 19 East Esplanade, Manly, ((02) 977-4668 or fax: (02) 977-6308, offers bed and breakfast.

Located in a line of nineteenth century terrace houses is the **Kendall Hotel** at 122 Victoria Street, Potts Point, ((02) 357-3200 or fax: (02) 357-7606, another boutique hotel with lots of character.

The **Garden Studios** at the corner of Bourke and Plunkett Streets, Woolloomooloo, ((02) 356-2355 or fax: (02) 356-4943, are self-contained units ten minutes walk from the city which can be reached through the Domain.

Barklay Hotel at 17 Bayswater Road, ((02) 358-6133 or fax: (02) 358-4363.

Established in 1873, the **Wynyard Hotel** at the corner of Clarence and Erskine, ((02) 299-1330, is well placed for access to most of Sydney's major attractions.

There are also quite a few places in Kings Cross, Bondi and Coogee that cater solely to backpackers.

WHERE TO EAT

When you have a city with such a beautiful

Opposite the University of NSW is **Barker Lodge Motor Inn** at 32 Barker Street in Kingsford, ((02) 662-8444, (008) 252-094 or fax: (02) 662-2363, mid-way between the city and airport. Near the University of Sydney and close to good inexpensive restaurants is the **Rooftop Motel** at 146-148 Glebe Point Road, Glebe, ((02) 660-7777 or fax: (02) 660-7155. The **Metro Inn** at 1 Meagher Street, Chippendale, ((02) 319-4133 or fax: (02) 698-7665, is close to Chinatown and close to Central Station.

Inexpensive

Close to everything in lively Kings Cross are the **Astoria Hotel** at 9 Darlinghurst Road, ((02) 356-3666 or fax: (02) 357-1734, and

harbor is it little wonder that some of the most exclusive restaurants are on the water, nor that many of them specialize in seafood. They have the advantage of splendid views and that is considered justification for a bill which may seem unreasonably high. Beware!

Ask any Sydneysider to name his city's best seafood restaurant and **Doyles on the Beach** at 11 Marine Parade, Watsons Bay, ((02) 337-2007, is sure to be his response. Situated near the Heads it looks back along the length of the harbor, and while Doyles may no longer be the best seafood restaurant

OPPOSITE: A well preserved terrace in The Rocks. ABOVE: An old façade for a modern business.

it remains a local institution. Another watering-hole gaining in reputation is **The Bather's Pavilion** at 4 The Esplanade on Balmoral Beach, ((02) 968-1133, with great · views over the beach. **Freshwater** on Moore Road, Harbord, ((02) 938-5575, resembles a rambling old guesthouse and looks out over a surf beach.

A number of good restaurants serve dishes other than seafood, and are close to the city to boot: most are located in The Rocks and around Darling Harbour and have good water views. Kept full by a constant flow of tourists some have become blasé. Not so at **N°7 at the Park** in the Park Hyatt Sydney at 7 Hickson Road, ((02) 241-1234. This establishment takes particular care in the presentation of its food with unusual combinations of Japanese ingredients. You need connections to get a window seat but the views are still good from anywhere in the restaurant. The view from of **The Wharf** at Pier 4 Hickson Road, Walsh Bay, ((02) 250-761, is uninspiring, a factor which appears not to have discouraged its patrons, actors by and large; its atmosphere is Bohemian.

What better way of enjoying the Harbour at night than aboard a catamaran fitted out as a restaurant? **Sail and Dine**, ((02) 262-3595, leaves Circular Quay each evening for a cruise of the Harbour.

The best view of the city is from the **Centre Point Tower** revolving restaurant, ((02) 233-3722, which provides an a la carte menu upstairs and has a more reasonably priced bistro below. On a clear day you can see as far as the Blue Mountains and also have a bird's-eye view of Sydney harbor.

Three restaurants situated in or near the Opera House provide the chance to dine before attending a concert or the convenience of a late supper afterwards. **Bennelong**, ((02) 250-7578, is located under the smaller sails at the back of the Opera House and offers special pre-theater meals. The **Forecourt**, ((02) 250-7300, is less formal and provides a wide selection of meals, from snacks to a full dinner. The view from the **Harbour Restaurant**, ((02) 250-7191, takes in the harbor and the Bridge but it caters mainly for pre-theater diners and the kitchen closes at 9:30 pm.

To find restaurants which are both good and moderately priced you will have to get away from the water.

Chinatown in the city has some of the best Chinese restaurants around, although Melbournians would challenge this claim.

For Cantonese cuisine try **Marigold's** at 299-305 Sussex Street, ((02) 281-3388. You'd better believe that the seafood is fresh at this restaurant, as you can choose your dish (alive) from large tanks: a few minutes later the lobster or crab will appear (cooked) in front of you. It brings tears to your eyes.

Cantonese *yum cha*, consisting largely of steamed and fried dumplings, has become very popular in Sydney and is traditionally served as a brunch. **East Ocean** at 421 Sussex Street, ((02) 212-4198, offers a wide selection of dishes which come around on trolleys for you to select. Just point to what you fancy. For food typically sold from stalls in Southeast Asia try **Travellers**, opposite the Chinese Gardens where dishes from a dozen Asian countries are served with prices in the $6 to $7 price range. There is no cheaper, nor more interesting place to dine in Chinatown.

On the lower North Shore are a number of sensibly priced establishments, with more expensive ones around Crows Nest. **Pino's** at 49 Willoughby Road, ((02) 439 2081, a humble pizzeria, has some of the best pasta in town. The place is usually full, which is its own recommendation. **The Red Centre** at 70 Alexander Street, ((02) 906 4408, serves pizza with a difference: they use deliciously unusual toppings. Moving away from Crows Nest to Mosman, the restaurants along Military Road generally become more pricey. **Cafe Sante** at 174 Military Road, Neutral Bay, ((02) 953-0569, is elegant and serves excellent food containing only the freshest ingredients.

The choice of restaurants widens around Oxford Street between the city and Paddington, where the best places to eat have good views of Oxford Street and watching the passing parade of trend-setters adds interest to the meal. **La Passion du Fruit** at 100 Oxford Street, ((02) 361-5487, is a good spot for a light meal or a *cafe au lait* while you watch the world go by. **The Golden**

Dog at 268 Oxford Street, ((02) 361-5157, is an Italian bistro serving both traditional pasta and some inventive specialities of its own. Off the main stretch is **Pegrum's** at 36 Gurner Street, Paddington, ((02) 360-4776, situated in a terrace house and definitely an "in" place.

The smell of Indonesian spices welcomes diners into the **Borobodur** at 263 Oxford Street, ((02) 331-3464, a small moderately priced outfit in Darlinghurst. Nearby is **Geronimo's** at 294 Crown Street, ((02) 331-3001, which has an identity problem. The

name suggests someone brandishing a tomahawk but the menu offers North Indian curries.

They must run the chefs on a roster at **Morgan's** at 304 Victoria Street, ((02) 360-7930, as the day starts at 6 am for breakfast and continues late into the night. The prices are very reasonable and the menu always interesting.

On either side of the University of Sydney are good cheap restaurants frequented by students. In Newtown are a various Thai restaurants which have sprung up in recent years, offering good value for money. Glebe Point Road is a bit of a mixed bag, offering a number of inexpensive ethnic restaurants.

HOW TO GET THERE

As well as being the major international gateway to Australia Sydney is also the hub of the transport network along the eastern seaboard.

By air Sydney is an hour from both Melbourne and Brisbane, and two hours from Adelaide. The bus takes 17 hours from Brisbane, 13 hours from Melbourne, 23 hours from Adelaide and two and half days from Perth on the other side of the continent. Sydney is the eastern terminus for the transcontinental *Indian Pacific*. If you fancy train-travel this 62-hour trip is one of the world's last great train journeys. As for Sydney's airports, the less said about them, the better. They are a disgrace, as is the road from the city leading to them.

DAY TRIPS FROM SYDNEY

KU-RING-GAI CHASE NATIONAL PARK

Sydney is fortunate to have at the edge of its suburban sprawl and 24 km (15 miles) from the city a National Park of great beauty. Visitors can take a scenic drive through it or stroll along its many tracks.

Bordered by Pittwater to the east, Broken Bay to the north and Sydney's suburbs to the south, the Ku-ring-gai Chase National Park covers 15,000 hectares (37,000 acres) and contains rivers, gorges and over 100 km (62 miles) of navigable water.

Caves and sheltered overhangs in sandstone provided protection for the Aborigines who once lived there: rock engraving of kangaroos, dolphins, emus and sharks are their memorial. Aboriginal paintings can be obtained from the **Bobbin Head and Kalkari Visitor Centre**, ((02) 457-9322.

How to Get There

A ferry to the park leaves from Palm Beach, or follow the signs from either the Berowra, Ku-ring-gai or Cowan railway stations to the National Park.

One of Sydney's many fountains, this one in Hyde Park.

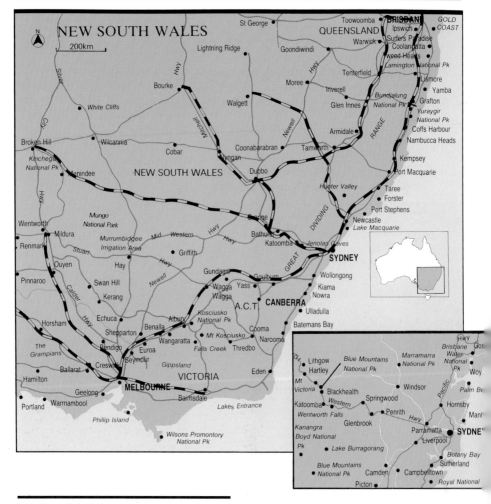

THE BLUE MOUNTAINS

The Blue Mountains, an easy hour-and-a-half's drive from Sydney, were *the* place for holidays for locals before the advent of inexpensive overseas air fares. Fifty years ago the Blue Mountains were lauded for the healthy "mountain air." Their vistas have been rediscovered by day-trippers from Sydney who continue to be attracted to this especially beautiful region. Make the day trip or stay there and enjoy the hills as a base from which to explore the surrounding countryside.

From a distance the mountains really appear blue, caused by the haze of eucalyptus vapor from the gum trees which absorbs the red component of sunlight.

General information

Information on touring around the Blue Mountains can be obtained from the **Blue Mountains' Tourist Authority** on the Great Western Highway, Glenbrook, ((047) 396-266, or by dropping into their booth at Echo Point. Walking maps can be obtained from the **Blue Mountains' Heritage Centre** on Govetts Leap Road, Blackheath, ((047) 878-877.

What to see and do

Man's encroachment on the sandstone ramparts is confined to the procession of small towns and villages straddling the Great Western Highway linking the mountains and Sydney. The mountains, despite their name, are really a 1,000 m (3,280 ft) sandstone plateau. Millions of years of erosion have created a scenic wilderness of valleys, ravines and cliffs.

Most of the area is a conservation region; numerous walking tracks run parallel to the edge of the escarpment and look-outs are clearly signposted. They provide breathtaking views of the harsh but spectacular land; walking tracks within the National Park lead to more than forty waterfalls.

There are several pretty villages on the Great Western Highway approach to the Blue Mountains: **Leura**, **Blackheath** and the village of **Springwood** are worth visiting.

The main town in the Blue Mountains is **Katoomba**, perched near cliffs which rise from the Jamieson Valley. What is claimed to be the world's steepest railway plunges 250 m (820 ft) down the cliff-wall on a 400 m (1,300 ft) track and a cable car sways out over the valley to give a truly heart-stopping ride. Both the **Scenic Railway and Skyway** start at the corner of Cliff Drive and Violet Street, ((047) 822 699.

At Katoomba is the **Three Sisters** rock formation with the best views from Echo Point or Queen Elizabeth Look-out. Rising

Author and artist Norman Lindsay lived at Springwood for over fifty years, etching and painting satyrs and nude women in compositions of Bacchanalian revelry. Although his works scandalized generations of prudes, his prints and paintings can be appreciated without the twitchings of that sanctimonious age. Lindsay also wrote the children's story, *The Magic Pudding* with his tongue in his cheek to prove that any stories about animals and food appeal to children. His house has been converted into the **Norman Lindsay Gallery and Museum** on Norman Lindsay Crescent, ((047) 511-067, where his paintings hang and memorabilia from his life are on display. His studio remains as it was when he died.

out of the Jamieson Valley, these three sheer rock columns are steeped in Aboriginal lore. To protect his daughters — Meenhi, Wimlah and Gunedu — from a witch-doctor, their father saw their plight from the valley below and turned them temporarily to stone using a magic stick. In his excitement the father dropped his stick and the witch-doctor turned him into a lyre-bird. The sound of the lyre-bird is believed by Aborigines to be their father looking for his magic stick so that he can turn his daughters back into flesh and blood.

ABOVE LEFT: Sandstone walls of the Blue Mountains National Park. These cliffs are perfect for abseiling ABOVE RIGHT.

While in town drop into the **Paragon Cafe** at 65 Katoomba Street for some tea or a meal. This *art deco* cafe was built in 1916 and appears not to have changed much in the intervening years, but nor has the menu. Try the home-made chocolates displayed in leadlight cabinets dating back to 1925.

Katoomba is also the place for a mid-year Christmas. Being in the Southern Hemisphere Australians are used to having Christmas at the height of summer, and the Christmas lunch is often a barbecue outdoors; the northern traditions are missed, so the tourist industry has come up with a solution. Between June and August more than 30 guest houses, restaurants, hotels and resorts in the Blue Mountains serve the full traditional Christmas dinner to the accompaniment of carol singing, open fires and mulled wine. How agreeable, having a mid-year Christmas devoid of squabbling relatives….

If all this indulgence niggles the conscience then play 18 holes of golf at the picturesque **Leura Golf Club** on Sublime Point Road, ((047) 825-011, or ride a horse through the Kanimbla Valley on day trips organized by the **Centennial Glen Horse and Sulky Hire**, ((047) 877-179.

One way of enjoying the scenery is from the lounge of the **Hydro Majestic Hotel**, ((047) 881-002, down the road at **Medlow Bath**. Windows fill the wall facing the Megalong Valley and the view is superb. The Hydro Majestic started out as a health resort. When the attractions of bowel kneading and centrifugal douching lost their appeal the resort was turned over to vacationers and the inside remodeled to take on the appearance of a grandiose hotel.

About an hour and half west of Katoomba are the limestone caverns of the **Jenolan Caves** which are open daily; the best way to see these cathedrals in lime is to join a guided tour, which leaves every thirty minutes from the **Jenolan Caves Reserve Trust**, ((063) 593-311.

Where to stay

There are some wonderful guesthouses and hotels in the Blue Mountains with prices ranging from moderate to expensive. The rates usually go up over weekends.

In Katoomba there is **The Cecil** at 108 Katoomba Street, ((047) 821-411, fax: (047) 825-364, a traditional guesthouse built for comfort rather than style. **Balmoral House** at 196 Bathurst Street, ((047) 882-264, was built in 1876: staying there provides a sense of history. Several motels in town provide moderately priced accommodation.

At Medlow Bath there is the famous **Hydro Majestic**, ((047) 881-002, fax: (047) 881-063, which as stated before is a hotel in the grand style.

The **Sky Rider Motor Inn**, ((047) 821-600, is at the corner of Scenic Cliff Road and the Great Western Highway, while in nearby Blackheath there is **Gardners Inn**, ((047) 878-347 and **Jemby-Rinjah Lodge** at 336 Lookout Road, ((047) 877-622, fax: (047) 876-230, set into the bush adjacent to the Grose Valley.

The **Jenolan Caves House**, ((063) 593-304, fax: (063) 593-227, has the relaxed atmosphere of a country homestead, and provides a chance to get away from it all.

Mid-year **Yulefest** packages are available at the Cecil Guesthouse, Hydro Majestic Hotel, Balmoral House and Jenolan Caves House.

How to Get There

Katoomba is about two hours by train from Sydney. Driving along the M4 motorway takes one and a half hours, and on the Great Western Highway slightly longer.

Trains to the Blue Mountains leave from Central Station in Sydney, stopping at Springwood, Katoomba, Mt. Victoria and Lithgow.

The local bus connects with some of the train services, running frequent services on weekdays and Saturday morning.

Daily tours are offered by **Australian Pacific Tours**, ((02) 252-2988, with stops at popular look-outs in the Blue Mountains and the Jenolan Caves.

THE SOUTH COAST

The coastal road south of Sydney passes through the industrial cities of Wollongong and Port Kembla and then onto rich pastoral country dotted with dairy herds. The road occasionally turns towards the coast to pretty fishing villages and small holiday resort towns.

GENERAL INFORMATION

Kiama's Visitor Centre at Blowhole Point, ((042) 323-322, is open daily from 9 am to 5 pm.

The **Shoalhaven Tourist Centre** at 254 Princes Highway, Bomaderry, ((044) 210-778, is open daily 9 am to 5 pm.

For information about the area around Bowral and Berrima contact the **Southern Highlands Information Centre** on the Hume Highway at Winfred West Park, ((048) 712-888, and which is open daily 9 am to 4:30 pm.

The **Eurobodalla Coast Tourism** office is at the corner of Princes Highway and Beach Road in Batemans Bay, ((044) 726-900, and is open daily between 9 am and 5 pm.

WHAT TO SEE AND DO

Kiama, 17 km (73 miles) south of Sydney, is famous for its blowhole that can spurt water as high as 60 m (200 ft) into the air when the sea is rough and the wind blows from the south-east. **The Terrace**, a row of historic timber cottages built in 1886, has been restored as a home for art galleries, craft shops and restaurants.

The walks along the cliffs to Cathedral Rocks and Kaleula Head are recommended. Maps of walking trails are available from the Visitor's Centre.

Inland from Kiama are the small towns of **Berrima** and **Bowral**, both of which merit a detour from the coastal route.

Berrima has changed very little since it was settled and virtually no buildings have been erected there since 1890. One that still functions as it did when built in 1834 is the sandstone **Surveyor General Inn**, although the food is more upmarket and these days Guinness is on tap. There are numerous restaurants, tea rooms, antique shops and galleries in town and to appreciate it best, go for a stroll around its streets.

Bibliophiles should not miss **Berkelouws' Antiquarian Books**, ((048) 771-

370, fax: (048) 771-102, located on the Hume Highway towards Mittagong where there are shelves filled with second-hand and rare books.

Bowral has retained its buildings from the late nineteenth century, many of which can be seen on Wingecarribee and Bendooley Streets. The town and surrounding area have traditionally been used as a resort by affluent Sydneysiders, as a consequence of which many fine restaurants and places to stay are in and around town.

Bowral is frothing with tributes to its favorite son, Donald Bradman — the greatest batsman Australia has ever produced. A **museum** in St. Jude Street dedicated to this cricketing immortal has an impressive collection of memorabilia which includes an oak bat from the mid-eighteenth century, and mementos from the current test team. An admission-fee is charged and the museum is open daily 10 am to 3 pm.

Back on the coast, **Nowra** is the main agricultural and business center of the Shoalhaven River district. The high escarpment and plateau immediately inland are bounded by high sandstone cliffs which can be seen to the west of the road into the village, from which there is easy access to the high tableland just 28 km (17 miles) away, preserved as the **Morton National Park**. This features the spectacular **Fitzroy Falls** and is a haven for a large number of indigenous animals and wild birds.

Batemans Bay is located on the Clyde River estuary and is a popular seaside resort where rumor has it that you can pick up oysters on the shore, but it may be easier to buy a couple of dozen — or a crayfish — for which the area is famous, and picnic with a bottle of Chablis on the foreshore. On the coast north of Batemans Bay is **Murramarang National Park**, known for its broad beaches and cliff-like headlands.

Frozen in time is **Central Tilba**, 79 km (50 miles) south of Batemans Bay. Surrounded by rugged coastal mountains this village of 25 wooden buildings was built in the 1890s and has remained unaltered to this day.

OVERLEAF: A drought scene in New South Wales.

WHERE TO STAY

In Kiama moderately priced accommodation is offered by the **Kiama Inn Hotel** at 50 Terralong Street, ((042) 321- 166, fax: (042) 323-401, within easy walking distance of all the sights of note, and the **Grand Hotel** at the corner of Manning and Bong Bong Streets, ((042) 321-037. The **Berrima Bakehouse Motel** is at the corner of the Hume Highway and Wingecarribee Street, ((048) 771-381, fax: (02) 771-047. Staying in Bowral can be expensive but the accommodation available is quite special. **Milton Park** on Hordern's Road, ((048) 611-522, fax: (048) 614-716, is on a 300-hectare (740-acre) estate and serves excellent meals to its guests, with wine from its cellar. The **Craigburn Resort**, ((048) 611-277, fax: (048) 621-690, has been providing accommodation since 1910 and has its own 9-hole golf course.

Excellent value weekend packages in Nowra can be obtained at the **Riverhaven Motel** at 1 Scenic Drive, ((044) 212-044, fax: (044) 212-121, located on the banks of the Shoalhaven River. A little out of Nowra but well worth the trip, is the **Coolangatta Historic Village Resort**, ((044) 487-131, fax: (044) 487-997, which was the site of the first settlement on the South Coast in 1822. Suites are moderately priced. Located in the Murramarang National Park, 10 km (6 miles) from Batemans Bay are self-contained cabins on the beach at the **Murramarang Caravan and Camping Resort**, ((044) 786-355, fax: (044) 786-230. In Batemans Bay itself a range of accommodation is offered by the **Coachhouse Tourist Van Park**, ((044) 724-392, fax: (044) 724-852, from inexpensive cabins to moderately priced villas. For a little luxury try the **Old Nelligen Post Office Guest House** at 7 Braidwood Street, ((044) 781-179, which provides a weekend package including meals in its admirable restaurant.

HOW TO GET THERE

Pioneer Motor Services of Nowra operate a bus service connecting with trains from Sydney and following the route along the 325 km (200 miles) coastline to the Victorian border.

Most of the worthwhile sights on the south coast are on or near the Princes Highway, a good route by car and easy to connect from town to town using local buses. The train from Sydney stops at Kiama and Nowra.

SNOWY MOUNTAINS

While most parts of Australia are hot and dry, the alpine areas which suffer winter snow are much visited by skiers who flock to the higher peaks along the Great Dividing Range, from Victoria to southern New South Wales. The best skiing is in the Snowy Mountains 200 km (125 miles) south of Canberra along the Monaro Highway.

GENERAL INFORMATION

The **Tourist Information Centre** is on the Snowy Mountains Highway at Tumut, ((069) 471-849, and provides useful advice on current road and skiing conditions. The Centre is open daily from 9 am to 5 pm. The **Cooma Visitors' Centre** is at 119 Sharp Street, Cooma, ((064) 501-742, and is open 9 am to 5 pm.

WHAT TO SEE AND DO

The slopes of **Thredbo, Perisher Valley, Smiggin Hole, Charlotte Pass** and a few other resorts on the mountains are packed between June and September with skiers. There is also cross-country skiing throughout the whole area, the major ski fields being in the **Kosciusko National Park**, covering 690,000 hectares (1,700,000 acres), thus making it the largest in New South Wales.

Glacial lakes, limestone caves, windswept moors and the head-waters of the Murray River all contribute to the park's scenic beauty. In summer the slopes are a carpet of yellow, white and purple flowers, delighting nature lovers and photographers, making this alpine area as popular in summer as during the winter skiing season. The moment the snow melts hikers take to its tracks, climbers head for sheer rock walls and anglers cast their lines into clear alpine streams and lakes for trout.

Dominating the Snowy Mountains is **Mt. Kosciusko**, 2,228 m (7,307 ft) above sea level. Although modest by world standards, this is Australia's highest peak. Take a chair lift, which operates year-round, from Thredbo or walk up to the peak, an easy eight kilometer (five mile) hike through alpine meadows. A more challenging 20 km (12 mile) walk starts at the information office at Sawpit Creek making its way up Perisher Valley. What's fun is to explore the Alps on a mountain bike, which you can rent from **Paddy Pallin** on Kosciusko Road, **Jindabyne**, ((064) 562-922; he also sells topographical maps of the area.

Australia's most ambitious engineering undertaking, the Snowy Mountain Scheme, involved the construction of 16 large dams and 160 km (100 miles) of tunnels re-routing water formerly running to waste into the Pacific Ocean, to irrigate land west of the Great Dividing Range. On its way west the drop of some 1,000 m (3,000 ft) is utilized to drive the hydroelectric turbines feeding south-eastern Australia's power grid. At **Tarbingo** on the New Dam Road, take a guided tour of the **Tumut N°3 Power Station** to gain an idea of the magnitude of the engineering involved.

WHERE TO STAY

During the winter it is essential to book well ahead. Rooms above the snow line can be expensive and some places will only accept bookings in blocks of a week or more. The tariffs during summer can be 50 percent cheaper than during winter.

There are several services offering a selection of accommodation both on and off the mountains which can save a lot of bother hunting around for somewhere to stay. Contact the **Snowy Mountains Reservation Centre** at Shop 16, Town Centre, Jindabyne, ((064) 562-633, (008) 020-622 fax: (064) 561-207, **Kosciusko Accommodation Centre** at Shop 2 Nugget's Crossing, Jindabyne, ((064) 562-022, (008) 026-354, fax: (064) 563-945, or the **Thredbo Accommodation Services** at Shop 9 Mowamba Place, Thredbo Village, ((064) 576-387, (008) 801-982, fax: (064) 576-057.

In the center of Thredbo Village, luxury accommodation is available at the **Thredbo Alpine**, ((064) 576-333, (008) 026-333, fax: (064) 576-142, and **Berntis Mountain Inn**, ((064) 576-332, (008) 026-316, fax: (064) 576-348. **Punchinello Lodge**, ((064) 576-315, is moderately priced.

At Jindabyne there are the **Alpine Resort** at 22 Nettin Circuit, ((064) 562-522, fax: (064) 562-854, and the less expensive **Lakeview Plaza Motel** at 2 Snowy River Avenue, ((064) 562-134, fax: (064) 561-372.

The **Kosciusko Chalet**, ((064) 575-245, (008) 026-369, fax: (064) 575-362, is a rambling guesthouse in Charlotte Pass, above the snow line in winter. The Chalet is also popular in summer.

If you have a car then you can save on accommodation by staying in one of the towns in the lowlands near the Alps. In **Cooma** is inexpensive accommodation at the **Bunkhouse** at 28 Soho Street, ((064) 522-983, and **Hawaii** at 192 Sharp Street, ((064) 521-211.

HOW TO GET THERE

Car access is by way of the Snowy Mountains Highway, the Alpine Way and Kosciusko Road. During winter it is advisable to carry tyre-chains.

There are Skitube trains to Perisher, Smiggin Hole and Blue Cow Mountain which leave Bullock's Flat in Jindabyne every twenty minutes in winter and on the hour in summer. Savings can be made by purchasing a return Skitube pass and chair-lift ticket-package.

There are daily flights to Cooma from Sydney by Eastern Australian Airlines and from Melbourne by Kendall Airlines.

Coach companies include a stop-over in the mountains on their itineraries, and day trips from Canberra can be arranged.

THE FAR WEST

The north and west of New South Wales are flat, arid and sparsely populated, making it

---

OVERLEAF: Outsize promotion in the banana-growing region.

part of the **Outback**. In 1883 Charles Rasp discovered rich lead, silver and zinc deposits near **Broken Hill**, which became the center for mineral exploration in this part of the State. The company formed to exploit the mine was The Broken Hill Proprietary Company which used its wealth to invest in steel manufacture and petroleum exploration. Today BHP is Australia's largest multinational company.

GENERAL INFORMATION

Information is available from the **Broken Hill Regional Tourist Association** at the corner of Bromide and Blende Streets, ((080) 876-077. Its staff will handle bookings for local tours and provide information on Outback attractions, while its information booth is open daily from 8:30 am to 5 pm.

WHAT TO SEE AND DO

Broken Hill could justifiably be known as *Silver City*; its mines once produced a third of the world's silver. The town itself is dreary beyond words, but explore **Delprats Underground Tourist Mine** in Crystal Road, ((080) 881-604. A 120 m (400 ft) drop in a cage takes you to the start, from which visitors are herded through a labyrinth of tunnels. One tour a day — 10:30 am takes place on weekdays and at 2 pm on Saturday.

The abysmal landscape around Broken Hill has inspired a generation of bush painters who have created styles unique to the area. Best known are Pro Hart who has a gallery at 108 Wymam Street and Jack Absalom whose gallery is at 638 Chapple Street. Works by other painters calling themselves "brushmen from the bush" can be seen at the **Ant Hill Gallery** at the corner of Oxide and Chapple Streets.

To gain some understanding of the wealth generated in the area visit the **Broken Hill City Art Gallery** at the Entertainment Centre in Chloride Street, ((080) 889-252. Silver craftwork is on display, and the pride of the collection is the *The Silver Tree*, commissioned by Charles Rasp. An admission fee is charged, the gallery being open Monday to Saturday.

If you really want to get off the beaten track, book a seat on the **Bush Mail Run**, the light aircraft which delivers post and supplies to 25 remote sheep stations in Outback New South Wales. The plane can hold up to five passengers and bookings are made with **Crittenden Airlines**, ((080) 885-702. Traveling only a few thousand meters above the endless plain you gain an appalling insight into the hinterland, forbidding, harsh and bereft of beauty. Morning tea and lunch at a homestead are included for passengers. The plane leaves Broken Hill Airport every Tuesday and Saturday morning and the round trip of approximately 1,100 km (680 miles) takes about ten and half hours. (Read Patrick White's epic novel, "Voss.")

Another way to explore the Outback is to take a safari tour out of Broken Hill. **Alf's Outback Tours**, ((080) 876-077, fax: (080) 878-108, takes small groups out in a four-wheeled drive vehicle to explore the surroundings. Alternatively, hire a 4WD from **Silver City Vehicle Hire** at 320 Beryl Street, ((080) 873-266, fax: (080) 885-775, and explore the Outback at your own pace.

About 25 km (16 miles) from Broken Hill is the "ghost town" of **Silverton**, deserted when silver mines in the area were exhausted. The population is now about 100 and it is not unusual to see a camel walking down the main street. Check out the **Silverton Hotel**, a typical Outback pub with the usual collection of Outback characters. The **Silverton Horizon Gallery** features contemporary art from the West Darling Ranges, while the **Peter Browne Gallery** is more eclectic.

White Cliffs is a town built underground to avoid the searing heat of the Outback. Located about 100 km (62 miles) north-west of Wilcannia, this area is Australia's oldest opal field and it has been known for visitors to pick up valuable opals by fossicking around the old diggings. While in White Cliffs improve your golf game on the local course which has no green fees because it has no greens, having the distinction of containing not one blade of grass. The sandtraps, however, are something else! Indeed, the whole place is something else.

WHERE TO STAY

There is a good choice of moderately priced motels in Broken Hill. The **Charles Rasp** at 158 Oxide Street, ((080) 883-355, fax: (080) 883-856, and the **Old Willyama Motor Inn** at 30 Iodide Street, ((080) 883-355, fax: (080) 883-856, are near the center of town. Budget accommodation is offered by **The Tourist Lodge** at 100 Argent Street, ((080) 882-086.

In White Cliffs it is not possible to go past the **Underground Motel**, ((080) 916-677, (008) 021-154, fax: (080) 916-654, which may not have any views (as there are no windows) but will provide a memorable stay. The owner, Leon Hornby, excavated its 32 rooms himself, and vertical shafts provide natural light to rooms.

HOW TO GET THERE

A number of airlines fly into Broken Hill. Monarch Air Services has a service from Sydney via Mildura, and Kendall fly in daily from Adelaide from Sunday to Friday.

THE NORTH COAST

Traveling north along the New South Wales coast the countryside becomes increasingly lush and sub-tropical as it runs the 900 km (560 miles) from Sydney to the Queensland border.

Broad cultivated valleys mark a succession of wide sluggish rivers which flow to the east, with names like Big River Country and Summerland.

Farming and timber bring prosperity to the towns in the valleys while small fishing villages cluster around the river mouths. During the summer months these villages see an influx of thousands of holiday-makers from the south who come to the excellent beaches or to try their hands at angling along the coast or in the rivers. Finding accommodation during the summer and school holidays may not be easy but for the rest of the year hotel and motel prices are competitive.

There are also untouched sections of coast preserved as national parks. **Yuraygir**

and **Bundjalung National Parks** stretch 80 km (50 miles) along the shore north of Coffs Harbour and feature secluded beaches, untouched coastline and wetlands full of water birds; there is good surfing at Angourie Beach. The area can be explored from one of the many tracks that meander along the coast.

GENERAL INFORMATION

Port Macquarie-Hastings Tourism has an office at the corner of Hay and Clarence Streets, ((065) 830-500 or (008) 025-935, which is open daily between 9 am and 4:30 pm.

Coffs Harbour Tourism in Urara Park, ((066) 528-824, is open weekdays between 8 am and 5 pm, and between 8 am and 6 pm on weekends.

The **Byron Bay Tourist Association** has an office at 69 Jonson Street, ((066) 858-050, which provides visitors with maps and brochures about the local sites of note.

WHAT TO SEE AND DO

To the north of Sydney is **Port Macquarie**, a major holiday town which can be a little on the pricey side but has all kinds of attractions and activities sure to appeal to the whole family.

The town started as a penal settlement in 1821 and several examples of colonial architecture have survived: at the corner of William and Hay Streets stands **St. Thomas Church**, built by convicts between 1824 and 1828 and open to the public weekdays between 9 am and 12 noon and 2 pm to 4 pm.

Sea Acres Rainforest Centre in Pacific Drive, ((065) 823-355, provides excellent educational displays on rain forest ecology: a broadwalk gives visitors an opportunity to wander through our last remaining pocket of coastal rain forest. The reserve is open daily between 9 am and 4:30 pm and an admission-fee is charged. **Fantasy Glades** in Parkland Close, ((065) 822-506, is a theme park introducing children to the wonders of this vanishing phenomenon, opening from 9 am to 5 pm daily.

Another 150 km (95 miles) to the north is the self-proclaimed **Banana Coast**. Just to prove it there is a monstrous banana north of **Coffs Harbour**, the capital of the Banana Coast.

At this point a word of warning about what Australian tourist promoters consider irresistible to visitors: make a concrete model of a local attraction, at least 10 m (32 ft) high, and tourists will simply be unable to help themselves as they flock through the doors. So be ready to be tempted by the Big Pineapple, the Big Prawn and even the Big Merino, which measures 15 m (50 ft) high and 18 m (60 ft) long, as you travel around the countryside.

For all its crassness, behind the **Big Banana** is a **theme park** which provides interesting information about the admirable banana, as well as aspects of Australia including displays on the Aboriginal Dreamtime and re-creations of scenes from Australia's early colonial history.

Coffs Harbour itself is ringed with banana groves with bunches of fruit covered in blue or white plastic bags to accelerate the ripening process from two years to 18 months.

Just 10 km (6 miles) north of Coffs Harbour is **Woolgoolga**, where a little piece of India has been transplanted into Australia. Sikhs have established themselves here and turbaned men and women in saris are part of local color now, with their white domed temple at the top of the hill. (You may visit it by arrangement.)

An area only recently discovered by tourists is **Byron Bay** which has the advantage of the climate and facilities of many of the larger resorts to the north and south, but without the crowds. Its coastline has been called the Rainbow Country because hippies flocked into the area in the 1970s: a decade later they were followed by disciples of the New Age. From their farms and communes in the hinterland they come into Byron Bay to shop, do business and meet friends. The result is a relaxed and laid-back place which does also cater to visitors who have no inclination to chant or meditate, but seek an attractive beach to lie on and a cocktail to lubricate the way into their personal nirvana. Byron Bay's atmosphere and charm attract celebrities: Paul Hogan and Linda

Kozlowski of *Crocodile Dundee* fame and Olivia Newton-John live nearby.

Nimbin, about an hour drive from Byron Bay, is the heartland of hippiedom. In 1973 an Aquarius Festival brought young people from around Australia to Nimbin for a counter-culture razzle and search for "oneness" with nature. Many stayed on and the town is an odd mix of aging hippies and good country folk. The **Rainbow Cafe**, its social hub, will get you into the groove.

There are some great **country markets** throughout Rainbow Country, seemingly at

least one on every weekend. King of these is at **Bangalow**, about 10 km (6 miles) from Byron Bay where handicrafts are on sale, and tropical fruit is inexpensive.

WHERE TO STAY

Staying at Port Macquarie can be expensive, particularly in the holiday season. Located on the river is **Sails Resort** on Park Street, ((065) 833-999, (008) 025-271,

The bleached landscape of Mungo National Park ABOVE where the earliest evidence of aboriginal man in Australia has been uncovered. OPPOSITE: Snow gums bent by the alpine winds at Mount Koscuisko National Park. Australia's snow fields are more extensive than those of Switzerland.

fax: (065) 840-397, a complex of luxury accommodation, restaurant and bars with sporting facilities for guests. Various motels offer a more basic and less expensive alternative, like the **Arrowyn** at 170 Gordon Street, ((065) 831-633, and almost next door **Bel Air** at 179 Gordon Street, ((065) 832-177, fax: (065) 832-177. For stays of more than a week self-contained units can be rented from **Col Collyer Real Estate**, ((065) 599-137.

A large choice of accommodation in Coffs Harbour can be booked through **Subtropical Holidays**, ((066) 515-255, (008) 809-592, fax: (066) 513-334. During summer demand is high so it is necessary to book early. If you want to make your own arrangements there is good moderately priced accommodation in Coffs Harbour. **Bo'suns Inn Motel** at 37 Ocean Parade, tel/fax: (066) 512-251 and **Midway Motor Inn** on the Pacific Highway, ((066) 521-444, are close to the city center.

Tucked away in 2.6 hectares (6.5 acres) of rain forest near Byron Bay is the **Wheel Resort** at 39–51 Broken Head Road, ((066) 856-139, fax: (066) 858-754, which consists of one and two bedroom self-contained cabins in a bush setting. If Byron Bay is not relaxed enough for you try **Cooper's Shoot Guesthouse**, ((066) 853-313, fax: (066) 853-315, a converted schoolhouse located on a quiet hilltop overlooking **Tallow Beach**.

How to Get There

The Pacific Highway runs along the north coast, and is a very good road for long distance driving.

There are daily flights out of Sydney to Coffs Harbour and Port Macquarie: Oxley Airlines has a service between Coffs Harbour and Brisbane. Coast to Coast flies into Port Macquarie from Brisbane, Lismore and Newcastle.

Lindsay Coach Service runs a daily shuttle between Sydney and Brisbane with stops at many major towns. The Pioneer service between Melbourne and Brisbane stops at Byron Bay and the Greyhound service at Port Macquarie, Coffs Harbour and Byron Bay, as does Bus Australia.

NATIONAL PARKS

General information on national parks in New South Wales can be obtained from the **National Parks and Wildlife Service** at 43 Bridge Street Hurstville, ((02) 585-6333. Information can also be obtained from the **National Parks Association of New South Wales**, ((02) 264-7994.

Within the boundaries of the **Barrington Tops National Park**, 96 km (60 miles) north-west of Newcastle are

widely differing ecologies, including a high plateau with its Snow Gums and Antarctic Beech, and a plain at 1,550 m (5,000 ft) with its sub-tropical vegetation. Contact the local ranger, ((049) 873-108, for further details.

Back towards the coast the **Myall Lakes National Park**, 32 km (20 miles) east of Bulahdelah, is the largest coastal freshwater and saline lake system in New South Wales where many tracks allow walkers to get a close look at the waterfowl drawn to the area. Alternatively take a boat out onto its waterways, half of which are navigable. Contact the local ranger, ((049) 873-108, for further details.

Brisbane Water National Park, 9 km (6 miles) south-west from Gosford is off the Pacific Highway and has a number of Aboriginal art galleries. Contact the local ranger, ((043) 244-911, for further details.

In the north-west corner of the State is the Sturt National Park, 330 km (205 miles) north of Broken Hill with examples of desert ecosystems from red dunes to stony plains over which red kangaroos range. There are about 300 km (185 miles) of dirt roads to explore and a four-wheel vehicle is essential. The Sturt National Park can be unpleasantly

The Australian Country Music Festival is held at Tamworth at the end of January. Tamworth, 440 km (275 miles) north of Sydney, is to Australian country music what Nashville is to American, and 600 events are programmed over ten days. Every pub, street corner and shopping mall is full of young hopefuls strumming "good old country music."

FEBRUARY The Sydney Gay and Lesbian Mardi Gras takes over Oxford Street, where 250,000 people come out to watch outrageous floats and those of the Persuasion

hot in summer, so try to visit in winter or spring. Contact the local ranger, ((080) 913-308, for further details.

FESTIVALS AND SPORTING EVENTS

JANUARY The whole month is turned over to the Festival of Sydney. An estimated four million visitors come for the music, theater and dance, much of it outdoors to take advantage of Sydney's great weather. The festival is launched with a spectacular computer controlled fireworks display over Sydney Harbour, starting on the stroke of the New Year.

dressed in (or out of) flamboyant costumes. The parade is followed by a party in the Showgrounds where almost 20,000 people razzle well into the next day.

MARCH Over three days in the second weekend of March the Myall Prawn Festival takes place in Tea Gardens, 250 km (155 miles) north of Sydney, near the coast. Highlights are the World Prawn Eating Competition, a parade and the Prawn Masquerade Ball.

APRIL During the Deniliquin Easter Jazz Festival the town is turned over to an orgy of jazz. On Saturday musicians who usually

The Festival of Sydney OPPOSITE and ABOVE lasts all January. Hundreds of events are on the calendar, many of them informal occasions during which anyone can join in the fun.

play gigs around town come together in the swinging jazz parade, and on Sunday they get together for jam sessions. Deniliquin is 790 km (490 miles) south-west of Sydney where the Riverina and Cobb Highways meet.

Sydney's **Royal Easter Show** is the foremost agricultural exposition in Australia. Lasting ten days it gives all an opportunity to see the best livestock in the land and the finest rural produce. Show jumping and rodeo events as well as fireworks display make it a happy event.

APRIL/MAY   The **Festival of the Falling Leaf**

JUNE   The Sydney Opera House is the focus of the **National Folkloric Festival** which allows Australia's immigrants to share their musical heritage with everyone. On the Sunday before the Queen's Birthday there is a parade from First Fleet Park to the Opera House forecourt.

The **Sydney Film Festival** is a binge of feature films, shorts and documentaries leaving movie buffs gasping for air after two weeks. It is necessary to book tickets, ((02) 660-3844.

JULY   During the **Tweed Banana Festival**, in

celebrates the coming of autumn, during which the Tumut's deciduous trees put on a brilliant show of red and yellow foliage. **Tumut**, 442 km (275 miles) south-west of Sydney, is on the Snowy Mountain Highway. Visitors can enjoy a street parade, band recitals, a billycart derby and a canoe relay on the Tumut River.

MAY   At the **State of Origin** league matches between Queensland (known as the "Maroons") and NSW (the "Blues"), fanaticism reaches its zenith when State pride is at stake.

Murwillumbah near the Queensland border the humble banana is celebrated.

SEPTEMBER   **Bathurst 1000 Festival** is for petrol-heads who enjoy production car and motor cycle racing. Bathurst is 221 km (137 miles) west of Sydney on the Great Western Highway.

OCTOBER   The **Australian Bush Music Festival**, at Glen Innes 670 km (415 miles) from Sydney on the New England Highway is a chance to hear the best bush bands play traditional songs and new compositions.

OCTOBER   More than 60,000 tulips flower every spring in Bowral. The **Tulip Festival** is a chance to see this pretty little town, a couple of hours' drive from Sydney, at its most beautiful.

A Dutch touch among the spring blooms at Bowral's Tulip Festival in New South Wales.

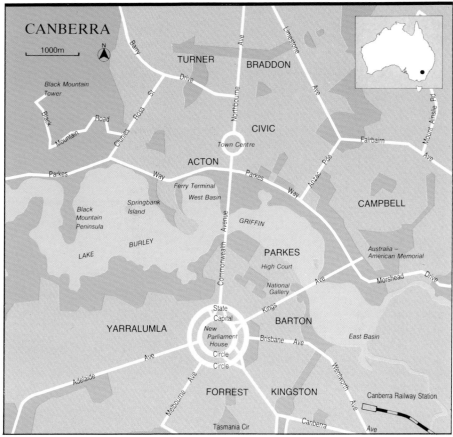

CANBERRA: THE NATIONAL CAPITAL

Running down their politicians is a popular pastime among Australians, and it is no surprise at all that the public ranks them as less honorable than real estate agents and marginally more than used-car salesmen. Despite the malicious slur on used-car salesmen, is it not distinctly peculiar that the national parliament, home of Australia's federal politicians, is not further from the two major population centers, — 286 km (177 miles) from Sydney and 653 km (404 miles) from Melbourne?

Canberra has been slated as overplanned with its broad thoroughfares and manicured suburbs, where the placing of every public edifice has been carefully predetermined. Buildings are well set back from the roads, numerous parklands break up the neat rows of houses and no building

exceeds six storeys. Even outdoor TV aerials are forbidden lest they mar the clean outlines of houses.

Only to the extent that it is a pre-planned capital has Canberra something in common with Brasilia, Islamabad and Washington. Critics of the town consider that the concept has been wasted by cluttering a beautiful layout with cheap buildings devoid of taste or elegance. Being the capital of Australia, politicians ensure that plenty of hot air keeps the tourist warm in winter, but in spite of them there is much to be seen and enjoyed.

BACKGROUND

When the first federal legislature met in 1901 in Parliament House in Melbourne the understanding was that in future a new and permanent location would be found between that city and Sydney.

The selection of a site by a committee of politicians established standards of behavior which successive generations of federal politicians have striven to perpetuate: in 1902, these people toured the countryside being lavishly wined and dined by locals who hoped to benefit from having the national capital on their doorstep. Their pattern of behavior has stood the test of time; a contemporary newspaper ridiculed the junketing politicians in verse. It wrote:

Each hill and dale, each stream and lake,
Seems all the more alluring,
When sandwiches and bottled ale,
Alleviate the touring.

It appears that the Federal Capital Committee had ample opportunity to indulge this predilection for bottled ale and sandwiches because nowhere was agreed upon until 1908 when a compromise site in the Molongo Valley was selected. This they named Canberra, after the Aboriginal word for "meeting place."

A competition to design the national capital was won by 35-year-old American architect Walter Burley Griffin. Griffin was a student of the Chicago School of Architecture, and forerunner in the Australian tradition of not trusting local architects to do anything of value. In designing Canberra, Griffin was aware of the natural amphitheater formed by the surrounding mountains, and the street plan and placement of buildings were designed to integrate these features. The excellent Griffin began work turning his vision into reality when he was appointed Federal Capital Director of Design. His task was made difficult by the spite and venom of envious architects, public servants and politicians to whom courage, taste and vision were alien. Often his plans and drawings were "lost" by the Works Department, causing deliberate, endless delays. Not surprisingly, Griffin eventually gave up in frustration. The momentum he had created, however, was sufficient to ensure that the enduring local tradition of mediocrity did not modify his original layout too much. He left much that is good there, evidence of a vision wasted on a nasty, smug, myopic succession of "bottled ale and sandwich" guzzlers.

On May 9, 1927 the Duke of York opened Parliament House and the national capital was all set for the business of government. At the time, the population of Canberra was

less that 6,000, most of which were construction workers. As the city grew construction workers were replaced by public servants, today the largest occupational group in Canberra's population of 220,000. Who knows? Perhaps one of these days government will begin.

GENERAL INFORMATION

There is a **Tourist Information Centre** in Northbourne Avenue, ((06) 205-0044 or (008) 026-166, and the **Queanbeyan Tourist**

Information Centre is in Farrer Place, ((06) 298-0241.

For information and timetables on bus services contact **Action Bus Service**, ((06) 207-7611; on trains to Sydney phone ((06) 239-0111, and to Melbourne phone ((06) 247- 6355.

WHAT TO SEE AND DO

Dominating Canberra is **Lake Burley Griffin**, which was created artificially in 1964 by damming the Molongo River. The best way to get a feel for the city is to hire a bike from **Mr Spoke's Bike Hire**, ((06) 257-1188, located near the Acton Ferry Terminal and Commonwealth Avenue Bridge. The circum-

New South Wales

ference of the lake is 35 km (22 miles), an easy ride.

Roads in Canberra form a series of circles, linked by radiating boulevards.

The lake is bisected by Commonwealth Avenue, running through the two foci of the city, — Civic, the main business and shopping centre, and Capital Hill, which is dominated by the new **Parliament House**, ((06) 277-5399. The center-piece of the new Parliament House, opened in time for the bicentennial in 1988, is an 81 m (265 ft) flag pole which towers over the landscape. The build-

and watch Australian democracy at work from the public gallery, if Parliament is sitting. "Debate" consists of abuse, where words like "scumbag" are standard Australian political jargon, alternating with a mind-numbing drone from back-bench hacks. The best time to gaze is during Question Time at 2 pm, when the Opposition is given the opportunity to interrogate the incumbents who are judged by how well they defend themselves before attacking the Opposition. The contents of the responses are beside the point, it seems.

ing itself is understated, with part of it underground to maintain the original topography of Capital Hill. In the forecourt a 100,000 mosaic by Northern Territory artist Michael Tjakamarra Nelson represents an Aboriginal meeting place. The mosaic is surrounded by water, symbolizing Australia as an island-continent. In the Great Hall hangs a magnificent tapestry designed by Arthur Boyd, while in the Foyer and scattered around the building are paintings by leading Australian artists, Sidney Nolan, Albert Tucker and Tom Roberts amongst them. In a display cabinet in the Members' Hall is a detailed copy of the *Magna Carta*. There are tours of the building, leaving every 30 minutes. Alternatively, visitors can take time out

The **National Gallery of Australia** in Parkes Place, ((06) 271-2519, overlooking the lake, holds an outstanding collection of over 70,000 Australian paintings, Aboriginal works including bark paintings and the works of foreign masters, like Jackson Pollock's controversial *Blue Poles* and paintings by Picasso, Warhol and Matisse. The gallery has eleven halls over three levels, and the top one is invariably devoted to indigenous art. Opening hours are between 10 am and 5 pm daily, and an admission-fee is charged. Major visiting shows are hosted, and an additional

Australia's new Parliament House and its setting on the shore of Lake Burley Griffin.

entrance fee is charged for a view of these exhibitions.

Next door to the Gallery is the **High Court** in King Edward Terrace, Parkes, ((06) 270-6811, where judges deliberate constitutional disputes; their decisions have shaped the changing relationship between the state and federal governments. Organized tours of the High Court are possible.

Further around the lake shore is the **National Library of Australia** in Parkes Place, ((06) 262-1111, which is required by law to receive a copy of every book, newspaper

and magazine published in Australia. In its keeping are one and a half million books and thousands of audio recordings. A changing exhibition of rare and historic documents in the library's collection is on display in the Exhibition Gallery.

The nearby **Royal Australian Mint** in Dennison Street, Deakin, ((06) 202-6999, provides a glimpse of the past with its rare coin collection dating back to the days of Spanish galleons. On a more up-to-date note visitors can also watch the mint make the country's money. Unfortunately no free souvenirs are offered.

To gain an appreciation of the early contributions made by Australia to cinema from its genesis at the turn of the century, visit the **National Film and Sound Archive** in McCoy Circuit, Acton, ((06) 267-1711. The exhibition hall has continuous screenings of newsreels and films from its collection; the Archive is housed in an Art Deco building

designed by Walter Haywood Morris in 1929, constructed of Hawkesbury River sandstone and featuring a foyer stained glass skylight with a stylized platypus as its center-piece. Opening hours are 9:30 am to 4 pm daily.

The **Australian National Botanic Gardens** is on the lower slopes of Black Mountain, three kilometers (two miles) west of the business district. The largest collection of native flora in Australia can be seen in the gardens. About 170,000 plant species from every corner of the country are on show. Visitors can walk through a rain forest that thrives in a former gully thanks to hundreds of fine mist sprays controlled by a time-switch. One of several trails leads past trees labeled to explain how they were used by the Aborigines.

Above the gardens is the **Black Mountain Tower**, a 195 m (640 ft) telecommunication tower and major Canberra landmark open to the public, and providing a panoramic view of Canberra and the surrounding landscape. The best place to go is the revolving **Tower Restaurant**, ((06) 248-6152.

More than 60 countries have diplomatic representation in the national capital. Missions have been built in the style of the country in question. For example, the Japanese embassy is set in traditional gardens, the Thai embassy is a landmark with its elevated roof and gold-colored tiles and the Italian embassy blends modern design with inspiration from ancient Rome. Lovers of kitsch will find themselves in Paradise.

WHERE TO STAY

Expensive
Canberra has few distinguished hotels, but an exception is the **Hyatt Hotel Canberra** in Commonwealth Avenue Yarralumla, ((06) 270-1234, (008) 222-188, fax: (06) 281-5998. The hotel has an exterior in the so-called garden pavilion style, its interior containing many Art Deco features. Another hotel with character is the **Olims Canberra Hotel** at the corner of Ainslie and Limestone Avenues, Braddon, ((06) 248-5511, (008) 020-016, fax: (06) 247-0864, set around a pleasantly landscaped courtyard.

The Snowy Mountains, near Canberra, are popular in spring and autumn for outdoor recreation.

Moderate

The **Forrest Motor Inn** at 30 National Circuit, ℂ (06) 295-3433, fax: (06) 295-2119, and **Regency Motor Inn** at 47 McMillan Crescent, Griffth, ℂ (06) 295-2700, fax: (06) 295-0827, are modern hotels on the Parliament side of Lake Burley Griffin.

Inexpensive

Not far out of the city is the **Red Cedar Motel** at the corner of Stirling Avenue and Aspinall Street, Watson, ℂ (06) 241-3222, (008) 020-621, fax: (06) 241-2355, off the main highway in a quiet suburban setting. A little further out of town, in Queanbeyan, is the **Burley Griffin Motel** at 147 Uriarra Road, ℂ (06) 297-1211, fax: (06) 297-3083.

WHERE TO EAT

A popular pastime in Canberra is going to restaurants frequented by political figures and watching them engage in the character-assassination of a party leader or plotting the destruction of a Minister. Some guides even include a list of politicians who frequent listed restaurants. You can usually identify the politicians as they spend most of dinner whispering across the table and are usually accompanied by a following of flunkies, although I may be confusing these acolytes with food tasters, a wise precaution employed by most politicians.

Fringe Benefits at 54 Marcus Clarke Street, ℂ (06) 247-4042, is one of the best restaurants in Canberra with an imaginative menu of Mediterranean dishes.

Jehangir Indian Restaurant at 15 Swinger Hill Shops in Mawson, ℂ (06) 290-1159, specializes in dishes from Northern India and the service is friendly. Joseph Cotter is a Canberra institution and widely respected as a top Indian chef. Unfortunately the location of his latest venture, **Geetanjali** in Duff Place, Deakin, ℂ (06) 285-2505, is out of the way but at least bookings are only required at weekends. It is rumored that at one dinner party, members of the governing party concluded a deal to overthrow the incumbent Prime Minister over *gulub jamun* and coffee.

The **Hyatt Hotel Promenade Cafe** in Commonwealth Avenue, ℂ (06) 270-1234, has excellent food and their desserts are just wonderful.

HOW TO GET THERE

Both major domestic airlines run regular flights into Canberra from Melbourne and Sydney: there are less-frequent flights from Brisbane and Adelaide.

Bus Australia, Pioneer and Greyhound stop at Canberra on their Melbourne- to-Sydney route: Greyhound also connects with Adelaide. Trip durations are four and a half hours to Sydney, nine hours to Melbourne and sixteen and half hours to Adelaide.

By car Canberra is 286 km (177 miles) from Sydney along the Hume Highway: turn off just after Goulburn.

Canberra is 653 km (404 miles) from Melbourne, and the turn-off from the Hume Highway is near Yass. If you are not in a hurry it is possible to take the scenic route to Canberra from Melbourne on the Princes Highway east through Gippsland to Cann River, and north onto the Cann Valley Highway which passes the **Coopracambra National Park**. There is a short unmade section of road (12 km or 7 miles) after crossing the New South Wales border, where Monaro Highway leads over the Great Dividing Range and into Canberra.

FESTIVALS AND SPORTING EVENTS

MARCH   The **Canberra Festival** is a ten-day party featuring concerts in the parks and outdoor art exhibitions. A highlight is the Birdman Rally, where would-be aviators try out their home-made man-powered flying machines over Lake Burley Griffin. While the winner gets $20,000 prize money — the losers encounter a degree of humidity as their creations plunge into the lake.

SEPTEMBER/OCTOBER   Commonwealth Park is transformed for the **Floriade**, when 2.3 hectares (5.6 acres) are planted with about half a million flowers in a floral display unmatched anywhere in the country. Private gardens are opened to the public and there are talks and demonstrations on every aspect of gardening.

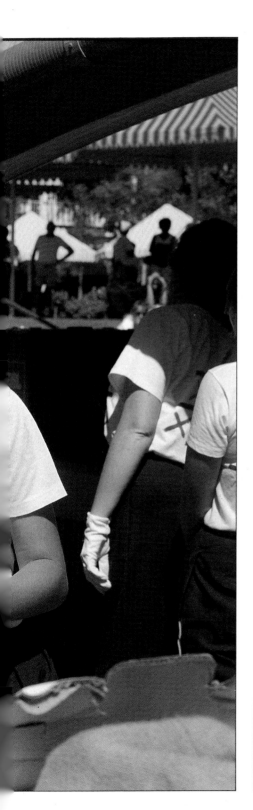

Queensland

Paradise and
Beyond

TO MOST southerners, Queensland is another country. Its inhabitants are stereotyped as slow-talking and ultra conservative. There is a hint of truth in this: the contrary north-east shares similarities with the Deep South in the United States. The government until quite recently was run by an incorrigibly independent and ruthlessly canny politician called Joh Bjelke-Petersen. Before him there was the reactionary Labor premier, Vince Gair.

Despite Queensland's reputation for archaic politics its people are as warm and friendly as the climate. Southerners come north and are quickly seduced by the informality and kindness of the Queenslanders.

BRISBANE

Brisbane is a sub-tropical city, and mango trees and banana palms adorn many front gardens: the older houses are built on stilts to allow cooling breezes to circulate on sweltering days.

In the afternoon children scamper home from school barefoot, their shoes in their school bags, while in the evening men return home from the office wearing shorts and long socks, most likely without their ties. As the final rays of sunlight penetrate the jacaranda foliage heavy with lavender flowers, the first fruit bats arrive to feast on ripe mangoes.

BACKGROUND

Brisbane began its days as a penal settlement for convicts who had re-offended after exile to Australia. Soldiers and recalcitrant convicts first established a settlement on Moreton Bay in 1824, an unsuitable site; the following year they moved up the Brisbane River to the spot where the city center stands today. The convict population never exceeded 1,000 and by 1839 their number had reduced to 29; on 11 February 1842 it became a free settlement.

In 1859, Moreton Bay District, as Queensland was then known, separated from New South Wales to become a colony in its own right.

In the early days there was constant friction between the local Aborigines and the

white settlers: in 1845 several tribes forged an alliance under the leadership of Dundalli, who led a guerrilla campaign against the colony for the next nine years.

Once the hinterland had been opened in the face of sometimes determined opposition from the Aborigines, the rural wealth helped Brisbane grow. Cattlemen from New South Wales drove their herds north to the wide plains and tableland, occupying large tracts of grazing land. The discovery of gold and the establishment of a successful sugar industry added to the colony's wealth, but

the expansion of coal exports after World War II, and the more recent tourist boom have make Queensland an important powerhouse in Australia's economy.

GENERAL INFORMATION

The **Queensland Government Travel Centre** at the corner of Adelaide and Edwards Streets, ((07) 221-6111 provides information and takes booking on attractions anywhere in Queensland. The **Brisbane Visitors and Convention Centre** is located on the ground floor of the Town Hall opposite King George Square, ((07) 221-8411, and services Brisbane only.

Information is also available about public transport:

Buses   ((07) 13-22-32.
Trains   ((07) 13-12-30.
Ferries   ((07) 235 1632.

ABOVE and OPPOSITE: Australia's favorites entertain the kids at Brisbane's Lone Pine Sanctuary.

WHAT TO SEE AND DO

Central City Precinct

The shopping and business districts are bounded by a bend in the Brisbane River, with the cultural and recreational attractions concentrated on the opposite south bank.

Overlooking the city in Wickham Terrace is **The Old Windmill**, a reminder of the city's convict past. Built in 1828 to crush corn it did not work because of a

Edward Street intersects **Queen's Street Mall**, a major shopping precinct. It continues along Queen Street down to the river where you can see the French Renaissance-style **Parliament House**, built in 1868.

Behind Parliament House are the **Old Botanic Gardens**, first used by convicts for vegetables. The southern tip jutting into the river is still known as **Garden Point**. The first Director of the Botanic Gardens laid them out much as they appear today, and you can still walk down the avenue of bunya pines he planted.

design fault: the sails were removed and convicts put to work on a treadmill to crush the corn. Offenses as trivial as using "disgusting language" and "insolence" earned convicts 14 hours of back-breaking shifts on the treadmill.

Walk down the hill to Edward Street which leads into the city. Just over the railway bridge running between Ann and Adelaide Streets is **Anzac Square**, the focal point of which is a rotunda of Doric columns. Built in 1930, the **Shrine of Memories** is dedicated to Australian soldiers who died during the First World War.

ABOVE: The Mall, LEFT Brisbane's traffic-free thoroughfare. RIGHT: One of the four bridges which link the center with the south of the city.

Queenslanders love the beach; for many years Brisbanites envied the southern capitals of Perth, Adelaide, Melbourne and Sydney their beach suburbs, when the solution to this shortcoming arose in the form of **Southbank**: located on the opposite side of Brisbane River from the city is Kodak Beach, part of a 16-hectare (40-acre) recreational development. Within the parkland displays of different ecosystems can be explored, where it is possible to walk through the **Gondwana Rainforest Sanctuary** or swim in a giant lagoon. The **Butterfly House** can be entered, giving literal meaning to "butterfly kisses," and the **Formal Gardens** with beautiful displays have ornamental fountains. On weekends, concerts and street theater entertain visitors and in the **Sun-**

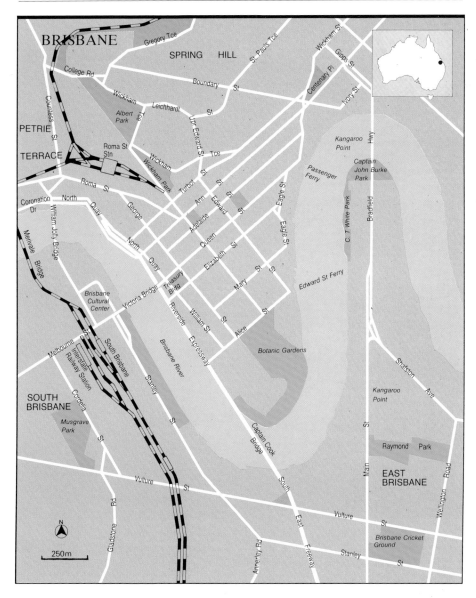

corp **Piazza** you can choose any one of the 18 restaurants or cafes for a good meal or just a coffee. Admission to Southbank is free, although there may be a charge for some events and exhibitions. For information on entertainment, ring ✆ (07) 867-2020.

Just north-west of the complex is the **Queensland Cultural Centre**, including the **Queensland Art Gallery** with a good collection of colonial paintings. Next door is the **Queensland Museum**, **Performing Arts Complex** and the **State Library of Queens-**

land. Tours leave on the hour from 10 am to 4 pm, Monday to Saturday.

Historic houses

Unfortunately not much of early Brisbane survives within the city. For examples of colonial architecture travel 4 km (2 miles) from the center to see the **Early Street Historical Village** in Norman Park at 75 McIlwraith Avenue, ✆ (07) 398-6866 with examples from a slab hut to **Auchenflower House**, described as a Victorian gentleman's residence. The village is open daily and an admission-fee is charged. The Discalced Carmelite Nuns once inhabited Auchenflower House but in the 1960s moved to **Ormiston House**, built in 1854. After the interior was restored Ormiston House on Wellington Street was opened to the public; the house and grounds can be inspected on Sundays between 1:30 pm and 4:30 pm from March through November. An admission-fee is payable.

Newstead House is situated in parkland overlooking the Brisbane River at Breakfast

Elsewhere in the park are over 80 types of native wild animals, all in a natural bushland setting. You can hand-feed the kangaroos and flightless emus, an ostrich-like bird, or get a close look at hedgehog-like echidnas or wombats. A launch leaves Hayles Wharf at North Quay on the Brisbane River daily at 1.15 pm, with additional departures on Sunday. Alternatively take a bus from "Koala Platform" that leaves the Myer Center hourly.

A few kilometers past the sanctuary is the **Mt. Coot-tha Reserve and Botanic Gardens**

Creek, ((07) 252-7373. Built in 1846, it has been totally restored and was once the unofficial Government House, being the Government Resident's home. Sit out on the verandah and enjoy a Devonshire tea of scones, jam and cream. Again, an admission-fee is charged.

Parks and Sanctuaries

Can anyone resist cuddling a koala bear? Eleven kilometers (seven miles) upriver of the city at Fig Tree Pocket live more than a hundred of them in the **Lone Pine Koala Sanctuary** on Jesmond Road, ((07) 241-4419. You can have your photograph taken holding one—but watch those claws which can make the cuddling rather less cuddly.

on Mt. Coot-tha Road. A mixture of parklands and forest, the 57-hectare (140-acre) reserve is Australia's largest sub-tropical Botanic Gardens in which the collection includes plants from native rain forests set around lagoons and ponds connected by streams, and vegetation found in the more arid zones of Queensland. Opening hours are from 8 am to 5 pm.

BRISBANE BY NIGHT

A few years ago a copy of *Playboy* magazine was banned in Queensland, as a result of which Queenslanders were thought by southerners to be prissy and straight-laced, but once the sun sinks below the horizon,

Brisbane kicks up its heels and starts to party.

C.L.U.B. Obsession in the Charleton Hotel at 688 Ipswich Road, Annerley jives until 3 am, and in Petrie Terrace the **Brisbane Underground** features live music on Friday, Saturday and Sunday. **Lexington Queen** at the corner of Albert and Queen Streets, and **Friday's** at Riverside centre in Eagle Street are two of Brisbane's classier nightspots.

Several pubs and clubs have excellent jazz. The **Brisbane Jazz Club** in Annie Street, Kangaroo Point, has live music on week-

The main shops are on **Queen Street** which is closed to traffic between George and Edward Streets. Converted into an imaginative mall it has an information kiosk for visitors, and off it is the **Myer Centre**, whose atriums, balconied walkways and large choice of shops make it a delight.

A rash of redevelopment has resulted in several new shopping complexes such as the **City Plaza** on the corner of Ann and

ends; for rock music try the **Mary Street Nightclub** at 138 Mary Street, or **St. Paul's Tavern** on Wharf Street.

The best way to find who is playing where is to consult Thursday's *Brisbane Courier-Mail* for its "What's on in Town" section.

For something more racy, **The Red Garter** at 693 Ann Street in Fortitude Valley has what are politely called "exotic dancers."

There is theater at the **Culture Centre**, with a full program of plays and concerts and the **Brisbane Arts Theatre** is on Petrie Terrace.

Several tours of the city are on offer; **Sunstate Day Tours**, ((07) 236-3355, takes you to a woolshed bush dance or nightclub tour.

George Streets, which has almost 60 specialty shops and open-air cafes. **Rowes Arcade**, off Post Office Square, has an Edwardian charm with dark cedar paneling and stained glass windows. A good place to buy Australiana is **Riverside Centre** and **Waterfront Place** on Eagle Street. There are also good restaurants here.

Every Sunday a **market** sets up outside the Riverside Complex, where stallholders sell a variety of arts and crafts and food-stall vendors provide sustenance to shoppers at the end of their tether.

OPPOSITE: The domes of Australia's largest planetarium in Brisbane's Mt Coot-tha Botanic Gardens. ABOVE: View south from the city center.

Queensland has its own opal fields and a number of shops in Brisbane specialize in these; black and white opals are on sale at **Opal World** in the Queen Street mall, ((07) 229-9589.

SPORT

Basketball is popular in Queensland, where the Brisbane Bullets attract a good crowd when they play National Basketball League games at the **Boondall Entertainment Centre**.

Queenslanders are torn between the three codes of football. None predominates. Rugby league is played at **Lang Park** at Milton and at the ANZ Stadium at Nathan, and the "Gabba" is the home of the local Australian Football League team, the *Brisbane Bears*. Rugby union is played at Ballymore Park at Herston.

During winter Brisbane's climate is perfect for horse racing, unlike the south which goes into virtual hibernation. Race meetings are held at **Eagle Farm** and **Doomben**, with several major race meetings occurring in between June and August.

WHERE TO STAY

Luxury

For a treat stay at **The Beaufort Hotel** in Edward Street, ((07) 221-1999, (008) 773-700, fax: (07) 221-6895, which couldn't be in a nicer spot: it overlooks the Brisbane River and Botanic Gardens. The hotel has three restaurants and two bars to choose from at night.

Stay in a quintessential Brisbane house with its white wooden verandah, set in a tropical garden. **Boomajarril** at 58 Derby Street, Hendra, ((07) 268-5764, fax: (07) 268-2064, is a colonial guesthouse which provides accommodation and meals.

Self-contained and in the center of town, is the **Mayfair Crest** on King Street Square, ((07) 229-9111, (008) 777-123, fax: (07) 229-9618. It has restaurants, bars, the nightclub **Spillanes** and shops all under one roof.

As you walk into the **Brisbane Hilton** at 190 Elizabeth Street, ((07) 231-3131, fax: (07) 231-3199, you immediately notice its atrium which is covered a towering 25 floors above the lobby.

Moderate

At 239 Wickham Terrace is the **Tower Mill Motor Inn**, ((07) 832-1421, (008) 806-553, fax: (07) 835-1013, a multi-storey motel with good views from the balconies off its rooms. Closer to the center of town is the **Wickham Terrace Motel** at 491 Wickham Terrace, ((07) 839-9611, (008) 773-069, fax: (07) 832-5348, in a quiet parkland location.

Six kilometers (four miles) from the city and a convenient walk to the Eagle Farm Racecourse is the **Raceways Motel** at 66 Kent Street, Hamilton, ((07) 268-4355, (008) 077-474, fax: (07) 868-1640.

Inexpensive

There are several economical hotels and backpacker hostels in New Farm. **Atoa House** at 143 Nugee Road, ((07) 268-2823, and **Bridge Inn** at 196 Bowen Terrace, ((07) 358-5000, provide basic accommodation.

WHERE TO EAT

The **Bays Seafood Restaurant** at 147 Alexandra Road, Clayfield, ((07) 262-5250, is located in a fine old building with the wide verandahs, typical of Queensland. Local mud crabs are a speciality of **Gambaro's** at 33 Caxton Street, Perrie Terrace, ((07) 369-9500. For spectacular views of Brisbane take Sir Samuel Griffith Drive to Mt. Coot-tha and enjoy a top meal at the **Summit Restaurant**, ((07) 367-2568.

Opposite the Botanic Gardens in the Heritage Hotel, is **Kabuki**, ((07) 221-2333, in the Heritage Hotel a *teppan-yaki* restaurant where the food is cooked in front of you.

Across the river on Southbank's broadwalk is **Ned Kelly's Tucker Restaurant**, ((07) 846-1880. It serves such local dainties as emu, crocodile and witchetty grubs if you dare, which enthusiasts describe as tasting a little like chicken. There are many more good restaurants at Southbank to choose from, most of which are moderately priced.

Several inexpensive restaurants are in South Brisbane. Vegetarian meals can be obtained from **Squirrels** at 190 Melbourne

OPPOSITE: Exuberant Gold Coast garden shop TOP, and BOTTOM a king size chess game at Surfers' Paradise.

Street, ((07) 844-4603, and honest pub food at the **Sly Fox Hotel** at 73 Melbourne Street, ((07) 846-5930, a favorite hang-out for backpackers.

HOW TO GET THERE

There are daily train services to Brisbane from Sydney taking about 14 hours and air services from most state capital cities, while the bus from Sydney takes 16 hours.

By car Brisbane can be reached from Sydney via the Pacific Highway or inland on the New England Highway: the trip takes about 15 hours.

GOLD COAST

An hour's drive south of Brisbane along the Pacific Highway is Australia's answer to Miami. Located just 42 km (26 miles) from Brisbane, the Gold Coast is Australia's most famous playground. It provides visitors with an abundance of sun, surf and sand. This glitzy, brash and unashamedly hedonistic resort caters to all the needs of both the well-heeled and the average holiday-maker.

GENERAL INFORMATION

There are several sources of information about attractions along the Gold Coast. The **Gold Coast Visitors and Convention Bureau** at 105 Upton Street, Bundall, ((075) 931-199, and information kiosks in Cavill Mall, Surfers' Paradise, as well as in Marine Parade, Tweed Heads, have a wide range of information about the region.

WHAT TO SEE AND DO

The Gold Coast runs southwards from Brisbane to the New South Wales border through a string of resort towns.

For decades it has been colonized by southerners seeking escape from the rigors of winter. More recently, people retiring are moving north seeking a permanent place in the sun. During the 1970s and 1980s this led to an explosion of development along the magnificent beaches of the Gold Coast: some would say too much development.

The number of visitors attracted annually to this popular holiday destination now exceeds the permanent population of Queensland.

Centered on **Surfers' Paradise** (known as just "Surfers"), high-rise buildings have sprouted along the sea-fronted highway, as though a slice of a major metropolis had been transplanted on the beach. With this ugly development have come streets jammed with traffic, unable to cope with ill-conceived, uncontrolled development. In consequence, behind the main highway it has now be-

come necessary to have a system of canals allowing more people access to the water. At private jetties are boats moored at the ends of the gardens backing onto canals. It may be pleasant but is scandalous neglect of a scenically beautiful asset.

Despite its frenetic pace and indiscriminate development the influx of so many visitors to the Gold Coast has its benefits: the area has more major man-made attractions than any other tourist region in Australia. The whole family can be kept constantly entertained here.

Watch dolphins jump through hoops, skiers perform acrobatics on water or divers hand-feed sharks at **Seaworld** at The Spit Main Beach, 3 km (2 miles) north of Surfers'

Paradise, ((075) 882-222. You can observe sea lions and whales from close-by and plenty of rides are available to keep children (and adults) of all ages amused. A monorail takes visitors around the 150-hectare (370-acre) park. Admission is $30 for adults and $19.50 for children.

The revival of the Australian motion picture industry has inspired **Movie World**, located 16 km (10 miles) north-west of Surfers' Paradise at Oxenford, ((075) 733-999. There are tours of special effects studios, where all is revealed and stuntmen thrill the assem-

A wildlife reserve worth visiting is the **Currumbin Sanctuary** at Currumbin Beach 19 km (12 miles) south of Surfers', ((075) 341-266, where you can help feed the flock of brightly colored wild lorikeets. Feeding times are from 8 am to 9:30 am and 4 pm to 5 pm. Kangaroos, wallabies and other Australian wildlife wander freely around the reserve where there are educational displays for children. On the way back into Surfers' is the **Burley Heads National Park** with its easy walking tracks: in winter humpback whales can be seen off this part of the coast as well.

bled multitudes with death-defying feats. Anyone who goes on the $13 million Batman Adventure ride will not readily forget the excitement, admission being $31 for an adult and $20 for children up to the age of 13.

Dreamworld is another theme park, located 17 km (10 miles) north of Surfers' Paradise at Coomera, ((075) 731-133. On this 24-hectare (60-acre) site visitors can take a cruise on Captain Sturt's paddlewheeler, enter the excitement of exploring the Eureka gold mine or be totally immersed in the spectacular Coca-Cola IMAX Theatre with its six storey screen, where the visual effects makes viewers feel part of the picture. Admission costs $30 for an adult and $19 for children.

At night Surfers' goes into high gear with its restaurants dotting the sidewalks and catering for every taste from gourmet to junk foods. There are many choices of what to do after dinner: take in a show, go nightclubbing or have a fling at **Jupiter's Casino**.

Where to Stay

Packages to the Gold Coast fly tourists from any state capital cities to Surfers' and provide a week's accommodation at discounted prices.

Despite miles of high-rise development, the vast expanse of soft surf and sand dominate the shoreline at Surfers' Paradise.

There are a large number of luxury hotels and apartments along the Gold Coast. Most are highrise and although they may lack character, the sea views from the upper floors are quite magnificent. In Surfers' Paradise **ANA Hotel Gold Coast** at 22 View Avenue, ((075) 791-000, (008) 074-440, fax: (075) 701-260, and **Ramada Hotel** at the corner of the Gold Coast Highway and Hanlan Street, ((075) 793-499, (008) 074-317, fax: (075) 398-370, provide a high standard of accommodation.

At least the motels are not highrise, and the **Chelsea Motor Inn** at 2990 Gold Coast

Highway, ((075) 389-333, 132-400, fax: (075) 923-709, and the **Pink Poodle Motel** at 2903 Gold Coast Highway, ((075) 399-211, fax: (075) 399-136, are just 150 m (500 ft) from the beach.

Outside the school holiday period there is keen competition between motels in the lower price bracket, and driving down the Gold Coast Highway you should be able to pick up significant out-of-season discounts.

For budget accommodation good deals can be obtained by shopping locally. If you decide to stay on the Gold Coast for a week

or more, renting a self-contained apartment is an inexpensive option. Prices start at $200 a week for a two bedroom unit. Bookings for apartments can be made through **Broadbeach Real Estate** at 2703 Main Place, ((075) 390-000, fax: (075) 383-280, and **Coolangatta Realty** at 72–74 Griffith Street, ((075) 352-000, fax: (075) 361-084. It is best to book well in advance.

HOW TO GET THERE

The Gold Coast Highway branches off the Pacific Highway at Gaven, and Surfers' Paradise is an hour's drive from Brisbane. There is an airport at Coolangatta at the southern end of the Gold Coast which receives direct flights from Brisbane, Melbourne, Sydney and Adelaide. There are also regular bus services from Brisbane.

SUNSHINE COAST

The Sunshine Coast lies to the north of Brisbane and is more sedate than its brash counterpart to the south. Several resort towns, a string of beaches and rocky headlands make up the 56 km (35 miles) of Sunshine Coast. There has been some development modeled on Surfers' Paradise, but mercifully restricted. The Sunshine Coast, therefore, has many of the benefits of the Gold Coast without the crowds and the pace is more relaxed.

The Mecca in the Sunshine Coast is **Noosa**, with its chic restaurants and exclusive boutiques. Hasting Street, lined with exotic flowering trees, is where people promenade or just sit outside in a sidewalk cafe, being really for the well-off. It also attracts younger people and those in search of good surf; some less expensive accommodation and eating houses are available to meet their needs.

The main beach runs parallel to Hasting Street, with the best restaurants and hotels on the east side of the road overlooking the ocean.

The **Noosa National Park**, at the northeast end of Hasting Street, has a path which takes you along the cliffs to Granite Bay with its pebble beach and the popular nudist beach at Alexandria Bay.

Flocks of rainbow lorikeets fly in to be fed by visitors to Currumbin sanctuary on the Gold Coast.

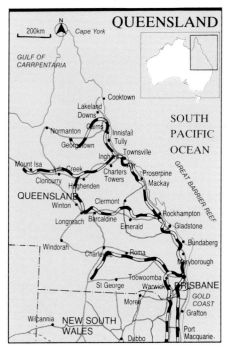

QUEENSLAND

200km Cape York

GULF OF
CARRPENTARIA

Cooktown

Lakeland
Downs

Normanton Cairns Innisfail
Geotown Tully
Townsville

SOUTH
PACIFIC
OCEAN

Mount Isa
Creek
Cloncurry Hughenden
Charters
Towers
Proserpine
Mackay

QUEENSLAND
Winton Clermont
Longreach Barcaldine Rockhampton
Emerald Gladstone
Windorah Roma Bundaberg
Charlev Maryborough
Toowoomba
St George Warwick BRISBANE
Moree GOLD
COAST
Grafton
Wilcannia NEW SOUTH
WALES Port
Dubbo Macquarie

race, ((074) 497-311, and **Noosa Riverside** at 175 Gympie Terrace, ((074) 497-551.

HOW TO GET THERE

There is a regular bus service to Noosa Heads, the trip taking about two hours.

THE SUGAR COAST

North of the Sunshine Coast plantations of sugar cane grow on the flat coastal plain. At harvest time the sky is alight with cane burning, clearing the fields for mechanized harvesting. Most of the work is done by machines but once this was a labor intensive industry. Before Federation in 1901 and the implementation of the White Australia Policy, many cane-cutters were Melanesian or Asian. This made for interesting days on the Sugar Coast, as town names like Melekula and Tanna remind us.

GENERAL INFORMATION

The **Maryborough Tourist Information Centre** at 30 Ferry Street, ((071) 214-111, is open daily.

Open only weekdays, however, the **Bundaberg District Tourism Centre** at the corner of Mulgrave and Bourbong Streets, ((071) 522-343 provides general information on the area.

The **Hervey Bay Information Centre**, ((071) 289-387, will advise on the best times to view whales.

WHAT TO SEE AND DO

To get a feel of what it must have been like in those boom times when sugar built fortunes, visit **Maryborough**, founded in 1865. A fine example of its early architecture is **Baddow House** at 364 Queen Street which is open to the public. Built in 1883, this two storey mansion lost some of its features during the war but there is enough left to justify a visit. Walk around the streets to see other examples of Maryborough's early architecture, featuring ornate wooden verandahs.

Bundaberg on the Burnett River is one of the few sugar towns that all Australians

Inland from the Sunshine Coast are the **Glasshouse Mountains**. These curiously-shaped rocky peaks rise some 500 m (1640 ft) out of the surrounding scrub. Dedicated rock climbers will find challenges among the sheer faces and there are walks to the lower reaches of the mountains along rough paths. Shrouded in mist, the Glasshouse Mountains have a mysteriousness when viewed from a distance.

WHERE TO STAY

Noosa generally attracts up-market visitors and most of the accommodation is priced accordingly. The best hotels are along Hasting Street facing Laguna Bay. The **Sheraton Noosa**, ((074) 494-888, (008) 073-535, fax: (074) 492-230, and **Netanya Noosa**, ((074) 474-722, offer luxury accommodation and direct access to the beach.

Moderately priced accommodation is available in **Myuna Holiday Apartments** set back from the beach at 19 Katharina Street, ((074) 475-588.

If you are willing to travel five kilometers (two miles) from Noosa, stay at Noosaville which has inexpensive motel accommodation at **Palm Tree Lodge** at 233 Gympie Ter-

have heard of because of one of its other products — Bundaberg Rum, a hearty dark spirit from a distillery attached to one of the town's five sugar mills. A visit would not be complete without a visit to the **Rum Distillery** in Avenue Street. The storage shed attached to the mill is the longest in Australia, being the length of four football fields. There are guided tours on the hour from 10 am to 3 pm weekdays and 10 am to 1 pm on weekends. An admission fee is charged.

The Sugar Coast has two attractions unrelated to sugar which draw thousands of visitors to the region every year.

Fraser Island is the largest sand island in the world, being 120 km (75 miles) long and between 25 and 50 km (16 to 31 miles) wide. The island takes its name from Eliza Fraser, who, with her husband Captain Fraser were shipwrecked there in 1836. Captured by Aborigines, the survivors were used as slaves. Only Eliza got away, escaping after three weeks. Her ordeal so unhinged her that she was eventually committed to a lunatic asylum.

As you would expect, Fraser Island has excellent beaches. There are colored dunes, some towering 240 m (790 ft) above the island, while inland are scrub and over forty small freshwater lakes which attract all manner of birdlife. Many people explore in four wheel drive vehicles or just take to its walking tracks. The **Great Sandy National Park** preserves 184,000 hectares (454,500 acres) of the northern part of the island.

Fraser Island is opposite **Hervey Bay**. Between June and October humpback whales migrate along the coast towards warmer waters in the north to mate and give birth. They can be seen off Hervey Bay, one of the best places anywhere to see these great mammals.

A third of Australia's sugar crop is grown in the canefields surrounding **Mackay**, 334 km (210 miles) from Rockhampton. As the "sugar capital of Australia" it would be amiss not to have a look at a working sugar plantation while in the region. **Poistone Cane Farm** on Homebush Walkerstone Road is 20 km (12 miles) inland from Mackay, ((079) 597-359. Visitors can see every stage of sugar production on this farm and finish the day with a cool drink of sugarcane juice. Back in

town see the exquisite blooms of orchids in the conservatory at **Queens Park**, which is also a showcase of ferns and exotic tropical flowers.

Mackay, together with **Proserpine**, 130 km (80 miles) to the north, are the departure points for the popular Whitsunday Passage islands. Tourist information on them can be obtained at nearby **Airlie Beach** from **Tourism Whitsunday** at the corner of Shute Harbour and Mandalay Roads, ((079) 466-673, open weekdays only. Airlie Beach is also a good place to learn scuba diving and there are a number of schools to choose from.

Crocodiles were sunning themselves on the banks of Ross Creek when the first settlers arrived to establish **Townsville**. Today, only 120 years later, the city is the third largest in Queensland and the crocodiles have had to find a more secluded river bank to bask. Visitors can get the best view of Townsville from **Castle Hill**, a 300 m (980 ft) red granite outcrop which rises steeply immediately behind the business district. The vantage point looks down upon on the growing city which has nonetheless managed to retain much of its colonial elegance.

The **Great Barrier Reef Wonderland**, on Flinders Street East, ((077) 211-793, contains the world's largest coral reef aquarium and a touch tank where some hardier marine specimens can be handled.

For great food, the restaurants along **Fisherman's Wharf**, ((077) 211-838, in Townsville allow diners to enjoy a meal under the stars, or watch street theater and live entertainment. On Sunday morning, wander along Flinders Malls' **Cotters Market**, ((077) 220-380, North Queensland's largest arts and craft market.

From Townsville travel to **Paluma**, an hour's drive north. Discover **Crystal Creek**, a clear mountain stream which is fed from a waterfall half way up Mount Spec, and walk through its peaceful rain forest.

WHERE TO STAY

Moderately priced accommodation on Fraser Island is available at **Happy Valley**, ((071) 279-144, and **Eliza Sands**, ((071) 279-132.

At Mackay the **Dolphin Heads Resort** on Beach Road, ((079) 546-666, (008) 075-088, fax:

(079) 548-341, is surrounded by palms and has its own pool.

Staying on Magnetic Island is an attractive alternative to Townsville. **Arcadia Hotel Resort** at 7 Marine Parade, ((077) 785-177 or fax: (077) 785-939, is moderately priced, while **Picnic Bay Holiday Hotel** at 1 The Esplanade, is good value for money accommodation.

How to Get There

Townsville has an international airport which

coast, covering an area of approximately 215,000 sq km (83,200 sq miles) and consisting of 3,000 individual coral reefs.

The Reef is indisputably one of the natural wonders of the world.

The Reef is built on the calcium skeletons of billions of minute coral polyps laid down over thousands of years. Above the calcareous remains of its predecessors new coral grows, nurtured by the unique conditions on the eastern coastal strip — warm, clear, shallow waters rich in nutrients which promotes the diverse aquatic life in the coral:

receives twice weekly services from Europe and the United Kingdom, and Garuda Airlines flies in from Indonesia. There are frequent daily flights from the southern States.

Buses run along the Queensland coast, stopping at the major towns.

The Bruce Highway, starting at Brisbane, links all the towns along the north coast.

THE GREAT BARRIER REEF

Off the coast near Bundaberg is **Lady Elliott Island**. This marks the southern edge of the Great Barrier Reef which stretches a staggering 2,000 km (1,250 miles) up the

there are an estimated 1,500 types of fish and 400 species of coral polyps within its boundary. The colors of this underwater wonderland are stunning. Fish, as brilliant as jewels, glide between waving sponges and delicate coral formations. On the sea floor starfish and sea urchins forage in the underwater grottoes.

In and around the Reef are about 900 islands.

Cays are sterile coral outcrops which over the centuries have acquired a fertile surface layer on which grasses and shrubs have established themselves. Sand-filled

Some of the varieties of coral on the Great Barrier Reef. About 300 species are to be found.

lagoons have formed on these, providing a platform for exploring the underwater swirl of color and movement.

Only a handful of islands are cays, and only three — **Lady Elliott Island** 80 km (50 miles) from Bundaberg, **Heron Island** 81 km (50 miles) off Gladstone and **Green Island** 27 km (16 miles) from Cairns, have facilities for visitors. There are also a number of uninhabited low-lying coral cays around the Reef that can be visited. Many of the islands are national parks and permits are required to camp on them.

Along the Reef are ordinary islands unconnected with it and covered with thick vegetation. Resorts have been established on a number of these and the Reef is usually only a short trip away.

Scuba diving provides freedom to explore the sea bed at will. If you ever thought about taking up scuba diving, what better time to start than during a visit to the Great Barrier Reef? There are schools in all the major resorts catering for learners. A simpler way to explore is with a snorkel, and glass-bottomed boats can be hired to see the Reef without getting wet.

There are major resorts on the larger islands, most of which are owned by one specific company. Each offers total packages that include accommodation, meals (but not alcoholic drinks), use of aquatic sports equipment, scuba lessons and entertainment. Contact numbers are included below for each resort managed by a single company.

The **Keppel Island Group** are continental islands near Rockhampton. On **Great Keppel Island** guests can relax on one of its seventeen beaches, skip over the water on skis or go parasailing. At night there is leisurely dining in the **Admiral Keppel** and afterwards discoing at the **Anchorage Bar** or **Neptune Nightclub**. The resort is run by Qantas, ((079) 395-044, fax: (079) 391-775, and marketing is aimed at the younger crowd. **Wapparaeurra Haven**, ((079) 391-907, fax: (079) 393-464, provides inexpensive accommodation and appeals to families.

At **Middle Island**, 1.5 km (1 mile) from Great Keppel Island, is an **Underwater Observatory**, ((079) 394-191, which provides a fish-eye view of the hundreds of colorful species that swim these waters: it is open daily between 9 am and 4:30 pm, and an admission-fee is charged. Nearby **North Keppel Island** is more for locals looking for an inexpensive camping holiday.

Between Mackay and Proserpine is **Linderman Island**, ((079) 469-333, fax: (079) 469-598, a Club Med resort with a wide range of activities for holiday-makers of all ages. There are good walking tracks around the eight-square-kilometer (three-square-mile) island and good safe beaches.

The **Whitsunday Passage Islands** are a collection of about 70 islands with some of the best-developed resorts on the Great Barrier Reef, definitely not off the beaten track. If you want sights of the Reef handed to you on a platter then **Hamilton Island**, ((079) 469-999, (008) 075-110, fax: (079) 469-425, is the place. The resort facilities provide a good choice of restaurants and accommodation. See the Reef from a glass bottomed boat or hover over the coastline in a helicopter.

A seven kilometer (four mile) trip from Shute Harbour, and the main jumping-off point for the Whitsunday Passage, **South Molle Island**, ((079) 469-433, fax: (079) 469-580, provides a good range of activities and children are well looked after. Casual visitors and guests are welcome.

At the top end of the market is **Hayman Island**, ((079) 469-100, fax: (079) 469-410, which recently underwent a $250 million redevelopment and is well positioned for visits to the outer reef. The Whitsunday resort sits on the island's only flat area and looks out over a lagoon. At adjacent **Hook Island** there is an **Underwater Observatory**, ((079) 514-644, providing some of the best views of coral on the Reef. It is open 11 am to 2 pm, and an admission fee is charged.

Across Cleveland Bay lies **Magnetic Island**, a suburb of Townsville which takes just 40 minutes to reach by boat. Most of the island is a national park with 22 km (14 miles) of walking tracks. The cane toad is an introduced species which has reached plague proportions in Queensland. These ugly amphibians are raced at **Arcadia Hotel**

OPPOSITE: Flying low TOP over a tiny island resort and the turquoise waters of the Great Barrier Reef is an exciting taster to a visit to this great natural wonder. BOTTOM Sunning at Surfers' Paradise.

Resort, ℂ (077) 785-177, every Wednesday at 8 pm. Before the race, toads competing are auctioned off, so anyone can participate. There is a prize for the winner, but first he or she has to kiss the winning toad, none of whom to date has turned into a prince or princess. You can cap off the evening at **Trix** nightclub, which rocks on into the early hours.

One of the most beautiful islands along the coast, and one that hasn't suffered from inappropriate tourist development, is **Hinchinbrook Island,** ℂ (070) 688-585. The island can be reached by ferry from either Cardwell or Lucinda: it covers an area of 39,350 hectares (97,200 acres) and is the world's largest island national park. Exploring by foot has its rewards, as the terrain changes from coastal mangroves and sandy beaches to mountains in the interior, **Mt. Bowen** at 1142 m (3,745 ft) being the highest point. Camping is also possible.

Lizard Island is the most northerly resort on the Great Barrier Reef, 90 km (56 miles) north of Cooktown, ℂ (070) 603-999. Captain Cook visited the island in 1770, seeking a way through the reef. From the highest point on the island Cook saw the outer reef, only 15 km (9 miles) away where waves pound the edge of the continental shelf. Lizard serves as a base for marlin fishermen between September and November.

HOW TO GET THERE

The best time to go to is between April and October. Contact the Government Tourist Office for the most convenient hopping-off points to the various islands, some of which can be reached by air. It takes about 22 hours by train from Brisbane to Proserpine, nearest rail town to the Whitsundays.

To tour the reef take a launch or catamaran, leaving daily from Mackay. Airlie Beach is the main embarkation point: a visit to the Reef is on the itinerary of many long-distance coach tour operators.

FAR NORTH QUEENSLAND

Cairns is the perfect base from which to explore far north Queensland. It offers the Great Barrier Reef on one side, while inland are many attractions to cater to all tastes.

GENERAL INFORMATION

The **Far North Queensland Tourism** office is at the corner of Alphin and Sheridan Streets, ℂ (070) 513-588, and is open daily. The **Gulf Local Tourism** office at 55 Macleod Street, ℂ (070) 311-631, provides information on attractions in the Gulf of Carpenteria.

WHAT TO SEE AND DO

Going north, Cairns is the last stop of any consequence. Easily accessible, it has its own airport and is therefore a popular base from which to explore far north Queensland, Cape York and the Gulf Country. The main rail line ends at Cairns, as does the Bruce Highway.

Life in Cairns is casual and its inhabitants take it at a leisurely pace, advisable in a climate so often hot and humid.

From Trinity Harbour, cruise boats depart for the Great Barrier Reef which is at its closest point to the coast. The **Great Adventure Cruises** on Wharf Street, ℂ (070) 510-455, provides two trips a day to Green Island, Lizard Island and other attractions along the Reef.

Big game fishermen from around the world congregate in Cairns for the **Marlin Meet,** which coincides with the migration of these fighting fish along the outer side of the Great Barrier Reef. Celebrities of the ilk of Greg Norman are known to keep an annual appointment with the giant Black Marlin ready for battle off the Cairns coast.

These marvelous creatures can reach 4 m (14 ft) in length and weigh over 1000 lb, in which case they are known as "granders." The fishing season is from mid-September to mid-December, and at approximately $1,200 per day this is not a cheap pastime; packages include luxury accommodation aboard the mother ship and a floatplane to take you to where the fish are biting. At night, over cocktails, you can wind your companions up with yarns about the "one that got away." If you do happen to catch a Black Marlin, unless you insist on having it stuffed the captain will suggest that you release it so it can fight another day. It is important to have a good skipper on fishing expeditions and Ross McCubbin of **Lucky Strike Charters**, ((018) 735-570, comes highly recommended.

A leisurely way of seeing the attractions inland of the coast is on the **Kuranda Scenic Railway**, ((070) 526-249. From Cairns Railway Station, the 100-year-old train sluggishly winds its way up through 15 tunnels to the **Atherton Tableland**, a trip of 34 km (21 miles). The track clings to the face of the escarpment, passing through lush forest and over 40 bridges. The old beast wheezes past the edge of **Barron Falls**, after heavy rain a thundering torrent which plunges hundreds of meters into a gorge colored with rainbow-flecked mist. When in full flow, the **Stoney Creek Falls** is so close to you that its spray envelopes the track. There are several trips each day; you can take organized tours to the surrounding national park from **Kuranda**, described as the "village in the rain forest."

There are two roads to the isolated town of **Cooktown**. Going via Cape Tribulation requires a four-wheel drive because parts of inland road are rough tracks.

Cooktown is where Captain Cook first landed on the mainland: he had put in to land to repair the *Endeavour* after running aground on a coral reef. Not surprisingly, the main attraction in town is the **James Cook Historical Museum** at the corner of Helen and Fureaux Streets, ((070) 695-386. This has several displays and relics to acquaint visitors with the early history of the town.

Cape York Peninsula, the northernmost part of Australia, once formed a land bridge to New Guinea when the sea level was lower and Torres Strait shallower. As a result, its flora and fauna are closely related to those found in New Guinea.

The area starts at Cooktown on the east coast and takes in some of the wildest, most isolated country in Australia, the best way of seeing which is on an organized safari.

In the heart of the Gulf Country is one of the most curious train tracks in the world. It leads nowhere and serves no practical purpose. Starting at **Normanton**, the **Gulflan-**der winds 152 km (94 miles) inland to **Croydon**, once a gold town. It is a leisurely journey, and unscheduled stops are not because of mechanical breakdowns but rather the driver's desire to show his passengers something of interest near the track. The train leaves Normanton on Wednesday and returns from Croydon on Thursday. Bookings can be made at Normanton Station, ((077) 451-391, or at the **QR Travel Centre** in Cairns, ((070) 526- 249. In 1993 the Queensland Government tried to close down this line but decided otherwise in the face of the ensuing public outcry.

At the north of the Cape are approximately 5,000 **Torres Strait** Islanders occupying 17 **islands**. Pearling was a major industry in the nineteenth century and pearls are still a source of income among the islanders. Permission to visit them should be obtained from the traditional land owners.

WHERE TO STAY

As you would expect in a large tourist center like Cairns, there is a wide choice of accommodation to choose from.

Most of the luxury hotels are along the Esplanade overlooking the harbor. The **Pacific International** is at the corner of Spence Street and the Esplanade, ((070) 517-888, and **Tuna Towers** is at 145 Esplanade, ((070) 514-688. Moderately priced motels close to the center of town are the **Flying Horseshoe** at 281–289 Sheridon Street, ((070) 513-022, fax: (070) 512-761, and the **Inn at the Pink Motel** at 261–269 Sheridan Street, ((070) 514-800, fax: (070) 311-526. Inexpensive accommodation is available from **Compass** at 232 Mulgrave Road, ((070) 515-466.

About 75 km (47 miles) from Cairns is **Port Douglas**, a popular holiday spot. For total luxury stay at the **Sheraton Mirage Port Douglas** on Port Douglas Road, ((070) 995-888, (008) 073-535, fax: (070) 985-885.

There are several choices of moderately priced accommodation in Kuranda. The **Cedar Park Rainforest Resort** at 1 Cedar Park Road, ((070) 937-077, fax: (070) 937-841, is about 15 km (9 miles) out of town. Being off the main road this resort is filled only with the noises of the rain forest — gurgling of the Clohesy River, wind in the trees or the occasional screech of a sulfur crested cockatoo flying overhead. In town there is a mixture of good quality cabins and inexpensive bunkhouse-type accommodation at the **Kuranda Rainforest Resort** at 2 Greenhills Road, ((070) 937-555.

Most of the accommodation in the Torres Strait islands is on **Thursday Island**, the largest in the Torres Strait group. The **Jardine** at the corner of Normanby Street and Victoria Parade, ((070) 691-555, provides luxury accommodation, while the **Grand Hotel,** ((070) 691-557, claims that Somerset Maugham stayed there.

How to Get There

There are direct flights to Cairns from Townsville, Mackay, Gladstone, Alice Springs, Brisbane, Perth, Melbourne and Sydney.

There are four Qantas Australian flights a week out of Cairns to Thursday Island.

The train runs between Melbourne, Sydney, Brisbane and Cairns, the final leg of the journey taking 32 hours and leaving Brisbane on Saturday, Sunday, Tuesday and Thursday.

NATIONAL PARKS

General Information

For details of National Parks phone the **Queensland Department of Conservation and Heritage,** ((07) 227-7111 and the **National Parks Association of Queensland,** ((07) 870-8086.

What to See and Do

Lamington, 110 km (68 miles) west of Brisbane or 54 km (33 miles) from Surfers' Paradise is the State's first national park. It features dense sub-tropical rain forests and wet eucalypt forest. The best way to see the park is on foot by way of its numerous paths, taking time to visit some of its 500 waterfalls. Contact the local ranger, ((075) 333-584, for further details.

Mountainous, often mist-shrouded, **Eungella National Park** is a 45-minute drive

west from Mackay and takes its name from the local Aboriginal word for "land of cloud." The sound of water is ever-present as sparkling creeks splash over rocks and plunge down inaccessible mountain slopes into deep ravines. The luxuriant rain forest is carpeted with ferns, which thrive in this damp atmosphere. There are 25 km (16 miles) of walking tracks in the park for those who want to take a closer look at its beauty or the profusion of delicately colored birds that come to feed on berries and fruit.

Daintree, 111 km (69 miles) north of Cairns and 5 km (3 miles) north of Mossman is a wilderness area with limited access even for walkers. Winter is the best time to visit this park, and further information can be obtained from the park ranger, ((070) 519-811.

Girraween National Park, 34 km (21 miles) south of Stanthorpe is inland from the Gold Coast. **Balancing Rock**, a large spherical boulder that defies gravity, balances on level ground. Further information can be obtained from the park ranger, ((076) 845-157.

FESTIVALS AND SPORTING EVENTS

The Queensland Tourist and Travel Corporation sells an annual **Events Calendar** for $2, which provides details of all festivals and sporting events.

JANUARY At Alexandra Headland on the Sunshine Coast the **XXXX Surf Craft Carnival** provides a chance to see life-saving boats race through the surf.

MARCH For a long time the parochialism of Queensland's politicians made them a laughing stock, but since they have cleaned up their act the **Brisbane International Comedy Bonanza** will have to suffice.

APRIL Over the Easter holidays the Brisbane-to-Gladstone yacht race ends with the **Gladstone Harbour Festival**. Gladstone is 580 km (360 miles) north of Brisbane off the Bruce Highway.

MAY/JUNE **State of Origin** rugby match between Queensland and NSW.

MAY/JUNE The **Queensland Winter Racing Carnival** runs for a month from mid-May. Visitors can watch thoroughbreds pounding their way to the finishing line, and afterwards enjoy classical and jazz music put on for the festival around Brisbane.

MAY/JUNE The **Wintersun Festival** is held in the twin cities of Tweed Heads and Coolangatta on the border of NSW and Queensland. It reminds southerners that there is somewhere in Australia warm in June. In 1993 Miss Wintersun was won by Mr Damien Taylor, showing the world that Australia is not sexist.

JUNE Cooktown, 332 km (206 miles) north of Cairns, celebrates its namesake in the **Cook-**

SEPTEMBER The **Birdsville Picnic Races** is well known around the country. Birdsville is 1,569 km (973 miles) west of Brisbane near the South Australian border, and is in the middle of nowhere. In September this tiny non-town with a population of about 30 attracts over 3,000 race fans who fly in from all over Australia.

OCTOBER The **Fun in the Sun Festival** is held in Cairns, which is 1,717 km (1,065 miles) from Brisbane.

The Gold Coast lets down its hair during the **Tropicarnival Festival,** which climaxes

town Discovery Festival by re-enacting Cook's landing on this part of the coast.

JULY The **King of the Mountain Festival,** ((074) 851-164, in Pomona 150 km (93 miles) north of Brisbane features country "sports" such as tug or war, iron-man competitions and wood chopping.

AUGUST The **Mount Isa Rodeo** allows men to test their strength and skill against bucking and rearing animals who would certainly rather be quietly grazing in a field somewhere else.

AUGUST/SEPTEMBER The **Festival of Arts** has grown in stature since it opened at the Brisbane Cultural Centre and attracts leading performers from Australia and abroad in all spheres of the arts.

in a grand parade through the streets of Surfers' Paradise.

The **Warwick Rodeo** is a month long festival that culminates in the rodeo itself, which attracts rough-riders from Australia and overseas. Warwick is 160 km (99 miles) southwest of Brisbane.

ABOVE: Station hands LEFT in rodeo garb at Warwick Rodeo. RIGHT Aboriginal boy in ceremonial paint.

Northern Territory

It's All Outback

"CROC THREAT" screamed the headline in *The News*, the Northern Territory's main daily newspaper. The stories below told of a two-meter (6 ft) salt-water crocodile trapped in a pool at the foot of Twin Falls, of water buffalo bulls hunted from helicopters, and of a Greek migrant celebrating Easter by letting off sticks of dynamite. All these appeared in *The News* on a single day, revealing the wild and untamed nature of the region. There is more than a little truth in the old Australian saying that "all madmen travel north and once there can't get away."

There are few towns in the Territory, but 80,000 of its 130,000 population live in Darwin and Alice Springs. It is a place of great distances, where the doctor comes by plane, children take their classes by short wave radio and cattle are rounded using motorbikes or helicopters. The weather is tropical and can change from drought to flood overnight.

The landscape of the Territory can only be described as bizarre; over the aeons nature and geological forces have played with the earth's surface to create flamboyant rock masterpieces in red and ochre. Rivers have cut deep gorges through sandstone plateaux. Spectacular waterfalls tumble down vertical rock faces. And there is a lot of very flat land too: an awful lot!

DARWIN

There have been two major attempts to demolish Darwin. The first occurred during World War Two when the Japanese conducted 64 bombing raids with the loss of 243 lives. The second was on Christmas Eve of 1974 when Cyclone Tracy unleashed four hours of fury, flattening much of Darwin, injuring thousands and leaving 65 dead.

Darwin recovered from both these catastrophes, a tribute to the spirit of its inhabitants. Such persistence in the face of repeated disasters is evidence, for many Southerners, that its inhabitants are truly "madmen." But for the people of Darwin, to live anywhere else is unthinkable. Every setback only reinforces their links with this bizarre tropical town.

Set on a peninsula, Darwin's lusty fertility, tropical nonchalance and suburbs set in a colorful sea of bougainvillea, frangipani and poinsettia have an attraction that even an outsider can feel.

The best time to visit the Territory is during the Dry season, between May and October when the days are warm, the weather stable and the humidity relatively low. The rest of the year is the Wet season, when the monsoons bring rain and attendant lightening storms late in the afternoon and overnight, making the days humid.

GENERAL INFORMATION

The **Darwin Information Centre** at 33 The Smith Mall, ((089) 814-300, is open on weekdays between 8:45 am and 5 pm, on Saturdays between 9 am and 12:30 pm and on Sundays between 10 am and 1 pm from May to October. Accommodation can be arranged by the staff at the center.

WHAT TO SEE AND DO

Much of Darwin has been rebuilt since Cyclone Tracy. Although the city and its suburbs look relatively new this northern city, in reality a provincial town, does not lack attractions.

Surrounded on three sides by water Darwin's central business district is at the northwest corner of the peninsula jutting into Darwin Harbour. The main shopping area

OPPOSITE: A road train, workhorse of the north. ABOVE: hand feeding stock during a drought.

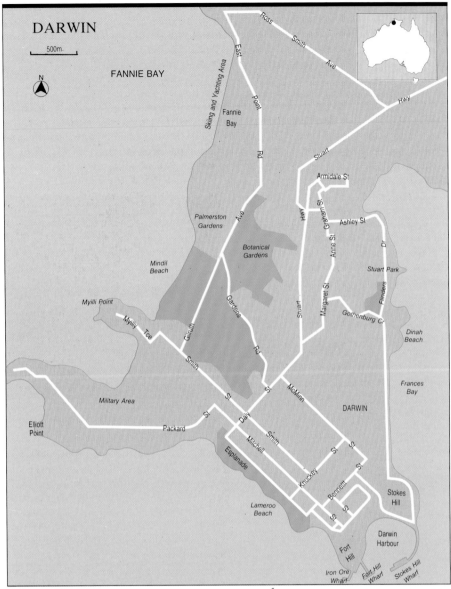

DARWIN

500m.

N

FANNIE BAY

is along Smith Street mall, between Bennett and Knuckey Streets. A stroll through town is the best way to get a feel for the place.

Start at the north-east end of Smith Street where the modern **Christchurch Anglican Cathedral** stands. Built after the devastation of Tracy the design incorporated the original porch, all that survived the cyclone.

The Chinese community was also devastated when its temple was ripped apart by Tracy's 280 km/h (175 mph) winds. However, a new **Chinese Temple** has been erected at

25 Woods Street; its lines retain the feel of the original structure of 1887 formerly situated on the same spot. It is open to the public on weekdays from 8 am to 4 pm and on weekends from 8 am to 3 pm. Admission is free. The temple is still used by the local Chinese who have had a long and at times troubled association with Darwin: tourists are requested to respect the sanctity of this place and the dignity of its worshipers.

Head towards the harbor end of town where most of the historic buildings spared by Cyclone Tracy are to be found. **Government House** is on the Esplanade overlooking the harbor. It is not open to the public, but by peering through the gate you will see a reminder of more gracious times. The century-old building has lived through Japanese bombing raids, a succession of cyclones and even an attack of white ants. Nevertheless, with its grand verandahs and gables the whole edifice has a colonial elegance now rare in Darwin.

At the other end of Esplanade is Doctor's Gully. At high tide hundreds of fish swim into the shallows where they know that they will get a free feed from visitors. **Aquascene** at 28 Doctor's Gully provides visitors with the opportunity of participating in this unique spectacle. It is advisable to ring first, ((089) 817-837, to find out feeding times. An admission fee is charged.

Picnic on the lawns of the **Botanical Gardens** off Gilruth Land, or wander among its collection of over 400 species of tropical and sub-tropical plants. It contains an amphitheater which serves as the setting for cultural events varying from concerts to Aboriginal dance performances.

A superb collection of Aboriginal artifacts and Oceania art are on show at the **Museum of Arts and Sciences** on Conacher Street, Fanny Bay, ((089) 898-211, about 4 km (2.5 miles) out of town. There is also a good collection of modern Australian works in the gallery, open daily free of charge.

Off the Stuart Highway on the Cox Peninsula Road, Berry Springs, is the **Territory Wildlife Park**, ((089) 886-266. It consists of 400 hectares (990 acres) of bushland where the Territory's animals can be seen in their native habitat. A special treat is to watch Wedge-tailed Eagles and other birds of prey soar around Park handlers at 10 am each day. Give yourself at least three hours to look around this immense reserve open daily from 8:30 am to 6 pm.

Some tours include a visit to the **Crocodile Farm**, along the Stuart Highway, ((089) 881-450, 40 km (25 miles) out of Darwin. More than seven thousand reptiles can be seen at various stages of growth, from eggs to jaw-snapping monsters. If you are frightened by the belligerence of these ancient beasts then you will probably suffer no qualms about purchasing a handbag or belt from the farm's shop, or having your revenge by dining on a Croc Burger in the kiosk.

DARWIN AFTER DARK

If the thrills of Darwin by day with its spectacles revolving around the dining habits of giant reptiles have not jaded you, get ready to enjoy Darwin by night, where the weather is kind to night-owls.

If it's Thursday, start the evening on **Mindil Beach** where there is a sunset market,

open throughout the Dry season. Shop for local crafts or try the food from one of the 60 stalls.

Innovative plays can be seen at **Brown's Mart Theatre** at 12 Smith Street and bookings made by phoning ((089) 813-728. The 1885 stone building is also of historic significance.

The squat pyramid-shaped **Diamond Beach Casino Hotel**, ((089) 462-666, is popular with tourists: if you don't want to gamble there are cabaret shows to watch or loud music to dance to at **Crystals**. The casino also provides jazz on its lawns at sunset.

Friday's edition of the *Northern Territory News* has a "Gig Guide," which summarizes what's on at night in Darwin.

SPORT

First thing in the morning is the best time to play an energetic game of golf. The **Gardens**

Diamond Beach Hotel Casino ABOVE is the focus of Darwin's nightlife.

Park Golf Course, ((089) 816-365, opposite the Casino has eighteen holes, and clubs and buggy can be hired.

The best sport in town is fishing, and the Top End is famous for its barramundi (known locally as "barra"). These freshwater fish provide anglers with a good fight, thrashing out of the water in an effort to escape. While there is reasonable *barra* fishing near Darwin, for anglers that are willing to travel to find the best, there are camping tours into the Outback where the prime spots can be found, and 18 kg (40 lb) *barra* caught. The best time of the year for this is from April to October.

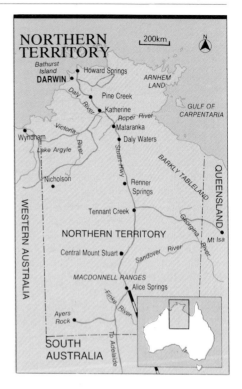

WHERE TO STAY

The **Diamond Beach Hotel Casino,** ((089) 462-666, and the **Beaufort** in The Esplanade, ((089) 829-911, offer luxury accommodation.

Moderately priced **Poinciana Inn** at the corner of Mitchell and McLachlan Streets, ((089) 818-111, fax: (089) 412-444, is in the center of town and close to everything.

There is also a good selection of budget accommodation in Darwin. Both the **Darwin City Lodge** at 151 Mitchell Street, ((089) 411-295, fax: (089) 813-720, and **Inner City Lodge** at 112 Mitchell Street, ((008) 808-365, are set in tropical gardens and reflect the informality typical of Darwin. Both guesthouses will pick you up from the airport.

WHERE TO EAT

Tourists have had a considerable influence over the standard of restaurants in Darwin, which have improved unimaginably over the last few years. One of the most popular places in town is **Christos** on Stokes Hill Wharf, ((089) 818-658, offering open air dining and serving local fish. The barramundi is recommended. For a menu that offers exotica such as buffalo, camel and crocodile try **The Magic Wok** at 48 Cavanagh Street, ((089) 813-332, or the **Safari Bistro** at the Travelodge on the Esplanade, ((089) 815-388.

If Darwin is not hot enough for you, try a curry from **Maharaja** at 37 Knuckey Street, ((089) 816-728, which is inexpensive.

HOW TO GET THERE

Ansett Australia provides at least one direct daily flight to Darwin from Sydney, Melbourne, Perth, Adelaide and Brisbane, but Qantas Australian has fewer services.

Driving to Darwin is a major undertaking, as the closest capital city is Adelaide, 3,215 km (1,993 miles) away. The road takes you past Uluru (Ayers Rock), Alice Springs and other attractions in the Outback. The other popular way to see the Top End is from Perth, traveling around the coast via Broome, a mere 4,430 km (2,750 miles).

There are coaches to Darwin from Brisbane and, via Alice Springs, from Adelaide.

KAKADU NATIONAL PARK

This is the showplace of the Top End — a spectacular and ancient wilderness of dramatic scenery, home of hundreds of species of birds and animals and a treasure house of Aboriginal art and lore. It is one of the world's great parks, justifiably on the highly prestigious World Heritage list.

Located 250 km (156 miles) east of Darwin, a three hour drive, it lies on the western fringe of Arnhem Land. The national park covers 19,000 sq km (7,350 sq miles).

GENERAL INFORMATION

At an information booth at the entrance of Kakadu on the Arnhem Highway visitors pay an admission fee that covers a visit of ten days. Children under 16 are allowed in

free of charge. It is a further 80 km (50 miles) to the **Park Headquarters Information Centre**, ℃ (089) 799-101, which is off the highway and provides visitors with a comprehensive collection of Park Notes, brochures explaining the ecology of the park and maps which locate major Aboriginal art galleries. There is also a tourist center in Jabiru, ℃ (089) 792-548.

WHAT TO SEE AND DO

The park includes a broad flood plain and is backed by the high ramparts of the Arnhem Land escarpment. In the Wet season, majestic waterfalls thunder off the plateau with the 200 m (650 ft) drop of the **Jim Jim Falls**

the most breathtaking. In the Dry season the water recedes to a series of lagoons and billabongs which attract thousands of birds. Along the coast, tidal mudflats and mangrove forests provide yet another habitat, so different from elsewhere in the park.

There are both freshwater and estuarine crocodiles in Kakadu. Take heed of crocodile warning signs, and you are strongly advised not to swim or paddle in natural waterways unless expressly told that it is safe. During the Wet season, swimming in small rock pools is no danger.

The best time to see Kakadu is at the beginning of the Dry season, between April and September. October and November can be uncomfortably humid, although the savage electric storms at this time of year, called the "build-up," are an unforgettable sight. During the Wet season many areas may not be accessible if the roads are washed out.

The Aborigines have lived in Arnhem Land for thousands of years; there is evidence of their rich culture in the galleries of rock paintings around Kakadu, a window on the past, a record of Dreamtime myths.

ABOVE: Beautiful Catherine Gorge LEFT makes the arduous journey south from Darwin worthwhile. Aboriginal children RIGHT play in Kakadu National Park, the "Top End's" showcase.

More than 300 galleries have been found and it is estimated that at least another 1,000 are known only to Aborigines. Accessible ones are found at **Ubirr** (previously known as Obiri Rock), an easy 45-minute walk from the visitors' center. The topography includes a number of overhangs and caves that made natural shelters for Aboriginal artists. Paintings include stick-like figures and X-ray drawings of animals showing their internal organs and bone structure. There is also a Tasmanian tiger drawn on an overhang of the main gallery, its antiquity assured because they became extinct in the Top End more than 3,000 years ago. Towards a look-out near the main gallery is another site with a series of hunters in motion painted in white on a black wall, and which may be over 1,000 years old. **Nourlangie Rock**, 28 km (17 miles) south of the visitor's center, also contains Aboriginal art galleries.

WHERE TO STAY

The best place to stay in Kakadu is in **Jabiru**, which is near the center of the park. **Gagudji Crocodile Hotel** in Flinders Street, ((008) 809-123, fax:(089) 790-148, is a luxury hotel in the shape of a crocodile. At the other end of the price range is the **Kakadu Frontier Lodge and Caravan Park** in Jabiru Drive, ((089) 792-422, fax:(089) 7922-254.

HOW TO GET THERE

There are quite a few package tours to Kakadu, ranging from one to six days. Another way to get a view of the park, particularly if you don't have much time, is from the air. **Kakadu Air**, ((089) 792-411, fax:(089) 792-303, has daily departures from Darwin and Kakadu itself, the flight covering Jim Jim and Twin Falls.

DOWN THE TRACK

The Stuart Highway, known simply as "the Track," bisects the Territory, running from Darwin to Alice Springs 1,530 km (950 miles) to the south and then another 290 km (180 miles) to the South Australian border.

Driving along the Track can be dry work, so take a detour off the highway and stop at **Daly Waters** for an ice cold beer in the oldest pub in the Territory.

Katherine, 345 km (214 miles) south of Darwin, is the next main town on the highway. Famous for its gorges it is worth making the arduous journey to see these wonders of nature. **Nitmiluk** (Katherine Gorge) is 32 km (20 miles) out of town, and access may be limited in the Wet season. The main geological structure is divided into thirteen gorges: on either side of the Katherine River are 70 m (230 ft) walls which change color according to the light and time of day. The best time to see them is first thing in the morning. In the other is the sheer face of Jedda's Leap, where legend has it that a couple jumped to their deaths because they were not allowed to wed. You can join a boat ride up the first two gorges, probably the best way to appreciate their awesome beauty; get hold of **Daly Gorge Boat Tours**, ((008) 089-103 or (089) 721-044, who offer trips ranging from two to eight hours.

About an hour and half south of Katherine is one of nature's little bonuses; if the heat and endless roads become too exhausting for you, jump into the brilliantly clear thermal pool at **Mataranka**, fed by spring water bubbling to the surface at a warm 34°C (93°F). The spring supports a veritable oasis, a small pocket of palms and lush tropical forest in a landscape otherwise almost bare of vegetation. This region is called the "Never never" — those who live here can never never leave it. The nearby Elsey Station is the location of the Australian classic novel by Jeannie Gunn *We of the Never Never*, which has been made into a film.

Thin woodland gives way to the scrub and red earth of the interior at **Renner Springs**, 500 km (310 miles) south of Katherine, this change marking the limit of the monsoons and the start of the dry center.

Near **Tennant Creek** is the site of the last goldrush in Australia that started in 1932; even today one mine is still operational. The creek itself is 11 km (7 miles) out of town because many years ago convenience overrode good intentions. In 1933, Joe Kilgariff made his way to the area with a cart carrying supplies and materials for the building of a pub. Caught in a sudden downpour and bogged in the mud, the publican unloaded his wagon and built the pub on the spot. The miners chose to build their town next to it rather than near the water supply of the creek, several kilometers away!

About 105 km (65 miles) south of Tennant Creek, straddling the highway are the **Devil's Marbles** — hundreds of huge spherical granite boulders, some of which are balanced precariously on others. Aborigines believe that these are eggs laid by the

In Katherine there is the **Pine Tree Motel** at 3 Third Street, ((089) 722-533, (008) 089-103, fax: 722-920, and the **Frontier Motor Inn**, ((089) 721-744, fax: 722-790.

The **Mataranka Homestead Tourist Resort** in Homestead Road, ((089) 754-544, fax: 754-580, provides accommodation that ranges from moderately priced motel rooms to inexpensive caravans. Guests can relax in the thermal pool filled with natural spring water.

The accommodation choices in Tennant Creek are limited, and **Safari Lodge** in

rainbow serpent during the Dreamtime, and so this is a registered sacred site for Aboriginals. The best time to view the Marbles is at dusk, when the sun's rays bring out the colors of red, yellow and brown minerals present in the granite.

You are more or less at the geographical center of the continent, marked by **Central Mount Stuart**, a low round hill to the west of the highway, about 65 km (40 miles) past **Barrow Creek**.

WHERE TO STAY

There is moderately priced accommodation along the Track, although the smaller places offer less choice.

Davidson Street, ((089) 623-188, offers both moderately priced rooms and bunkrooms for budget travelers.

THE RED CENTER

Alice Springs, known simply as "the Alice," is widely recognized as the unofficial capital of the Red Center.

In a country where the spirit of the Outback is revered Australians have a soft spot for the Alice.

An artist's impression of Alice Springs decorates the wall of the market town's shopping center.

The area started its life as a link in the first telegraph line across the continent, completed in 1872. Each repeater station was fortified against attacks by hostile Aborigines who hadn't heard that Europeans now "owned" the land which they had occupied for more than 40,000 years.

In 1933 the original name, Stuart, was changed to Alice Springs, after the wife of Sir Charles Todd who was responsible for the construction of the Overland Telegraph line. Sir Charles had the river named after

WHAT TO SEE AND DO

Alice Springs

Alice Springs is at the foot of the **MacDonnell Ranges**, and its ever-changing colors provide an attractive backdrop to the town. There are several points of interest worth exploring before going further afield to the MacDonnell Ranges.

Built between 1870 and 1872, the **Telegraph Station Historical Reserve** on the Stuart Highway, ((089) 521-013, contains a

him, which was no great honor as it runs dry for most of the year.

Up to twenty years ago the population had struggled to reach 4,000, when the Alice survived as a railhead to move cattle southwards.

Today the permanent population has grown to about 14,000, supported mainly by the tourism which has boomed since the world discovered the *Red Center*. The town receives an estimated 150,000 visitors a year.

GENERAL INFORMATION

The **Northern Territory Tourist Bureau** is located in the Ford Plaza Building in Todd Mall, ((089) 515-470.

reconstruction of the stone repeater station that was a vital link in the 3,000 km (1,860 mile) Overland Telegraph line. The historic Reserve is open daily and there are guided tours from May to September. To get a greater appreciation of the history of central Australia visit the **Old Timers Folk Museum** on the Stuart Highway, ((089) 522-844, which contains displays of relics from the early pioneers and is open between 2 pm and 4 pm.

At the **Old Pioneer Cemetery** on George Crescent only a few headstones remain: buried here are two men who are part of the Red Center's colorful history. One of them, Harold Lasseter, set out in 1930 with two camels into the desert, never to return. His last diary entry tantalizingly declared that he had found a fabulously rich gold reef, which no prospector has ever succeeded in finding. The other, Albert Namatjira, immortalized many features of the MacDonnell Ranges in watercolor paintings. Although his work is universally admired he died a tragic figure in 1959, unable to claim the fundamental human rights white Australians take for granted.

The area around the Alice is rich in geological features which will take your breath away. Be warned that traveling a few hundred kilometers a day is not considered excessive in the Outback, and certainly the best way to see it is by car or coach. Still, for the adventurous there are camel safaris into the MacDonnell Ranges offered by **Frontier Camel Tours**, ((089) 530-444, fax: (089) 555-015.

MacDonnell Ranges

Fifty kilometers (31 miles) west of Alice Springs in the MacDonnell Ranges is **Standley Chasm**, 9 m (30 ft) wide and 80 m (260 ft) deep. The best time to visit is at midday when sunlight reflects off the sides of the chasm and highlights the colors. **Ormiston Gorge** is another feature in the MacDonnell Ranges well worth visiting; its near vertical cliff face shimmers red in the sun, punctuated by white ghost gums rising from ledges.

A different view of the MacDonnell Ranges is at dawn from the air, and **Outback Ballooning**, ((089) 528-723, (008) 809-790, fax: (089) 523-869, offer a 30-minute flight for $110.

Chamber's Pillar is off the Gap Road, 165 km (102 miles) south of Alice Springs, a protuberance of sandstone eroded by wind over 350 million years standing 50 meters (164 ft) above the surrounding plain, and a landmark visible from very far away.

Uluru (Ayers Rock)

Uluru (once known as Ayers Rock) is the most famous feature of the Red Center. Its famous domed silhouette is as distinctively Australian as the pyramids are Egyptian or Eiffel Tower French.

There are fascinating Aboriginal legends about the crevices OPPOSITE in Uluru (Ayers Rock) told on a special tour round the rock. RIGHT the trail to the summit.

Ayers Rock was first sighted by Europeans in 1873, when surveyor William Gosse saw the Rock during an expedition to map the 2,400 km (1,500 miles) of desert between Alice Springs and Perth.

Uluru is on the World Heritage list and part of a 132,566-hectare (327,450-acre) park.

This single rock, actually the peak of a buried mountain, rises 384 m (1,260 ft) from the surrounding plain; the perimeter is some 9 km (5.5 miles) at its base. The flanks of the rock are etched with deep gullies which fill with rushing water when it rains.

The sandstone monolith is rich in the crystalline mineral felspar, giving the rock its colors which vary with the time and weather. On sunny days it can be any tint from red to orange, while when wet it changes to black, purple, white or any shade in between. Even a novice photographer can take the most stunning photographs at dawn or sunset when the colors are most vivid.

In 1985 the government handed the Pitjantjantjara and Yankunytjatjara people freehold title over the land which they leased back to the government for 99 years. They did, however, change the name back to its original "Uluru."

Sacred to local Aborigines, Uluru abounds in Aboriginal legends; every crevice and contoured shape has a Dreamtime story attached to it. For example, on the south side the indentations in the rock are where spears scored it in a battle between the poisonous snake people, the Leru, and the sleeping lizard people, the Loongardi. Learn more about Aboriginal mythology on a **Rod Steinert Tour**, ℂ (089) 555-000, around the rock.

It is possible to climb to the top: handrails and guide-chains help climbers on the more difficult sections. The round trip to the summit takes about two hours. About 75,000 people begin the climb each year, and most succeed. Some climbers turn back at a place dubbed "chicken rock," so don't be too embarrassed if you don't make it.

If you feel like traveling a bit on the wild side then **Uluru Motor Cycle Tours**, ℂ (089) 562-019, fax: (089) 562-196, will rent you a Harley Davidson for the journey from Ayers Rock Resort to Uluru.

Olgas

A range of domed rocks called the Olgas (or Kata Tjuta by Aborigines), lies 27 km (17 miles) to the west. **Mount Olga** itself is higher than Uluru, rising 546 m (1,790 ft) above the surrounding plain. They were best described by their European discoverer, Ernest Giles, who wrote "Mount Olga displayed to our astonished eyes rounded minarets, giant cupolas, and monstrous domes." Driving around the Olgas cannot beat walking through this strange collection of giant rocks, with its gorges and the **Valley of the Wind**.

WHERE TO STAY

Luxury accommodation in the Alice is available from **Media Alice Springs** at Barrett Drive, ℂ (089) 528-000. If you want to be close to the casino stay at the **Vista Alice Springs**, ℂ (089) 526-100, or **Lasseter's Hotel Casino** at 93 Barrett Drive, ℂ (089) 525-066.

The **Outback Motor Lodge** at South Terrace, ℂ (008) 896-133, fax: (089) 532-166, is moderately priced as is the nearby **Gapview Resort Hotel** at the corner of Gap Street and South Terrace, ℂ (089) 526-611 or (008) 896-124.

The **Old Alice Inn** on Todd Street, ℂ (089) 521-255, provides budget accommodation.

HOW TO GET THERE

Uluru is approximately 470 km (290 miles) south-west of Alice Springs and reached by taking the turn-off from the Stuart Highway onto the Lasseter Highway.

There are daily bus services between the Alice and Uluru, and many commercial package tours of Uluru and the Olgas are available.

NATIONAL PARKS

For details of National Parks contact the **Conservation Commission of the Northern Territory**, ℂ (089) 895-511 or its information center in Gaymark Building Palmerston, ℂ (089) 894-411.

OPPOSITE: The Olgas (TOP); Standley Chasm (BOTTOM LEFT) and baby-backpacking in Ormiston (BOTTOM RIGHT).

WHAT TO SEE AND DO

The oldest river in the world carved **Finke Gorge**, 155 km (96 miles) west of Alice Springs, into the surrounding plain. It is notable for its cabbage palms, a leftover from when the area was much wetter, and can only be reached by four wheel drive vehicles. Contact the local ranger, ((089) 518-271, for further details.

Henbury Meteorite Conservation Park, 150 km (93 miles) south-west of Alice Springs,

contains a series of craters formed 4,700 years ago when a shower of meteorites struck the Earth at about 40,000 km/h (25,000 mph). The largest is 183 m (600 ft) wide and 15 m (50 ft) deep.

Simpsons Gap National Park, 8 km (5 miles) west of Alice Springs, features several gaps and there are several walking tracks. A 17 km (10 mile) cycle track through the park makes access easy. Contact the local ranger, ((089) 518-211, for further details.

FESTIVALS AND SPORTING EVENTS

JANUARY To celebrate Australia Day a race is held around the country. The competitors

are cockroaches and the course is a model of Australia with a running track around the edge. The **Cockroach Race** is held in the Darwin Sailing Club, ((089) 811-700.

MARCH There is a theory that Australian Rules Football is an Aboriginal game adapted by the early colonists. It is therefore natural that Aborigines at the Top End have a passion for the game. The best of the season is the **Northern Territory League Grand Final**, played at Football Park in Marrara, where some players don't bother with boots and the skill levels are exceptional.

APRIL/MAY During the **Barra Classic** fishermen help themselves to 15 kg (33 lb) barramundi. The venue changes from year-to-year but is usually held near Darwin.

JUNE Darwin's **Bougainvillea Festival**, ((089) 896-642, is just a good excuse for a party and includes craft displays, music and a Grand Parade.

JULY/AUGUST The **Darwin Cup** is the Territory's main horse race meeting and held at the Fannie Bay Racecourse on the first Monday in August. It is preceded by a month of festivities.

AUGUST Northern Territorians have a powerful reputation for drinking beer, and rather than just throw the empties away they put them to good use in the **Beer Can Regatta**, in vessels made entirely of cans. The race takes place on Mindil Beach in Darwin.

AUGUST/SEPTEMBER The Henley-on-Todd **Regatta** in Alice Springs is one of those "don't miss" events where teams race along the dry bed of the Todd River in bottomless boats.

ABOVE: Larger than life display at the Grand Parade, part of Darwin's Bougainvillea Festival. OPPOSITE: This amazing array of chimney-like sandstone monoliths, known as the "Hidden City of Nathan", is part of the Abner Range on the Nathan River Property in the Gulf of Carpentaria.

South Australia

Hidden Treasures

SOUTH AUSTRALIA has lived under a heavy historical disability. As the one State that never accepted convicts, South Australia has no notable prisons, guard houses, police barracks or courthouses with which to interest tourists. To compensate, the industrious free settlers built churches and beautiful colonial sandstone buildings. In its capital, Adelaide, extensive parklands were established along the sluggish Torrens River.

In the twentieth century was added a love for culture, with the inauguration of the Adelaide Arts Festival, the first such event in Australia. To complete the picture of a thoroughly civilized place to live, South Australians acquired an appreciation of fine wines. The best, as any South Australian will quickly tell you, are made exclusively in his state's Clare Valley, McLaren Vale and Barossa Valley.

ADELAIDE

The city is set out in a grid pattern with broad streets and immaculate streetscapes which reflect Adelaide's graciousness. Across the Torrens River lies North Adelaide, both the city's first suburb and one of the more elegant in Australia. Surrounding Adelaide are 668 hectares (1,650 acres) of parklands, the pride and joy of the city. They are made for strolling through, playing on or just looking at.

Beyond the city, the suburbs stretch to the low sand dunes of the Gulf St. Vincent in the west, and up into the green folds of the Adelaide Hills to the east.

Once known as the "City of Churches," Adelaide's respectable exterior hides a more risque underside. Its nightlife swings, and during November the central city is turned over to the deafening snarl of the sleek racing cars that come for the **Grand Prix**.

BACKGROUND

Founded in 1836, South Australia was a reaction by its liberal founders to the convict base of other colonies. Social theorist, Edward Gibbon Wakefield, believed that colonies could grow on the capital raised from the sale of Crown land to free settlers.

He argued that a civilized community could only thrive with such colonists. Ironically, Wakefield hatched his scheme while in Newgate Prison for abducting a fifteen year old heiress. His proposal was initially rejected by the government. By the time it had been accepted in a modified form Wakefield had lost interest, but his supporters remained committed to his plan. On 15 August 1834 Westminster passed an Act for the Establishment of the Colony of South Australia.

In 1836 Colonel William Light, the first Surveyor-General, chose the site for Ade-

laide. Later that year Governor Hindmarsh arrived to administer the new colony. A raging quarrel erupted between the two men who disagreed where Adelaide should be sited. To an onlooker this squabble was out of place in the civilized colony both men wished to found. The volatile Hindmarsh followed his run-in with Colonel Light with petty disputes with land developers, and was recalled by the Imperial Government in 1838.

Surviving without convict labor proved difficult. It was only economic stimulation provided by copper discoveries, in Kapunda in 1842 and Burra in 1845 that allowed Adelaide to embark on an ambitious building program. Fortunately many of the churches, public buildings and houses built in the late nineteenth century survive today, adding to the city's charm.

Adelaide's Festival Centre ABOVE, home of the best arts festival in the country, and OPPOSITE pedestrian-only shopping precinct.

GENERAL INFORMATION

The Tourism South Australia Travel Centre at 1 King Street, ((08) 212-1505 or (008) 882-092, provides information, books accommodation and can arrange tours anywhere in the State. It is open every day although on weekends it closes at 2 pm. The **Royal Automobile Association of South Australia** at 41 Hindmarsh Square, ((08) 223-4555, has information about the condition of roads, sells maps and offers an accommodation booking service. In Glenelg there is a **Tourist Information Centre** on the foreshore at Bayworld Museum, ((08) 294-5833, which is open daily.

Information about Adelaide's public transport can be obtained by phoning ((08) 210-1000 between 8 am and 7:30 pm weekdays and 9 am and 4 pm weekends and public holidays. For information on country and interstate trains phone ((08) 231-4366.

WHAT TO SEE AND DO

Central City

The easy way to see Adelaide is on the **Adelaide Explorer Tram**. The two-and-a-half hour journey, starting at the Travel Centre, is a round trip of Glenelg and the city. Passengers can get on and off the tram as often as they like on the same ticket. However, Colonel Light's layout for Adelaide and its flat topography makes it a walker's delight.

After coming out of the travel center, turn into **North Terrace**, Adelaide's most charming boulevard. Along its dignified tree-lined length are South Australia's seats of political power, learning and culture. I'm uncertain into which of these categories to put the **Adelaide Casino**, ((08) 212-2811, which is also in North Terrace and housed in a renovated railway station, undoubtedly the most elegant in Australia. Its interior is crowded with tables set for blackjack, craps, baccarat and roulette, while video poker machines are located on the first floor of the Casino. Between Monday and Thursday it is open from 10 am to 4 am. These hours are extended to 24 hours a day at weekends, on holidays and during the Grand Prix.

Dress requirements are for smart casual clothes. For men, though a tie and jacket are not compulsory, jeans are definitely unacceptable.

East along North Terrace is the **Old Parliament House**, ((08) 212-6881, built in 1855, which has now been turned into a constitutional museum with constantly changing exhibitions.

Nearby is the **Art Gallery of South Australia**, ((08) 207-7000, with an excellent collection of Australian art. While there, make sure you see works by Hans Heysen who painted the rocks of the Flinders Ranges and mighty ghost gums.

The **University of Adelaide** is cramped between North Terrace and the river. The overcrowding, however, has not robbed the predominantly neo-Gothic campus of its academic repose. While on campus drop into the **Museum of Classical Archaeology** on the first floor of the Mitchell Building, ((08) 228-5239, which exhibits artifacts from ancient Rome, Greece and Egypt, some dating back 5,000 years. The museum is open weekdays from 12 noon to 3 pm.

Further along North Terrace are the **Botanic Gardens**, ((08) 223-3102, a relaxing 30 hectares (75 acres) of shady lawns. Down the center of the gardens magnificent 120-year-old Moreton Bay fig trees line the avenue to the Main Lake. Near the Plane Tree Drive entrance is the **Bicentennial Conservatory**, a giant glasshouse in which a fine mist of water nourishes lush rain forest, beautiful flowers and waterside plants. In the gardens, open daily, it is hard to imagine that a major city is just a few hundred meters away.

Ayers House at 228 North Terrace, opposite the Royal Adelaide Hospital, was built in 1855. Home to Sir Henry Ayers, who was elected Premier of South Australia for a record seven times, the mansion is open to the public Tuesday to Sunday.

Turn right after Ayers House into East Terrace, and after a couple of minutes walk there is the **Tandanya Aboriginal Cultural Institute** at 253 Grenfell Street, ((08) 223-2467. The center was established to foster Aboriginal culture, art and dance, and its activities and exhibitions are open to the public. Grenfell Street leads into **King Wil-**

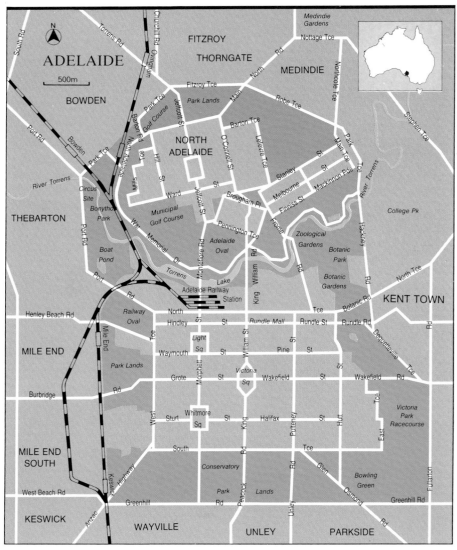

liam Street, which, at 42 m (140 ft), is the widest of any Australian city thoroughfare, bisecting the city and continuing into North Adelaide.

The center of Adelaide is marked by **Victoria Square**, located at the junction of Grote, Wakefield and King William Streets. Just north of Victoria Square is the **Post Office**, built in 1867, and the imposing Renaissance-style **Town Hall** built between 1863 and 1866, inspired by public buildings in Florence and Genoa. There are one-hour tours of the interior of the Town Hall every Tuesday and Thursday at 10:30 am and 2:30 pm.

Festival Centre

The **Festival Centre**, overlooking the Torrens River, is located off King William Street north of the city. Opened in 1973, the same year as the celebrated Sydney Opera House, the Centre is the focus of Adelaide's cultural life. Its admirers assert that while the Festival Centre cost one tenth of the Opera House it is ten times more successful. Spite may have motivated this claim, but what is indisputable is that the Festival Centre is made for comfort, its concert halls have excellent acoustics and its stages are functional, a claim that only the most boring chauvinist could make of the Sydney Opera House. The superb complex houses the Festival Theatre, an experimental theater, the Playhouse, an amphitheater for outdoor performances and a plaza for informal cultural gatherings, such as poetry readings.

The Festival Centre is the main venue of Adelaide's well-known **Arts Festival** which attracts top performers from overseas and Australia to sing, act, dance and perform for enthusiastic audiences. This was mainly a home town affair when it started in 1960 but today visitors attracted by its reputation pack Adelaide for the tenday Festival, a benchmark by which cultural festivals in other States are measured.

Port Adelaide

The Port was established in 1840 and boasts some of the finest historic buildings in South Australia. Solid stone warehouses, workmen's cottages and wharves are a reminder of an era when the port was home to clippers and steamships. Explore the area bounded by Nelson Street, St. Vincent Street, Todd Street and McLaren Parade for intact nineteenth century streetscapes. The area's history is on display in the **Maritime Museum** at 126 Lipson Street, ((08) 240-0200.

Glenelg

The first settlement in Adelaide was at Glenelg, which today is a pleasant seaside suburb. To get there take Adelaide's only tram, which starts at Victoria Square and is a pleasant 30-minute ride to Jetty Road, Glenelg's main thoroughfare.

In Macfarlane Street, Glenelg North, a plaque marks where Governor Hindmarsh proclaimed South Australia a British colony. The plaque can be seen next to the arched remains of an ancient gum tree. Nearby, in the **Patawalonga Boat Haven** in Adelphi Terrace, ((07) 294-7000, is a replica of Hindmarsh's ship, the *Buffalo*, which has been converted into a museum and restaurant.

The pub scene in Adelaide is busy, and there are several good places in Kent Town just east of the city which have live bands over the weekend. **The Hotel Royal** at 2 North Terrace, and the **Kent Town Hotel** at 76 Rundle Street, have different bands, playing anything from rock to reggae. On Sunday afternoon the Folk Club have a gig at the **Earl of Leicester** at 85 Leicester Street, Parkside.

The daily newspaper, the *Adelaide Advertiser*, is a good source of information on what is happening in Adelaide. On Thursday the

Guide section provides information on theater and which bands are playing at which clubs. The free newspaper *Rip It Up* is left lying around pubs and music shops, and contains a wealth of information on the local music scene. The *Adelaide Review* provides an excellent and critical guide to theater, concerts and dance and is distributed free of charge at better bookshops.

ADELAIDE BY NIGHT

The liveliest spot in the city is Hindley Street, with its clubs, pubs, restaurants and nightclubs. It also has one of the more infamous strip joints in Australia called the **Crazy Horse** at 145 Hindley Street.

WHERE TO SHOP

Rundle Mall is lined with department stores, boutiques, coffee shops and cinemas. Colorful flower stalls and a fountain make the mall a pleasant setting to shop, or to sit back in an outdoor cafe and be entertained by buskers. There are a number of arcades leading off the mall for those seeking even greater shopping variety. The **Myers Centre** fronts the Mall and it is worth dropping into its international food hall on the lower ground floor.

The **Central Market** has operated from its site in Grote Street for over 120 years and specializes in fresh foodstuffs. Kangaroo meat, which has been banned in other States for human consumption, can be purchased in the meat section. In Rundle Street near Frome Street is the **East End Market**, open

Mall, ((08) 211-7440, and black opals from **Bartram Opals** in Suite 106, 38 Grawler Place, ((08) 223-3684.

Adelaide supports a lively community of craftspeople. Turn a corner and more than likely you will come across the works of local artists. The **Jam Factory Craft and Design Centre** at 19 Morphett Street, ((08) 410-0727, is a government project. Some of the best local pottery, paintings, sculpture, weaving and glassware can be seen in its galleries. There are also some very good private galleries in Adelaide. Original Aus-

weekends. It has an enormous food hall that can seat 150 people, and offers a choice of Chinese, Italian and other cuisines from around the world, but its main attraction is its stalls selling crafts, clothing and souvenirs.

Opals are a popular souvenir. A form of silica, quality opals come in various colors — orange, red, yellow and the rare blue. The best opals have large areas of uniform color and no cracks or flaws: South Australia's come in light colors. The best place to learn more about them is **Opal Field Gems** on the third floor at 29 King William Street, ((08) 212-5300, where they can be seen being cut: they also have a video running on the history of opal mining. Opal jewelry can be purchased from **Olympic Opal** at 5 Rundle

tralian hand-made arts and crafts can be purchased from **L'unique** in the City Cross Arcade off Rundle Mall, ((08) 231-0030, while in North Adelaide **Greenhill Galleries** at 140 Barton Terrace, ((08) 267-2887, have regular exhibitions of paintings by Australian artists.

Outside the central shopping precinct are several streets in the suburbs with much to offer. **Melbourne Street** in North Adelaide is a lively avenue of trendy restaurants, boutiques and gift shops, while for antiques **Unley Road** and **Goodwood Road** should be explored.

ABOVE and OPPOSITE: Outdoor art at Adelaide's Festival Centre.

SPORT

South Australia supports a good basketball team, the Adelaide 36ers, who are part of the National Basketball League. When they play at home it is at the Clipsal Powerhouse in William Street, Beverley.

Football is taken seriously, and **Football Park** in Turner Drive, West Lakes is usually filled with a partisan crowd whenever the Adelaide Crows play at home. Cricket and football are played at the Adelaide Oval off King William Road.

If golf is your game then the **City of Adelaide Golf Links** has two 18-hole courses on which to play. For bookings ring either ((08) 267-2171 or (08) 231-2359.

WHERE TO STAY

Luxury

The Grosvenor at 125 North Terrace, ((08) 231-2961, (008) 888-222, fax: 231-0765, is conveniently located opposite the Casino. The **Adelaide Meridien** at 21–37 Melbourne Street, North Adelaide, ((08) 267-3033, (008) 888-228, fax: 239-0275, has spacious rooms and executive suites are available with separate lounge and bar.

For something a little different try the **North Adelaide Heritage Apartments**, ((08) 272-1355, fax: (08) 272-6261, which offers a choice of historic cottages dating from the turn of the century. Many of the apartments are fitted with colonial antique furnishings and the rooms are scented with fresh flowers.

There are great ocean views at the **Ramada Grand Hotel** in Moseley Square in Glenelg, ((08) 376-1222, (008) 882-777, fax: (08) 376-1111. The hotel is also handy for access to the airport, just five minutes away.

Moderate

Largs Pier at 198 The Esplanade, Largs Bay, ((08) 495-666, is an impressive three storey hotel with wide colonial verandahs. When built in 1883 it was able to offer the luxury of hot, cold and sea water on tap. Today it retains its stylish reputation but not the sea water on tap. Attached to the main building are 17 motel-style units. In North Adelaide

is the **Old Adelaide Inn** at 160 O'Connell Street, ((08) 267-5066, (008) 888-378, fax: (08) 267-2946, which is only about twenty years old: its name is misleading. Ask for a quiet room if the noise from the main road is likely to worry you.

Inexpensive

Princes Lodge at 73 Lefevre Terrace, North Adelaide, ((08) 267-5566, offers budget accommodation within walking distance of the city. At Glenelg there is **St. Vincent** at 28 Jetty Road, ((08) 294-4377, and a few blocks away is the **Norfolk Motel** at 69–71 Broadway, ((08) 295-6354.

WHERE TO EAT

Any visitor to Adelaide is dared by locals to try South Australia's national dish — the pie floater — which is a meat pie sitting in green pea soup. Should you feel both peckish and brave, **Cowley's Pie Cart** opens after 6 pm outside the Post Office on Franklin Street, while **Balfour's** is outside the Casino on North Terrace.

There are also more conventional places to eat. Adelaide has many good restaurants where meals can be enjoyed with a bottle of wine from the admirable vineyards of the Barossa Valley or McLaren Vale.

The western end of Hindley Street has good, inexpensive and moderately priced restaurants which are noisy and full of life. As this is also the entertainment center of the city, they keep filling with customers during the evening and meals can be obtained from late afternoon; alternatively, have a later supper after a show. For Lebanese food try **Quiet Waters** at 75 Hindley Street, ((08) 231-9137, or **Jerusalem Sheshkabab** at 131B Hindley Street, ((08) 212-6185. A tasty Sri Lankan meal, amazingly cheap, is available from the **Ceylon Hut** at 27 Bank Street, ((08) 231-2034. This simple cafe is located just off Hindley Street and is not open on Sunday. Run by Vietnamese Buddhists, the **Peaceful Vegetarian** at 167 Hindley Street, ((08) 212-7805, takes the humble bean curd and serves it in an amazingly varied number of interesting dishes.

Restaurants in North Adelaide are more upmarket. Overlooking the Torrens River is

Flannigan's on War Memorial Drive, ((08) 211-8555, specializing in seafood. Fine Italian cuisine is served in **Carlo's Place** at 73 Melbourne Street, ((08) 239-1655. If you like Cajun fish and the exotic flavors of Creole cooking try **Bacall's** at 149 Melbourne Street, ((08) 267-2030. Another restaurant area is in Gouger Street, which has a wide selection of Asian and European style restaurants. There is even an Australian restaurant that serves indigenous food: kangaroo, yabbies and (you lucky people!) witchetty grubs, when they can get them. The **Red**

from Alice Springs easy going, as the train is equipped with excellent dining facilities and a bar.

DAY TRIPS FROM ADELAIDE

ADELAIDE HILLS

The Adelaide Hills rise out of the central plain and provide a perfect view of the city to the west. Being so close by, a day trip to the Hills is an agreeable weekend activity.

Ochre at 129 Gouger Street, ((08) 212-7266, has an inexpensive cafe that opens up into a formal restaurant. For a simply delicious meal try the char grilled emu medallions.

HOW TO GET THERE

A number of international flights include stopovers in Adelaide, which is also a popular starting point for Central Australia.

There are regular bus services from Alice Springs, Canberra, Darwin, Perth, Sydney and Melbourne.

The *Indian Pacific* train, linking the Indian and Pacific Oceans, passes through Adelaide on its journey from Perth to Sydney. The *Ghan* makes the 20-hour journey

A popular destination is **Hahndorf**, just thirty minutes away from Adelaide, but many other picturesque villages and hamlets in the Adelaide Hills are also worth visiting.

In 1839, fifty-two Lutheran families fleeing Prussia settled on 60 hectares (150 acres) of farming land in the hills 30 km (19 miles) east of Adelaide. The settlement was named Hahndorf after the Danish captain of the *Zebra*, the ship that brought them to South Australia. The tightly-knit community prospered but when the First World War broke out German-speakers encountered hostility from other Australians. For a while Hahn-

Adelaide is renowned for its open spaces, here on the waterfront promenade at Glenelg beach near the Ramada Grand Hotel and town Hall clock tower.

dorf changed its name to Ambleside to disguise its German origins, but reverted to its original name in 1935. Other German villages in the Adelaide Hills also changed their names but not all were changed back to their original ones after the war.

General information
The **Tourist Information Centre** at 64 Main Street, Hahndorf, ((08) 388-1185, provides brochures on attractions in the Adelaide Hills.

What to See and Do
The architecture of many buildings and cottages in the Adelaide Hills is typically German with gables.

In Hahndorf many of the original structures have been preserved and the German atmosphere of the village is strong.

As the township was founded by Lutherans it follows that their faith was manifested in two fine old churches — **St. Michael's** built in 1858, and **St. Paul's**, built in 1890. Both are still used by the local community. The **Blacksmith's Shop** and neighboring buildings were also built in the nineteenth century. There are also German restaurants in town, and best of all the **German Cake Shop** which serves the sweet Sacher Torte.

Numerous other villages are scattered around the hills where many good galleries can be found. In Clarendon there is **The Old Gallery,** ((08) 383-6219, with regularly changing exhibitions, while in Meadows the **Paris Creek Pottery,** ((08) 388-3224, offers local craftware.

The unique **Warrawong Sanctuary** at Stock Road, Mylor, ((08) 388-5380, is home to an assortment of small indigenous animals such as brush tailed bettongs, tammar wallabies and rainbow lorikeets. Its main claim to fame is its breeding colony of platypuses, the only one in existence. The best time to see the wildlife is at dusk, and the management has organized walks each evening at sunset. Reservations must be made.

Where to stay
Rather than stay in Adelaide many tourists prefer one of the many guesthouses or houses providing bed and breakfast accommodation in the Adelaide Hills.

The **Apple Tree Cottage** at Oakbank, ((08) 388-4193, is a secluded self-contained settlers' cottage set in 70 hectares (170 acres) of farmland. **Cherryville Lofts,** ((08) 390-1375, is a renovated bluestone loft built in the 1870s that offers reasonably priced accommodation in the hills.

More conventional lodging is provided by the **Hahndorf Inn Motor Lodge,** ((08) 388-1000, (008) 882-682, fax: (08) 388-1092.

How to Get There
The Adelaide Hills are about 30 km (19 miles) from the city and can be reached by taking the sign-posted turn-off on the South Eastern Freeway. Several coach companies put on tours of the Hills which take in the main sights.

BAROSSA VALLEY

German Lutherans fled their native land because they found religious persecution by the King of Prussia intolerable. Lead by Pastor August Kavel, 468 Prussians and Silesians arrived in Australia from their homeland in 1838.

These immigrants had a profound influence on the new colony, with Barossa Valley villages looking like those of Prussia. The origin of the valley's name is Spanish but the local German population referred to it as "New Silesia" for many years.

They brought with them considerable knowledge of farming. When in 1847 grape vines were found to thrive in the valley many farms became vineyards. Today approximately 9,000 hectares (22,200 acres) are under cultivation and the Barossa Valley produces approximately a third of Australia's total output, known wherever people have been let into the secret that Australia produces excellent wines.

GENERAL INFORMATION

Information can be obtained at the **Barossa Valley Tourist Office** in Coulthard House at 66 Murray Street, Nuriootpa, ((085) 621-

OPPOSITE: Autumnal tones at Chateau Reynella winery.

866, at the northern end of the Barossa Valley. At the Adelaide end information can be obtained from the **Gawler Tourist Office** at 61 Murray Street, ℂ (08) 226-814.

WHAT TO SEE AND DO

The valley is 40 km (25 miles) long and 11 km (seven miles) wide and is easily accessible from Adelaide, just 50 km (31 miles) away.

The main attractions in the Barossa Valley are indeed its wineries, many of which are open for tours and tastings. Over fifty are situated in the area: usually signs along the road are sufficient to direct visitors. The main ones are concentrated along the Barossa Highway between Lyndoch and Nuriootpa.

Penfolds on Barossa Way, Nuriootpa, and **Seppeltsfield Winery** in Seppeltsfield are two of the oldest vineyards in the region and visitors are invited to taste their wines.

One of the more picturesque towns in the Barossa Valley is **Tanunda**, which features old buildings and cottages built in a style common in Germany in the mid-nineteenth century. Traditional games like German skittles are still a favorite pastime. Other evidence of the region's German heritage can be seen in the **Barossa Historical Museum** at 47 Murray Street, ℂ (085) 633-295, and open daily. A few kilometers to the west you can walk down the shady street of **Bethany**, the valley's oldest village founded in 1842, and pass the thatched barns and pretty rustic cottages of an earlier, more romantic period.

WHERE TO STAY

For luxurious accommodation stay at the **Woodlands of Lyndoch** at the corner of Barossa Valley Way and Altona Road, ℂ (085) 244-511.

In the heart of the Barossa is the **Nuriootpa Vine Inn** at 14–22 Murray Street, ℂ (085) 622-133, fax: (085) 623-236, and the **Karawatha Guest House** in Greenock Road, ℂ (085) 621-746, both of which are moderately priced.

In Tanunda **Stonewell Cottages** in Stonewell Street, ℂ (085) 632-019, and **Norma's Place** at 50 John Street, ℂ (085) 630-100, are full of character. On the sprawling **Lawley Farm**, ℂ (085) 632-141, fax: (085) 632-875,

Bruce and Sancha Withers do everything they can to make their nineteenth century stone cottages comfortable for guests who are invited into the elegant farmhouse for a hearty breakfast.

HOW TO GET THERE

The Barossa Valley can be reached from Adelaide by taking the Main North Road to Gawler, and then right towards Lyndoch. The first wineries appear along the road in about seventy minutes.

FLEURIEU PENINSULA

The Fleurieu Peninsula is just south of Adelaide, and has long been a favorite family holiday area with fishing and water sports the main activities.

GENERAL INFORMATION

There are tourist information centers at Victor Harbour in Torrens Street, ℂ (085) 524-255, at Goolwa in Cadell Street, ℂ (085) 551-144, and at Strathalbyn, ℂ (085) 363-212.

WHAT TO SEE AND DO

At the northern end of the peninsula is **McLaren Vale**, a lesser-known wine making area than the Barossa Valley. As a result its streets are not clogged with tour coaches, the vineyards are smaller and the winemakers more likely to take time to chat about their favorite topic — making wine. The vineyards are scattered in the hills around the township of McLaren Vale, and most have tastings and sales on the premises.

Seaview Winery in Chaffey's Road is one of the best known in the area. Take some time to search out the small vineyards which rely on their reputations to sell wine from their own premises: they are able to produce some quite remarkable wines which shame the established brands. One is Noon's, tucked away on Rifle Range Road, where tastings are in a shed off the main homestead, and David Noon is more than happy to talk about his produce over a glass of his best Shiraz, cheese and biscuits. There is also a barbecue area in the vineyard where visitors can have a picnic and perhaps try a Noon's Riesling.

Low hills run down the center of the peninsula, where historic towns dot the landscape. Their placid appearance cloaks their past; smugglers once worked the area, evading customs officials as they landed spirits and tobacco illicitly. Many a gang of contraband runners have rowed their illegal merchandise up the Onkaparinga River and hidden in Old Noarlunga, where the old Horseshoe Inn was a favorite hideout.

About 40 km (25 miles) from McLaren Vale is the seaside town of **Victor Harbour**, a popular destination for holiday-makers from Adelaide. A causeway connects the town to **Granite Island** and visitors can take a horse tramway across the bridge. The service runs daily between 10 am and 4 pm.

Another way to explore the peninsula is to take the **Cockle Train**, ((08) 231-1707, along the coast from Victor Harbour to **Goolwa**. The 16-km (10-mile) journey takes about 30 minutes.

Victor Harbour overlooks **Encounter Bay** where Southern Right Whales can be seen swimming close to shore: the best time to see them is between May and September. More information can be obtained from the National Parks and Wildlife office at 57 Ocean Street, ((085) 523-677.

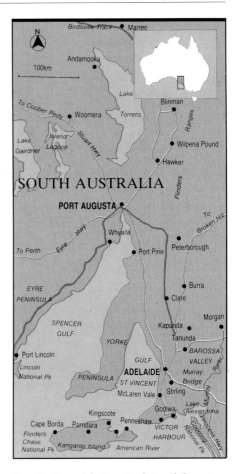

WHERE TO STAY

In Victor Harbour the **Warringa Guest House**, ((085) 525-970, is a warm, friendly place to stay. The luxurious **Whalers' Inn** at The Bluff overlooking Encounter Bay, ((085) 524-400, fax: (085) 524-240, welcomes guests with a complimentary bottle of champagne on their arrival; the view from its seafood restaurant of the bay and Granite Island is quite splendid.

HOW TO GET THERE

An enjoyable way to reach the Fleurieu Peninsula is aboard the *Southern Encounter*, a steam train that winds its way through the Adelaide Hills, stopping at Mt. Barker, and then onto Strathalbyn, Goolwa and Victor Harbour. It leaves from the Australian Na-

tional's Keswick Terminal two kilometers (one mile) from the city, and it is recommended that you book first by telephoning ((08) 231-1707. Departures are at 9 am, arriving at 12:40 pm.

KANGAROO ISLAND

At the tip of the Fleurieu Peninsula is Cape Jervis, where the ferry connects each day with Kangaroo Island, Australia's third largest. 140 km long and about 40 km wide (77 and 25 miles), there is an abundance of native wildlife and its beaches provide good viewing of penguins and seals.

BACKGROUND

The island was first sighted in 1802 when Matthew Flinders was circumnavigating the continent. He sent crew members ashore to shoot kangaroos for food when supplies ran low. The French, for a while, were also interested in south-east Australia and in 1803 Kangaroo Island was visited by their navigator, Nicholas Baudin, after whom several landmarks around the island were named.

Its early history is also closely connected with the sealing and whaling industries in the southern waters off Australia. Since these were banned the seal population is thriving and sightings of whales in the southern oceans are frequent.

The place abounds with indigenous wildlife. Kangaroos are everywhere, and in the **Flinders Chase National Park** at the western end lives a colony of **koalas** and Cape Barren geese. Off **Cape du Couedic** you can watch fur seals romp in the surf or bask on the rocks.

A good place to see fairy **penguins** is along the beach at **Penneshaw**. During May and June ungainly fluffy chicks wait in burrows for their mothers' return with fish for dinner. Arrive at sunset and take a torch, but don't use a flash on your camera because it

GENERAL INFORMATION

Tourist information can be obtained from the Dudley Council office in Middle Terrace, Penneshaw, ((0848) 31011, or the National Parks and Wildlife office in Dauncey Street, Kingscote, ((0848) 22381.

WHAT TO SEE AND DO

The best way around is by car, and you can take your own over on the ferry. Bike hire is also available but the number of unmade roads on the island makes cycling less attractive.

upsets them. As the night approaches they tumble out of the surf and dash to their burrows along the cliff to feed their hungry offspring.

At **Seal Bay**, a 45-minute drive from the main settlement of **Kingscote**, lives a colony of sea lions. Arrangements to see them must be made with the park ranger, ((0848) 28-233. Approaching the beach, its appearance is of large boulders scattered along the clean white sand. On closer inspection they are seals, immobile on the beach, exhausted by their fishing expeditions. Occasionally one of these large mammals gets the needle to a neighbour, a short altercation takes place, and then lethargy returns with the two combatants losing interest and returning to their solitary contemplation. If disturbed by human beings they can become aggressive, and the park ranger whose hut is above the beach will advise visitors as to a safe distance from which to view them.

There's also some good fishing off **Snelling Beach**, both in the surf and off the rocks.

WHERE TO STAY

The best place to stay on the island is the **Ozone Seafront Hotel** on the foreshore at

Kingscote, ((0848) 22-011, fax: (0848) 22-249, an old fashioned chalet that concentrates on creature comforts rather than style.

Ellson's Seaside House on Chapman Terrace, ((0848) 22-030, is an inexpensive guesthouse in Kingscote while the **Island Resort** in Telegraph Road, ((0848) 22-100, fax: (0848) 22-747, is moderately priced.

Amberlee in Parndana, ((0848) 37-239, offers a moderately priced bed and breakfast in a relatively modern house.

HOW TO GET THERE

The **Kangaroo Island Sealink**, ((08) 373-3722, and **Eastern Cove Traders**, ((008) 018-484, run ferries between Cape Jervis and

Penneshaw, and **Island Seaways**, ((08) 47-5577, links Port Adelaide with Kingscote. There are also daily flights from Adelaide.

BURRA

Burra, 156 km (97 miles) north of Adelaide, is one of Australia's oldest mining towns where many of the original buildings remain intact.

Approximately 50,000 tons of copper were extracted from the hills around Burra between 1845 and 1877. The boom attracted miners from Wales, Scotland and Cornwall; even small communities of Germans and Chileans came. In the mid-nineteenth century Burra was in fact the largest inland town in Australia.

GENERAL INFORMATION

The **Tourist Information Centre** at 2 Market Square, ((088) 922-154, has a wealth of historic information on the town. There are organized tours by the Centre if enough people show interest.

WHAT TO SEE AND DO

For the visitor who doesn't mind wearing out some shoe leather, the 11 km (7 miles) **Heritage Trail** around Burra is the best way to see most of the points of interest. Get a map from the Tourist Information Centre.

To familiarize yourself with its history pay a visit to the **Market Square Museum** at 9 Market Square, ((088) 922-154 which includes a re-creation of a general store and post office of the 1870s. A more extensive museum on the mining history of Burra is located in the **Bon Accord Mine Complex** in Railway Terrace, ((088) 922-056, once a working mine.

The scars of open cut mines are all around Burra, the water in them stained green by copper salts. The miners lived within their own ethnic communities; for example, the row of stone houses along Kingston Street is is where the Cornish miners lived, and **Paxton Cottage Number 1** has had its original

The ramparts ABOVE, and wind-etched shapes of Remarkable Rocks, OPPOSITE, in Mount Remarkable National Park on Kangaroo Island.

furnishings restored and is open to the public on weekends and public holidays.

The Welsh miners lived along the river, in caves dug into the bank. Extensions to accommodate additions to the family were easily accomplished by just digging out another room. Best of all, the Welsh miners had no rent to pay. It is estimated that 1,800 of these thrifty people lived along a 5 km (3 mile) stretch of river, where many of the homes remain intact and can be visited.

WHERE TO STAY

For a taste of the real Burra stay at **Paxton Square** in Kingston Street, ((088) 922-622, which provides refurbished 1850 miner's cottages at very reasonable tariffs. Other accommodation is at **Tivers Row** in Truro Street, ((088) 922-461, or the inexpensive **Burra Caravan and Camping Park** which has powered sites available.

HOW TO GET THERE

From Adelaide you can get there by car along the Main North Road and Barrier Highway.

FLINDERS RANGES

On a hot day, the Flinders Ranges shimmer in the distance, changing color — from reds and orange to blues and purple — depending on the time of day and the distance. These jagged mountains are not high but in places have a rugged beauty accentuated by the plain surrounding them.

They begin south of Adelaide and stretch north into the desert interior of South Australia — a distance of about 800 km (500 miles).

The history of the Flinders Ranges is geologically complex. Formed 500 million years ago, the mountains gradually eroded to low lying hills. About 50 million years ago new disturbances pushed up the old range, resulting in a profile of saw-tooth ridges together with the rounded hills of the earlier phase.

GENERAL INFORMATION

Tourist information and maps of walking trails can be obtained from tourist informa-

tion centers at **Peterborough** in the Main Street, ((086) 512-708, **Port Augusta** at 41 Flinders Terrace, ((086) 410-793, **Quorn** in the Council Offices on Seventh Street and **Melrose** in Sturt Street, ((086) 662-014.

WHAT TO SEE AND DO

Not far from Port Augusta is **Quorn**, which was an important junction for trains servicing inland South Australia. One way to get a feel for the romance of the long-past era of the steam train is to take the **Pichi Richi Railway**, ((08) 276-6232, through the Pichi Richi Pass to Woolshed. The round trip takes about three hours but the train only runs between March and November.

Hawker is the gateway to the northern Flinders Ranges. Ten kilometers (six miles) south of Hawker are the **Yourambulla Caves**, which contain fine Aboriginal rock paintings and carvings.

A singularly interesting place in the district is **Wilpena Pound**, a natural amphitheater whose rocky walls and cliffs encircle an oval bowl, 20 km (12 miles) long and 8 km (5 miles) wide. The only way in is along a track through the gap in the ramparts of the north-west corner. The bowl itself is covered with scrub, and in spring wildflowers grow in profusion. Five walking tracks snake across the basin, which although fairly flat will take a good day's hiking for the return trip. If you are willing to clamber up **St. Mary's Peak** (1,170 m or 3,840 ft) there is a marvelous view of the Pound from the top.

The Flinders Ranges are split by a number of gorges through which dirt roads wind; the sides are rich in yellows and ochres broken by the greens of the eucalypts that sprout mysteriously from the walls. **Kangaroos** inhabit the area, and you may be lucky enough to see a Mountain Kangaroo or a rare Yellow-footed Rock Wallaby hopping up steep slopes or stopping to graze on the ledges.

The area is rich in Aboriginal lore: legend has it that Arkaroom the serpent created the ranges and formed the gorges by wriggling across the countryside. He then slithered westward to Lake Frome and drank it dry, which explains the absence of water there. He now sleeps in the Yacki water hole in the Gammon Ranges.

Interesting walks abound along its 700 km (434 miles) length, with a variety of landscape types and ecosystems. Walking maps can be obtained from the State Information Centre at 77 Grenfell Street or from the National Parks and Wildlife Service at 55 Grenfell Street in Adelaide.

WHERE TO STAY

The **Rawnsley Park Tourist Park**, ((086) 480-030, provides moderately priced

cabin accommodation in the heart of the Flinders Ranges National Park. At nearby Hawker alternative accommodation is offered by the **Hawker Hotel Motel** at 80 Elder Terrace, ((086) 484-102, fax: (086) 484-151, and the **Outback Motel** in Wilpena Road, ((086) 484-100, fax: (086) 484-109.

At Quorn there is **The Mill Motel** at 2 Railway Terrace, ((086) 486-016.

HOW TO GET THERE

Take the coastal road along Spencer Gulf and the Flinders Ranges are to your right. Head inland to Hawker, about 400 km (250 miles) from Adelaide, and further

north you will come to the **Flinders Ranges National Park** which protects some of the wilder sections of the mountain range.

There are good roads leading through the Flinders Ranges but many are unmade; a four-wheel drive vehicle is recommended for a self-drive tour.

NULLARBOR PLAIN

Most people traveling from Adelaide to Perth prefer to fly in order to avoid the Nullarbor Plain, but not all.

The Latin meaning of Nullarbor — no trees — is appropriate as this arid plain supports only low lying bushes. Traversing it is as unforgettable as the endless tundra along the route of the trans-Siberian railway.

The Plain runs along the Great Australian Bight, between **Ceduna** in South Australia and the mining town of **Norseman** in Western Australia. Covering 200,000 sq km (77,400 sq miles), similar in area to the British Isles, it was once a seabed. It rose about 100 million years ago and is made of limestone.

Ooldea, at the eastern end of the Nullarbor Plain has a special place in Australian history. From 1919 until 1935 Daisy Bates camped on this site, caring for the Aborigines in what must be one of the most inhospitable places on Earth. Occasional passengers on the Trans-Continental train were astonished by the sight of an Edwardian lady in dark ankle-length skirts, black stockings, stiff collar, white gloves and holding a parasol traveling across the flat expanse in a camel buggy. In 1938, Bates wrote in *The Passing of the Aborigines* "The Australian native can withstand all the reverses of nature, fiendish droughts and sweeping floods, horrors of thirst and enforced starvation — but he cannot withstand civilization." She saw as her mission to arrest the contamination of civilization, but in the title of her book she admitted defeat.

Flinders Ranges ABOVE stretch into the desert interior of South Australia, a popular area for walks and drives among ochre cliffs, wildflowers and for seeing a wallaby.

WHAT TO SEE AND DO

The 1,300 km (800 miles) Nullarbor Plain is a featureless expanse of absolutely flat terrain. Its rust-colored earth is tinged grey-green by bluebush and saltbush and punctuated by one-house towns that exist solely to service the train and passing traffic.

Underground, carved out of limestone, are subterranean rivers, cathedral-like caves and large lakes. The Nullarbor is a treasure trove for archaeologists; a well preserved 4,600-year-old Tasmanian tiger, now extinct, was discovered in a cave called Thylacine Hole, and is on show at the West Australian Museum in Perth.

As the Eyre Highway is never far from the Great Australian Bight, sightings of **Southern Right Whales** add interest to the crossing. They come to this area to breed, and 20 m (60 ft) whales and their calves can be seen off the coast between June and October. The look-outs are off the highway on Aboriginal land and permits, costing $2 a person, can be obtained from **Yalata Roadhouse**, ((086) 256-807, and **Nullarbor Hotel-Motel Inn**, ((086) 256-271. Occasional sightings of albino whales are made in these waters by lucky people. The two motels just mentioned provide moderately priced accommodation, and bookings for August and September, when tourists arrive in coaches to see the whales, are advisable.

WHERE TO STAY

Most of the accommodation is along the Eyre Highway. Overlooking Murat Bay is the **Ceduna Community** on the corner of O'Loughlin and South Terraces, ((086) 252-008. In **Madura**, 1,254 km (777 miles) west of Perth you can stay at the moderately priced **Hospitality Inn**, ((090) 393-464 or **Madura Caravan Facility**, which can be booked through the Hospitality Inn. Further west the old mining area of Norseman has a reasonable range of accommodation: the **Great Western** in Princep Street, ((090) 391-633, is centrally located while further up the street is the **Gateway Caravan Park**, ((090) 391-500.

HOW TO GET THERE

Coaches between Adelaide and Perth regularly travel along the Eyre Highway. Further inland is the railway, which is the last leg of the Indian-Pacific from Sydney. With few barriers to circumnavigate the train track runs in an absolute straight line for 478 km (300 miles).

COOBER PEDY

Coober Pedy, 863 km (535 miles) north-west of Adelaide, is an opal mining town on the edge of the Great Victoria Desert and makes a fascinating stopover on the way to Alice Springs.

To start a conversation with a local just mention the weather, and watch him or her wax lyrical on whether the next day will be baking hot, blistering hot, scorching, or just hot. Such conversations should preferably be conducted over an ice cold beer, a local antidote to the heat.

Despite any boasts from the locals, Coober Pedy is not the hottest place in Australia. That honour goes to Cloncurry in Queensland which reached 53.1°C (127°F) in 1889. Nevertheless in a town where the temperature is often over 40°C (105°F) the quality of the heat is a topic worthy of very serious discussion; when the temperature drops below 30°C (85°F) locals are known to reach for a jacket.

The town was built on the wealth of opals, discovered in the area in 1915. With a permanent population of just over 2,000, it remains the largest opal mining town in Australia.

GENERAL INFORMATION

The **Coober Pedy Tourist Information Centre** is in the Council Office in Hutchison Street, ((086) 725-298, and is open 9 am to 5 pm weekdays, 9 am to 12 noon Saturday and 2 pm to 5 pm Sunday.

OPPOSITE TOP A tourist mine. Many people in the remote opal mining town of Coober Pedy have carved out underground homes OPPOSITE BOTTOM to avoid the heat.

WHAT TO SEE AND DO

To escape the heat and wind many miners chose in to live underground in caves or dug-outs, where the temperature is a steady 24°C (75°F). Approximately 40 percent of the population live underground.

On the surface the landscape is desolate; mines and diggings cover a radius of 50 km (31 miles) around the town. Thousands upon thousands of small pyramids of white sand two to three meters (12 to 18 ft) in

height are piled up beside old diggings. Care should be taken walking around Coober Pedy because old mines have been known to collapse in drops of up to 30 m (100 ft).

While not as close to the Almighty as they could be, the **Catacomb Church** in Catacomb Street and **Church of Sts. Peter and Paul** are underground and a good deal cooler than had they been built along more traditional lines, soaring to the heavens. Both can be inspected daily and services are conducted on Sunday. In 1993 the **Serbian Church** opened in Potch Gully, and its walls are covered in fine religious carvings by Norm Ashton.

Also underground is the **Umoona Opal Mine and Museum** in Hutchison Street, ((086) 725-288, which is a complex of chambers. Incorporated is a museum with exhibitions on opal mining and Aboriginal culture as well as an impressive display of opals. The **Old Timer's Mine** in Crowder's Gully Road, ((086) 725-555 is another museum which gives an intrigu-

in insight into opal mining and includes an original 1918 miner's home. Across the road is **The Big Winch**, a giant mine winch overlooking the town. Below it is an opal and art gallery, displaying famous black opals. Another way to explore Coober Pedy is to take the **Gem City Opal Tours**, ((086) 725-333, and Trevor McLeod, an ex-miner himself, shows you about the surrounding countryside.

In the **Breakaway National Reserve** is the **Painted Desert**, which draws visitors to its ever-changing colors. You can get there by taking the Alice Springs Road for 28 km (17 miles) out of Coober Pedy.

WHERE TO STAY

Very sensibly, there are several underground hotels in Coober Pedy. **The Underground** in Catacomb Road, ((086) 725-324, fax: (086) 725-911, and the **Desert Cave** in Hutchinson Street, ((086) 725-688 or (008) 088-521, are both moderately priced.

HOW TO GET THERE

Most coaches between Alice Springs and Adelaide which take the Stuart Highway stop over in Coober Pedy. Kendall Airlines has daily flights from Adelaide.

NATIONAL PARKS

For information on national parks contact the **Nature Conservation Society of South Australia**, ((08) 223-5155.

The **Simpson Desert Conservation Park** covers 692,680 hectares (1,710,920 acres) and access is really only by four-wheel drive vehicles. This is a desert of sand dunes, their subtle colors seen at their best at dusk and dawn.

The **Tantanoola Caves Conservation Park** is 21 km (13 miles) south-east of Millicent. They honeycomb the ancient limestone cliffs, where a walkway through the main cave is for visitors. For further details contact the park ranger on ((087) 344-153.

In the district are two lakes, each different in its own way, which merit a visit.

Near the border of Victoria is the **Blue Lake** at Mt. Gambier, which in November changes color from its winter-grey to the most startling blue; to date science has been unable to explain this. **Lake Eyre** blooms after rain, a rare event in this region, the driest in Australia with an average rainfall of 100 to 150 mm (4 to 6 inches). Once it was thought to be the edge of a great inland sea, but many explorers have been disappointed by what they found, a very large dry pan containing an estimated 500 million tons of salt.

It should be noted that visitors to the Simpson Desert Conservation Park or Lake Eyre National Park require an Overnight Pass at $15 or a Desert Pass at $50, both of which include maps of the area.

FESTIVALS AND SPORTING EVENTS

JANUARY The German origins of Hahndorf, just 30 km (19 miles) outside the city in the Adelaide Hills, are made manifest during the **Schutzenfest** where traditional German food and music are offered. On the Saturday there are shooting competitions.

A week or two after the Schutzenfest Hahndorf celebrates **Founder's Day**, with a parade through its streets.

FEBRUARY The **Adelaide Festival Fringe** allows avant-garde performers to kick off the Adelaide season of culture. This festival is held every even year.

MARCH The **Adelaide Festival** is the oldest and best known festival of culture and the performing arts in Australia. Much of it takes place in the Festival Complex on the Torrens River, and is also held every even year.

APRIL The **Opal Festival** in Coober Pedy celebrates the town's claim to fame and many of the events have a mining theme.

The **Barossa Valley Vintage Festival** is held biennially, every odd year. Needless to say a major theme is wine-making which, when combined with food and music, provides an excellent incentive to spend Easter there.

MAY Any opportunity to taste over 100 wines from **McLaren Vale**, with the added bonus of food stalls serving dishes usually only seen in good restaurants, is irresistible. Don't miss the **Gourmet Weekend** in McLaren Vale.

OCTOBER There are no race courses anywhere near Coober Pedy which is well and truly in the sticks. So don't miss out on their sport: the **Coober Pedy Races** is a meeting which attracts people from hundreds of miles around.

NOVEMBER Adelaide's most famous event is the **Australian Formula One Grand Prix**, when the city streets become the race-track,

and windows rattle as the racing cars whiz around the course at speeds of up to 300 km/h (190 mph).

The **Blue Lakes Festival**, coincides with when the lake at Mt. Gambier turns blue.

Advice for drivers OPPOSITE in the arid outback.
ABOVE A Coober Pedy miner washes for opals.

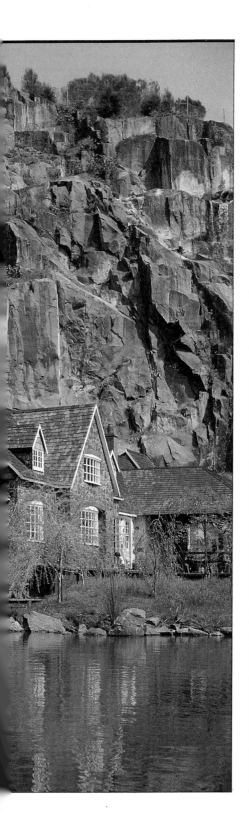

Tasmania
The Holiday Isle

A VISIT to Tasmania is not advised for the indecisive tourist, faced with numerous and diverse choices of what to see and do. Australia's smallest state has it all. And more.

Tasmania is blessed with countryside which changes from rolling hills in the north, reminiscent of picturesque English counties, to the rugged majesty of its west coast. It has cool untouched rain forests and wildernesses where you can walk for days and never see another soul. The State is quite compact, taking just two and half hours to drive from north to south; many of its attractions can be reached without having to travel great distances.

Tasmania is sparsely populated with just under half a million people in an area approximately the size of Ireland. In the largely undisturbed countryside, much of it reserved as national parks, are numerous opportunities to see animals in their natural setting. It is common for wallabies and possums to feed around the country cottages where you may be staying. Tasmania is also home of the Tasmanian Devil, extinct on the mainland, an animal usually about 30 cm (12 inches) tall, although males can grow to 90 cm (35 inches) and weigh 90 kg (200 lb). The Tasmanian Devil, named because of its fierce appearance, is shy, but if lucky you may see one feeding at night in the remoter parts of the north-west and central regions of the island. The Tasmanian Tiger is believed to be extinct, although sightings have been reported occasionally in remote regions.

As the second oldest colony, Tasmania retains many fine Georgian buildings and largely unchanged village streetscapes. Many colonial cottages provide accommodation, acquainting tourists with the history of the State. To complete the holiday experience eat at the fine restaurants which concentrate on local ingredients such as Tasmanian smoked salmon, King Island Camembert and freshwater and saltwater fish.

So self-contained is the island that Tasmanians refer to other Australians as "mainlanders" or remind them when they visit that they come from "Tasmania's northern island."

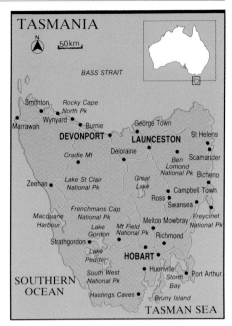

Above all, Tasmania does everything to cater to the tourist's needs. The State is known around Australia as the Holiday Isle.

HOBART

Hobart is confused by simple concepts like time and place. It knows that it is near the end of the twentieth century, but insists on giving the outward appearance of a nineteenth century city although the occasional luxury hotel or high rise building breaks the skyline as a gesture to modernity. The population of Hobart knows that it lives in the capital of a state but insists on maintaining the friendliness and intimacy of a country town, where everyone knows everyone else and nothing is rushed.

The climate is mild in summer but decidedly chilly in winter, being the only State capital that has any winter snow, albeit rarely. Above the city is Mount Wellington, its summit often hidden in cloud or dusted with snow, while the majestic River Derwent divides the city from surrounding green farmland and outlying suburbs. Hobart's

OPPOSITE: Sunset at Bicheno, busy little fishing port and charming old holiday resort.

landscape more closely resembles the European countryside than any other part of Australia's.

GENERAL INFORMATION

The **Tasbureau Office**, at 80 Elizabeth Street, ℂ (002) 308-233, will handle all your tour bookings and answer any queries. There are free counter copies of *The Treasure Islander* and *Tasmanian Travelways*, newspapers which provide up-to-date information about attractions around Tasmania.

BACKGROUND

Hobart was established only 16 years after Sydney, making it Australia's second oldest city, with the intention of forestalling French designs on Tasmania.

Governor Macquarie, when he gave instructions to build the settlement on the River Derwent, did not want to repeat the chaotic street plan of Sydney and the city center is laid out on a grid.

As transportation ended, Hobart became a backwater. Even today, Australia's second city is the smallest State capital with a population of just 180,000 people. However, being by-passed by progress has meant that Hobart retains much of it Georgian elegance and heritage.

WHAT TO SEE AND DO

The best place to start an exploration of Hobart is **Constitutional Dock**, where fresh fish are sold straight off the boats.

Adjacent is **Franklin Wharf** where river-cruisers set off each day for a tour of the River Derwent. A trip on the **Essalisa**, ℂ (002) 235-893, provides an opportunity to travel on an original vintage ferry. The boat runs a lunch cruise that lasts about one and a half hours.

South of the wharf area are the graceful lines of **Parliament House**, built by convicts in 1827 and originally used as a Customs House (although many alterations and additions have since been made). When Parliament is in session visitors can view proceedings from the public gallery, while on non-sitting days if you are fortunate an attendant will show you around.

Back down the hill, east of the Parliament House, is **Salamanca Place**. In the last century Salamanca was a busy area, with Clydesdales pulling drays along the cobbled street to load wool clippers and other vessels. Most of the warehouses along the street have been preserved but rather than storing wool they house galleries, restaurants and souvenir shops. On Saturday mornings Salamanca Place is abuzz with a colorful market catering to locals and tourists alike.

On the high ground at the back of Salamanca Place is **Battery Point**, a colonial-era village looking much as it did a century and half ago, with many fine Georgian cottages and houses. The Point took its name from the battery of cannons that in 1818 were placed on high ground to repulse the French should they try and take Hobart. Invaders never came, and the cannons were never fired in anger.

As Hobart's' first suburb, the winding narrow streets of Battery Point were home for the merchants, seamen, boat builders and fishermen who worked at the docks. The **Shipwright's Arms** at 27 Trumpeter Bay Point is a reminder of the kind of public house that served the locals. In the center of Battery Point is **Arthur Circus**, a charming little park surrounded by tiny stone cottages. The **National Trust**, ℂ (002) 236-236, has an organized walking tour of Battery Point which leaves every Saturday from the Wishing Well in Franklin Square and is good value at $5.

To learn a little more about the seafaring history of Hobart visit the **Maritime Museum** at Secheron House in Secheron Road, ℂ (002) 235-082, housing a unique collection of memorabilia from the colony's early seafaring days. The museum is open daily and an admission-fee is charged. Another interesting one in Battery Point is the **Van Diemen's Land Folk Museum** at 103 Hampton Road, ℂ (002) 342-791, accommodated in a historic Georgian house built in 1836. It is Australia's oldest folk museum, with furniture, clothing and prints from the penal colony's earliest days, and is open daily with an admission-fee charged. On your return to the city, observe that backing onto Hampton Street is **Anglesea Barracks**, Australia's oldest military establishment, built in 1811 and is still used by the army. The barracks are open daily and a guided tour is conducted ever Tuesday at 11 am.

The site of the first settlement, founded in September 1803 by Lieutenant John Bowen, was **Risdon Cove**. This site proved unsuitable and in February 1804 the settlement was moved to Hobart. Archaeologists have uncovered structures erected by the first party of convicts and soldiers, and these can be seen at Risdon Cove which is now a suburb of Hobart on the East Derwent High-

At the bottom of Mt. Wellington, should you have developed a thirst, drop into **Cascade Brewery** on Cascade Road, South Hobart, ((002) 241-144. Established in 1832, it is the oldest brewery in Australia. Visitors can learn more about the art of making beer in the museum attached to the Brewery before walking through the colonial gardens at **Woodstock**, across the road from the brewery. There are tours of the brewery, museum and gardens conducted on weekdays between 9:30 am and 1 pm: bookings are essential.

way. The visitors' center, ((002) 308-399, provides a guide to the area and should be contacted to obtain information on opening times.

Mt. Wellington, rearing 1,270 m (4,165 ft) above the city, provides great views of the surrounding countryside. From the top it is possible to see parts of the southwest corner of Tasmania. Choose your weather, however, as the peak is liable at any time of year to be wreathed in cloud. An imaginative tour operator recently launched a novel descent — by bicycle — which is fun but certainly not for the faint-hearted. Contact **Brake Out Cycling Tours**, ((002) 782-966, fax: (002) 781-056, to book.

HOBART BY NIGHT

Hobart has a lively nightlife for such a small place and on the weekend there are over thirty nightspots and pubs that provide live music.

Starting at about 10 pm, **Round Midnight**, at 39 Salamanca Place, swings through the night as does **The Lodge** on the first floor at 251 Liverpool Street, a recent addition to Hobart's night life. There are good bands six nights a week at the **Dog House Hotel** on the corner of Barrack and Goulburn Streets. Music ranges from gentle folk and blues to

Hobart's busy Franklin Wharf. From here river cruisers set off for tours of the Derwent.

"head-banging" music for the younger crowd, and the pub closes at about 1 am.

There is a Gig Guide in *The Mercury* newspaper every Thursday, which lists live music venues for the coming week.

The brightest lights shine at **Wrest Point Casino** on Sandy Bay, a five-minute taxi ride from the city. International stars appear in cabaret where there is a stylish revolving restaurant with views over the city and River Derwent. The gaming rooms offer all the usual gambling variations from poker machines to roulette, as well as "two-up".

manca Place. In the same arcade you will find **Roy Gilbert**, ℂ (002) 233-572, who makes wondrous fantasies in leather such as cribbage boards with dragons carved onto them and wall plaques inspired by *art nouveau*. The **Crafts Council of Tasmania** in Salamanca Place, ℂ (002) 235-622, has compiled a directory of other craft shops worth visiting.

SPORT

The highlight of the sporting calendar is

SHOPPING

Salamanca Place has a good selection of craft shops. Popular souvenirs are products made from local woods: Huon pine is particularly prized, being an almost indestructible wood growing only in the remote regions of the south-west today, although once it was common. The honey-yellow wood contains a pleasant-smelling resinous oil which preserves it and retains a distinctive scent for decades. There are many shops offering wooden crafts such as "eggs" and salt and pepper shakers, but for better quality wooden products have a look around **Handmark Gallery** at 77 Sala-

the Sydney–Hobart and Melbourne–Hobart yacht races. Both end around New Year's Day when the town is turned over to celebrations and the usual intemperate drinking. The **Royal Yacht Club of Tasmania**, ℂ (002) 234-599, can provide additional details of the races.

There are four 18-hole golf courses within a few kilometers of the city center and numerous 9-hole country courses beyond the city limits. The **Royal Hobart Golf Club** at Seven Mile Beach, ℂ (002) 486-161, welcomes visitors and clubs and bag can be hired. A *Guide to Tasmanian Golf Courses* is available free from any Tasmanian Travel Bureaux.

WHERE TO STAY

Luxury

Just above Salamanca Place in Battery Point is the imposing **Innkeepers Leena**, a stately mansion at 20 Runnymede Street, ((002) 323-900, fax: (002) 240-112, once the home of whaling magnate Alexander McGregor. Its sumptuous interior recalls how well one with some initiative could live in the colony.

Tantallon Lodge at 8 Mona Street, Battery Point, ((and fax) (002) 241-724, combines colonial decor with luxury accommodation, while the very modern **Sherridan Hotel** at 1 Davey Street, ((002) 354-535, fax: (002) 238-175, fronts the wharf area. The **Wrest Point Casino** at 410 Sandy Bay, ((002) 250-112, fax: (002) 253-909, towers above Hobart offering unsurpassed views of the city and easy access to the gaming rooms.

Moderate

The best place to stay if you want a taste of the real Hobart is at Battery Point where there is a good choice of colonial cottages providing bed and breakfast. The best rooms in **Cromwell Cottage** at 6 Cromwell Street, ((002) 236-734, are on the top floor and overlook the River Derwent. **Colville Cottage** at 32 Mona Street, ((002) 236-968, fax: (002) 240-500, is set in a beautiful English garden, while **Barton Cottage** at 12 Hampden Road, ((002) 241-606, fax: (002) 241-724, provides spacious accommodation in a double storey colonial building. There are quite a few other cottages to choose from, so make further inquires at the **Central Booking Office**, ((003) 317-900, or **Heritage Accommodation** on ((002) 241-612, fax: (002) 240-472.

Inexpensive

The **Waratah Motor Hotel** at 272 Murray Street, ((002) 343-685, and **Black Prince Hotel** at 145 Elizabeth Street, ((002) 343-501, offer inexpensive accommodation close to the city center.

WHERE TO EAT

Hobart has several excellent seafood restaurants which draw on the local catch for their kitchens. **Mure's Fish House** at 5 Knopwood Street, Battery Point, ((002) 312-121, serves good fish and chips from its bistro on the ground floor while the upstairs' **Upper Deck Restaurant**, ((002) 311-999, provides good quality seafood meals and wonderful views of the dock area. Nearby is the **Drunken Admiral Restaurant** at 17–19 Hunter Street Hobart, ((002) 341-903, which serves an excellent bisque, its interior a maze of nets and seafaring memorabilia.

There are several good restaurants in Salamanca Place which cater to tourists: at the far end N°87 is the seafood and steak

restaurant, the **Ball and Chain Grill**, ((002) 232-655, serving generous portions from its charcoal grill. In summer there is nothing nicer than sitting outside in its courtyard. **Panache** (N°89), ((002) 242-929, is a simple cafe with an outdoor dining area.

There are also good restaurants in Sandy Bay, 4 km (2 miles) from the city, near the Wrest Point Casino. At the Casino itself is the **Revolving Restaurant**, ((002) 250-112, with its panoramic view of Hobart and the River Derwent. **Mawson's Hut Restaurant** at 80 Queen Street, ((002) 233-969, uses fresh Tasmanian ingredients in its innovative cuisine. **Prossers'** on Beach Road, Long Point, ((002) 252-276, overlooks the River Derwent and its chilli prawns invite the accompaniment of a cool white wine from the restaurant's excellent cellar of Tasmanian wines.

Less expensive meals can be obtained in the city from **Singapore Eating House** at 7 Murray Street, ((002) 311-777, and **Marti Zucco**

ABOVE: Hobart restaurant. OPPOSITE: Restaurants, galleries and craft shops, which now line Salamanca Place were wool warehouses in the last century.

at 364 Elizabeth Street, ((002) 349-611, which serves stylish Italian food. There is a good choice of restaurants along Elizabeth Street.

HOW TO GET THERE

Hobart is served by two international air services from Auckland and Christchurch in New Zealand. The only direct Ansett and Australian Airlines flights are from Melbourne and Sydney, through which passengers from other departure points need to connect.

The *Spirit of Tasmania* ferry leaves Melbourne at 6 pm on Monday, Wednesday and Friday, arriving at Devonport the next morning. The bus connections arrive in Hobart at 1:15 pm the next day.

DAY TRIPS FROM HOBART

PORT ARTHUR

Port Arthur was established as a penal colony in 1830. In 1979 the Tasmanian and federal governments spent nine million dollars to make the site a premier tourist attraction by restoring parts of the penal settlement itself.

Port Arthur is 102 km (63 miles) southeast of Hobart and visitors usually make a day trip from Hobart to see it, although overnight accommodation is available locally.

The penal settlement was founded on a peninsula called **Eaglehawk Neck**. Across its narrowest point a line of ferocious dogs was chained to discourage prisoners from escaping. The dogs did their job well, and only a handful of convicts ever got away.

The only contact the prisoners had with the outside world was the icy blast of wind from the Antarctic. Despite the cold there was no doubt in the minds of the some 12,500 convicts who served time at Port Arthur that they had come to hell.

General Information

Tourist information can be obtained from the **National Parks and Wildlife Service**, ((002) 502-107 in Port Arthur.

What to See and Do

Now surrounded by pleasant lawns, the four-storey **Penitentiary** is still menacing. The last prisoners left in 1877 but ghosts remain of men sentenced to the hideous conditions from which some died or were driven insane.

Discipline was severe and misbehavior punished by placing the prisoner in solitary confinement in the **Model Prison**, which has also been restored. Prisoners were subjected to a form of sensory deprivation, as the cells were soundproof and dark. Wardens even wore felt slippers to mute their footfalls. The silence was complete. Disobedience resulted in more extreme deprivation, as transgressors were thrown into dumb cells that were separated from the world by a meter of solid rock and four doors. Many prisoners went mad and a **Lunatic Asylum** took these unfortunate souls. Its very existence is a stark reminder of the degradation to which Port Arthur subjected its inmates. The Asylum has been turned into a visitor's center and museum with displays on how the criminals lived.

In the middle of the bay is the forbidding **Isle of the Dead**, where 1769 convicts and 180 freemen lie buried. The headstones for the freemen, carved by the convicts (complete with spelling mistakes), can still be seen. The island is reached by a ferry which leaves the jetty at Port Arthur daily every hour, from 10:30 am to 4:30 pm.

How to Get There
Organized tours are available from **Hobart Coaches**, ℂ (002) 344-077 or (008) 030-620, leaving Hobart Monday, Wednesday, Friday and Sunday.

RICHMOND

Richmond is twenty minutes from Hobart

mons who was sent to Australia as a guest of His Majesty. This petty criminal is believed to have been the model used by Charles Dickens to create the character Fagin in *Oliver Twist*.

Prospect House, ℂ (002) 624-238, is in one of the nicest settings for a restaurant you could wish. Meals are served in the front rooms of the Georgian house built in 1830 by convicts. Accommodation is also provided at the back in airy rooms with louvered French doors opening on to a peaceful courtyard.

and is a fine example of an early nineteenth century village. Many of the original buildings are still intact and at night the streets are lit up by old lamps.

The Coal River is spanned by the **Richmond Bridge**, dating back to 1823 and making it the oldest in Australia. Its setting is quite beautiful as ducks swim in the placid waters under the bridge, and weeping willows shade its banks. A backdrop to the bridge is **St. John's Church**, built in 1824 and still used by those of the Catholic persuasion. In town visitors can see **Old Hobart Town** on Bridge Street, a scale model of Hobart as it was in the 1820s. See the restored jail house, built in 1825. It once held Izzy Solo-

How to Get There
Richmond is 26 km (14 miles) north east of Hobart and a regular weekday bus service takes 30 minutes to make the journey. There are four buses a day, two in the morning and two in the evening.

BRUNY ISLAND

Bruny Island is divided by a very narrow isthmus which at high tide is not much wider than the road. Driving along it at night requires care because penguins occasionally walk across.

ABOVE: Hobart and wintery Mt. Wellington. The Tasman Bridge is one of 5,000 bridges on the island. OPPOSITE: The guard tower at Port Arthur, the best preserved of Australia's convict past.

The island was first sighted by Abel Tasman in 1642 and has been visited by the "who's who" of Australian sea explorers, such as Cook, Furneaux and Bligh.

It is also a place of great sadness to Aborigines: there is a memorial on the island to Truganini, believed to be the last tribal Tasmanian Aborigine, a fact since disputed. That does not negate the tragedy of the Tasmanian native inhabitants who were effectively exterminated by white man's disease and white man's barbarism. There is a poignant verse to the people of Truganini, who was born on Bruny Island, at **Big Hummock**. It says "They roam no more upon this isle, so staying meditate awhile."

There are mini-bus tours provided by **Bruny Island Venture Tours**, ((002) 732-886, fax: (002) 730-269, for small groups of people. Accommodation and meals are included. Peter Watson, whose association with the island spans 45 years, introduces visitors to its rugged beauty and explains the history he obviously loves dearly.

If time is limited at least take a look at the **lighthouse**, built in 1838, and still operating.

There are few good eating places on Bruny Island, and at **Lyndenne Restaurant** at Barnes Bay, ((002) 606-264, the chef is particularly proud of his grilled steaks. The seafood platter at the **Penguin**, ((002) 723-170, in Venture Bay includes all the local delicacies such as Atlantic smoked salmon, smoked trout and crayfish.

How to Get There

Bruny Island is 34 km (21 miles) south of Hobart and can be reached by ferry from Kettering. The crossing takes about 15 minutes and the ferry takes cars across to the island.

HUON VALLEY

Tasmania was once promoted as the Apple Isle because it was Australia's main producer of them. The tourist authorities found that few visitors would travel to Tasmania for this reason alone. While Tasmania's other attractions are now more widely appreciated the fact remains that the state is still a major producer of apples, which is not as strong an industry as it once was. The home of the apple industry is the Huon Valley, south of Hobart. In this fertile region orchards line the roadsides and march up the hillsides; the prettiest time is during October when the trees are in blossom.

The Huon River opens out into a wide estuary, with picturesque villages such as **Huonville**, **Geeveston** and **Dover** lying quietly along its banks.

If this area is so famous for its fruit then it's quite logical that Huonville's main feature should be its **Apple Industry Museum**, where over 500 varieties of apple are on show. The museum is open daily between 9 am and 5 pm, and an admission-fee is charged. A favorite souvenir of the area is the Apple Folk, dolls with heads carved from apples, and then dried. The wrinkles created by the drying process makes each face quite

unique, a concept that the makers of Barbie Dolls are unlikely to appreciate. But then, their business may be more successful!

Geeveston is the gateway to the **Hartz Mountains National Park**, which is classified as a World Heritage area because of its rugged alpine scenery.

How to get there

The best way of touring the Huon Valley is by car, and most of the main attractions are close to the Huon Highway.

THE WEST COAST

The trip down the west coast is popular as it takes in some of the most spectacular scenery in Tasmania, with majestic mountains, fast flowing rivers and still lakes.

WHAT TO SEE AND DO

Tarraleah

Tarraleah is perched on the Central Highland Plateau, and is a convenient stop when touring the west coast or the lake region to the north. The town was built by the Hydroelectric Commission, a major employer in Tasmania and a power unto itself, paying little attention to the government.

Cradle Mountain ABOVE is the island's most popular destination, especially for hikers.

Typical of those settlements built by the Hydroelectric Commission, simple timber houses are provided for its workmen.

One of the best maintained nine hole golf courses in Tasmania is here with an indoor swimming pool, also naturally maintained by the Hydroelectric Commission.

In days gone by the guesthouse was reserved for the top brass of the Commission and a whole suite of rooms was kept ready in case the Commissioner should drop in for a breath of country air, but today the town is being privatised.

The guesthouse **Tarraleah Chalet,** ((002) 893-128, fax: (002) 893-177, was sold to Izzy Munoz in 1991 and is now open to all comers. See it before it is renovated, because it is a classical artifact of the 1930s. Rooms have names like Lake Echo, Laughing Jack Lagoon and Clumy Dam, the lounge is comfortable and the glass-enclosed verandahs are wonderfully warm in winter when the sun is out. A permanent resident of Tarraleah is Terry, who will tell you colorful tales about the early days when the people who lived and worked on the west coast were as rugged as the scenery. In more mellow moments he can turn into Terrance L. Emmerton who has a local reputation as a witty bush poet. Provided someone is buying him drinks, he is not adverse to giving a public reading at the bar.

Queenstown

Queenstown, on the west coast, is one of the most desolate places on Earth. Its lunar landscape is man-made by polluted fall-out from the copper smelter.

Either approach road to the town winds through bare red-brown clay, as all the topsoil has been washed away. Before mining began the steep hills were covered with dense rain forest. For 78 years the copper smelter in Queenstown belched sulfuric acid into the atmosphere, killing those trees not felled to feed the furnaces. Top-soil eroded off the bare hills, making the current attempts at regenerating the vegetation exceedingly difficult.

If the ozone layer finally decides to give up the ghost, atomic fission gets out of hand and sparks a nuclear winter or the greenhouse effect fries the earth, then I imagine the rest of the world will start to look like Queenstown. The place is a timely warning, and for that alone is worth a visit, albeit a short one.

Strahan

Strahan, standing on the shore of Macquarie Harbour, was once a major coastal port. Huge Huon pine logs were floated down the **Gordon River** for milling in Strahan and then export.

This small unassuming town is the starting point for cruises along the Gordon River, which runs through part of the World Heritage area. The **Gordon River Cruises,** ((004) 717-187, depart from the main wharf every day at 9 am and return at about 1:30 pm. The cruise moves up the Gordon River, past ancient Huon pines until at Heritage Landing there is an opportunity to get off and explore some of the 2000-year-old rain forest, via a walkway designed to prevent damage to the delicate ecosystem. The availability of day trips down the Gordon River is limited; to obtain an idea of the richness of the scenery, **Wilderness Air,** ((004) 717-280, fax: (004) 717-303, provides flights over the South-West Heritage Area. The seaplane touches down on the Gordon and a walk to **St. John Falls** allows visitors to look at the rain forest themselves.

Cradle Mountain

The **Cradle Mountain-Lake St. Clair National Park** is one of the most popular destinations in Tasmania, particularly with hikers.

It is possible to walk from Lake St. Clair to Cradle Mountain on the **Overland Track,** an 85-km (53-mile) hike that is both challenging and rewarding. The journey takes five or six days and the path is well signposted. It is important that walkers are fit because there are no access roads and the only way out in an emergency is by helicopter. The Overland Track passes glacial lakes and winds its way through alpine heathland and dense beech forests. In the distance jagged mountain ranges provide an impressive backdrop. There are huts along the way to provide shelter from bad weather, which can come upon the mountain quite suddenly. The best time to visit the area is from

December to April. Before starting out all walkers must register with the park ranger and a walking fee is payable.

There are also shorter walks around Lake St. Clair and Cradle Mountain for less experienced walkers that vary between one and eight hours, and provide a surprising variety of scenery within a short distance.

WHERE TO STAY

Once the only accommodation in mining towns was in pubs. In Queenstown three

commodation in log cabins, which are a perfect base for exploring the national park. Each cabin has a pot-bellied stove, and in the evening Potaroos, small wallabies, graze around the back of the cabins. There are also the **Cradle Mountain Campgrounds**, ((004) 921-395, nearby which offer budget accommodation.

HOW TO GET THERE

165 km (102 miles) from Hobart, along the Lyell Highway is **Derwent Bridge**, a pub

hotels still provide inexpensive accommodation. In Orr Street there are the **Empire Hotel**, ((004) 711-699, **Hunters Hotel**, ((004) 711-531, and the **Commercial Hotel** on Driffield Street, ((004) 711-511. The **Queenstown Motor Inn** at 54–58 Orr Street, ((004) 711-866, is moderately priced.

At Strahan **Franklin Manor**, ((004) 717-311, fax: (004) 717-267, overlooking Macquarie Harbour, offers colonial accommodation in a gabled guesthouse built in 1897. The restaurant attached to Franklin Manor gives preference to guests. **Sharonlee**, ((004) 717-224, fax: (004) 717-375, offers moderately priced self-contained cabins.

The **Cradle Mountain Lodge**, ((004) 921-303 or (008) 030-377, offers expensive ac-

and little else. It is the turn off for the Lake St. Clair entrance to Cradle Mountain-Lake St. Clair National Park. The Cradle Mountain entrance can be reached by turning off the Bass Highway at Wilmont and continuing south along a 58 km (36 miles) stretch of road, the last section of which is unmade.

Tasmanian Wildness Travel runs a daily bus to Cradle Mountain from Devonport and Launceston on Tuesday and Thursday, and a bus to Lake St. Clair on Wednesday. Buses run from Hobart to Lake St. Clair and Strahan on Saturday. The Tasmanian Redline Buses run from Hobart to Bernie via Queenstown and

The nursery rhyme place name animated with musical clock is an attraction at a Hobart shopping arcade.

Derwent Bridge from Tuesday to Saturday. Transport from Derwent Bridge to Lake St. Clair operates on demand and the charter service can be contacted at ☏ (004) 928-093.

UP THE MIDDLE

The **Midlands Highway** runs 198 km (123 miles) between Hobart and Launceston, and is Tasmania's main artery. It bypasses many of the historic villages along the route, allowing them to revert to a peace

that was lost with the advent of motor cars. Most townships which are just a short distance off the highway, have early histories as coaching stops and military depots and are rich in colonial character. The trip takes about two hours by car but there are sufficient places of interest to visit for it to be worth taking your time.

The route was first surveyed in 1807 by Surveyor-General Charles Grimes, and towns sprang up along its length, radiating out from the two major population centers. By 1830, there were 16 inns along the route providing refreshment for travelers between Hobart and Launceston. The road, built using convict labor, was not completed until 1850. At the time it was the best highway in the country on which the latest methods of road-making were used.

WHAT TO SEE AND DO

Ross

Ross, 122 km (76 miles) from Hobart, is situated on the Macquarie River. The village is splendidly preserved, and indeed a living museum of nineteenth century architecture. Its streets are lined with historic homes and public buildings, many of which have been restored and are now used as museums, hotels or shops to cater for tourists.

Spanning the river is the **Ross Bridge**, which is not quite as old as the one at Richmond, having been built only in 1836 with convict labor. It is, however, certainly one of the most beautiful in Australia. Over the sandstone arches the convicts added 186 carved stones which took their inspiration of Celtic folklore. It is rumored that some of the figures are caricatures of local colonial "deities."

The main crossroads of Bridge and Church Streets, was known locally as the "four corners of Ross" — Damnation (one corner was occupied by a women's prison, now gone), Recreation (Town Hall), Salvation (**Lady of Sacred Heart Catholic Church**) and Temptation (**Man O'Ross Hotel**). While not all four buildings remain, fortunately the 1817 hotel survives, its interior richly paneled with Tasmanian Oak and Blackwood.

Ross itself, with its leafy streets has the feeling of an English village. Opposite St. John's Church on the main street is the **Village Tea Room** that serves light refreshment and a display of fine Tasmanian craft gives visitors an opportunity to purchase a quality souvenir.

Evandale

Turn-off the main Highway at Breadalbane for Evandale, 20 km (12 miles) from Launceston. The village provides an excellent example of an intact Georgian streetscape. Off the main road 8 km (5 miles) from town is **Clarendon House**, ☏ (003) 986-220, which was built in 1838 by wealthy wool grower and merchant James Fox on his 5,700-hectare (14,000-acre) property. Approaching the house down the long drive it is difficult not to be impressed by the first appearance of the two-storey mansion, its facade supported by huge Ionic columns and an architectural style which would not have been out of place on a grand plantation in Virginia early last century. The house is furnished in the style of the period and is open for visits.

Perth

Perth, on the highway only 20 km (13 miles) south of Launceston, also has strong nineteenth century connections. The historic **Leather Bottell Inn**, ((003) 982-248, has been converted into an excellent restaurant, being open daily for morning and afternoon teas, lunch, and dinner from Thursday to Saturday.

Central Highland

An alternative route through the center of Tasmania takes you to the **Land of Three** region is of world standard, as was recognized in 1988 when the World Fly Fishing Championship was held on the Central Highlands. Reeling in a 2 kg (4.4 lb) trout is an everyday event and in some lakes 4 kg (9 lb) trout are not uncommon. The best times to fish is from the beginning of October to late March.

Many of the larger lakes also feed water to hydroelectric schemes connected to rivers that flow off the plateau. To get some idea of the massive engineering involved in these schemes visit the **Poatina Power Station**,

Thousand Lakes. The roads are not as good or fast as the Midlands Highway, but the scenery more than justifies getting off the beaten track to see this seldom-visited area.

From Launceston take the Bass Highway to Deloraine and then turn onto the scenic Lake Highway, which takes you onto the windswept central plateau with its scurrying clouds, gnarled pencil pines, moorland and mountains. The terrain is pock-marked with glacial lakes, some so shallow that it is possible to walk across them, and others no larger than a football field.

The lakes in this rarely-visited part are teeming with wild brown trout, much prized by fly-fishermen (who are trying to keep this great fishing ground a secret). Fishing in the

((003) 978-254, which is open for inspection on weekdays from 9 am to 12:30 pm and from 1 pm to 3:30 pm.

WHERE TO STAY

Ross has a good selection of colonial accommodation. The **Man O'Ross**, ((003) 815-240, is inexpensive and includes a hearty breakfast. **Hudson Cottage** and **Apple Dumpling Cottage**, ((003) 815-354, fax: (003) 815-408, are self-contained colonial cottages that date back to the 1850s and 1880s respectively.

ABOVE: Ringaroo River in Tasmania's northeast. OPPOSITE: The beautiful convict-built bridge at Ross. The convict who carried out the carving received his freedom as a reward.

Each is furnished with pieces from the mid-nineteenth century.

There are few places to stay along the Lake Highway, but some moderately priced accommodation is available in Bothwell. **Bothwell Grange** in Alexander Street, ((002) 595-556, is in town and the quaint **Mrs Woods Farmhouse**, ((002) 595-612, is 8 km (5 miles) out of town.

The **Compleat Angler Lodge** on Haddens Bay, **Great Lake**, ((002) 598-179 or fax: (002) 598-147, $IGreat Lake>is moderately priced. The hotel caters to fishermen and Peter Wilson will provide you with information on the best places to fish.

How to Get There

Tasmanian Redline Coaches run a daily service between Hobart and Launceston along the Midlands Highway. There are no regular buses for transportation along the Lakes Highway, and the only way to explore this area is by car.

LAUNCESTON

The first test any visitor has in gaining acceptance from the locals is if he or she pronounces the city's name correctly. *Lawn*-ceston will be greeted with hoots of protest, while *Lon*-ceston will elicit a sigh of satisfaction. Casually refer to the city as "Lonny" and you will be accepted as an honorary local and invited home for dinner to meet the family.

Despite its small size with a population of about 93,000, Launceston has an intense rivalry with Hobart. Both cities once reported separately to Sydney. In 1812, much to Launceston's horror, it came under the control of the colonial administration located in Hobart.

General information

In Launceston the **Tasmanian Travel Centre** at the corner of St. John and Paterson Streets, ((003) 373-122, is open from 8.45 am to 5 pm weekdays, and from 9 am to 12 noon weekends. The **National Trust** has an information center at The Old Umbrella Shop, 60 George Street.

What to See and Do

Tasmania's second largest city is otherwise known as the garden city because of its numerous parks in which European trees such as ash, oaks and elms thrive. It is an excellent base for exploring the northern part of Tasmania and also has some attractions in its own right to justify staying there a few days.

Launceston's outstanding natural beauty spot, only a few minutes walk from the center of town, is **Cataract Gorge and Cliff Grounds**.

The park that provides access to the gorge is an ideal setting for a picnic. The Cataract Gorge itself is a canyon through which the South Esk River plunges with spectacular ferocity after heavy rain. A walking path follows the cliff face and a 300 m (985 ft) chairlift, the world's largest single span lift, offers a breathtaking ride over the waters.

The natural beauty of Launceston — founded just a few months after Hobart — is complemented by a variety of historic buildings, a number of which line St. John and George Streets.

The best known commercial attraction is the **Penny Royal World** on Patterson Street, ((003) 316-699, which re-creates colonial industrial practices. A watermill has been restored to working order, along with a corn-mill, windmill, cannon foundry and arsenal.

Grindelwald, 15 km (9 miles) north of Launceston, is a Swiss village transported to the Antipodes. This does not appear as out-of-place as it may seem, as the landscape in this part of Tasmania with its green rolling hills resembles the foothills of the Alps.

WHERE TO STAY

Luxury

Eight kilometers (five miles) south-west of

agency ((003) 342-231at 121–129 Balfour Street, and visitors can lay themselves down at night on an old-fashioned four-poster bed. **Ivy Cottage** at 17 York Street, features an antique bath and its genuine feather eiderdowns are snug on the coldest winter night. Both cottages can be booked through the same agency, ((003) 342-231.

At the corner of Margaret and York Streets is the **Old Bakery Inn**, ((003) 317-900, fax: (003) 317-756, which has been restored to its nineteenth century condition, in which even some of the original ovens remain.

Launceston is the **Country Club Casino** at Prospect Vale, ((003) 355-777, (008) 030-211, fax: (003) 355-788. The hotel offers guests access to its 18-hole, par 72 golf course, dining in its classy restaurant, and at night live entertainment at the casino or gambling at its gaming tables.

For a quiet stay in Grindelwald, **Holiday Resort** on Lake Louise is a good choice. ((003) 301-799, fax: (003) 301-607.

Moderate

Launceston was founded in 1805 and many of its splendid nineteenth century houses and cottages have been converted into self-contained accommodation. A large weeping willow shades **The Shambles, booking**

Inexpensive

For comfortable motel-type accommodation try the **Great Northern** at 3 Earl Street, ((003) 319-999, fax: (003) 393-727, or **North Lodge**, ((003) 319-966, fax: (003) 342-810.

WHERE TO EAT

The **Gorge Restaurant** in Cliff Ground, ((003) 313-330, is perched in the grounds of Cataract Gorge. The view from the restaurant is of the surrounding cliffs, which at night are

ABOVE: St Andrew's Church. Launceston's many parks give it the sobriquet of Tasmania's garden city. OPPOSITE: A jolly boat ride at Penny Royal World.

illuminated. During the day light meals and afternoon tea are served on outside tables, where tame peacock strut, contemptuous of diners.

Dine in great style at **Fee & Me** at the corner of Fredrick and Charles Streets, ((003) 313-195, located in an elegant two storey mansion built in 1835. Nearby is **Elm Cottage** at 168 Charles Street, ((003) 318-468, a quaint restaurant near the center of Launceston. **Quigley's** at 96 Balfour Street, ((003) 316-971, is well-known in town for its game and fish dishes.

HOW TO GET THERE

Ansett and Australian Airlines have services from most state capital cities to Launceston. Airlines of Tasmania provide flights between Hobart and Launceston.

The *Spirit of Tasmania* ferry leaves Melbourne at 6 pm on Monday, Wednesday and Friday, arriving at Devonport the next morning. A bus connection arrives in Launceston at 10 am the next day.

THE EAST COAST

Tasmania is not well endowed with the Australian trilogy of sun, surf and sand; the nearest you get to it is on the east coast, where there is a string of small resort towns.

The Tasman Highway runs 435 km (270 miles) between Hobart and Launceston. From Launceston it loops through the northeast corner, skirting the rocky bastion of the Ben Lomond plateau and reaching the coast at **St. Helens**.

WHAT TO SEE AND DO

Bicheno

Once boats left Bicheno to harpoon whales in the Tasman sea or kill seals on the islands off Tasmania. This butchery is no longer acceptable and now the only quarry are crayfish, oysters and abalone.

This seaside village, a popular holiday destination, attracts surf fishermen. Bicheno is also a good base for exploring the nearby **Douglas-Apsley National Park**.

Coles Bay

Coles Bay is located at the neck of the peninsula that constitutes the **Feycinet Peninsula National Park**, with its pink granite peaks and vertical cliffs dropping straight into the sea. A 25 km (16 mile) walking circuit takes in a variety of coastal scenery, and tracks lead to **Wineglass Bay** and the **Lighthouse**.

Swansea

Situated on Oyster Bay, Swansea was settled in the 1820s and many of its original buildings still stand. The **Swansea Bark Mill**, ((002) 578-382, was built in 1886 and today is a museum which shows visitors the early industries in the area. Of particular interest is the display of how leather was tanned using black wattle bark. An admission-fee is charged and the museum is open daily. The bay has safe sheltered beaches and so is popular with families.

WHERE TO STAY

There is a good range of accommodation in Bicheno, a dedicated holiday town. The oldest building was built in 1845: the jail house. Following a long tradition of offering free accommodation to guests cunningly invited by the Crown, the **Gaol House Cottages** have upgraded standards and service, and now seek paying guests. For the curious, some of the original cells remain. The cottages are on the corner of James and Burgess Streets, ((003) 751-430, fax: (003) 751-368.

The modest **Wintersun Lodge Motel** at 35 Gordon Street, ((003) 751-225, is inexpensive while the **Diamond Island Resort** at 69 Tasman Highway, ((003) 751-161, is moderately priced.

Freycinet Lodge near Coles Bay, ((003) 570-101, is located in the National Park and provides moderately priced accommodation. Vans can be hired at the **Coles Bay Caravan Park**, ((003) 570-100, at very reasonable rates.

In Swansea the 1836 **Oyster Bay Guesthouse** at 10 Franklin Street, ((003) 578-110,

and **Schouten House**, ((003) 578-564, offer moderately priced accommodation.

How to Get There

Redline Coaches run buses along the east coast between Hobart and Launceston with stops at St. Helens, Bicheno and Swansea. Hobart Coaches run a service from Hobart to the east coast towns every day except Saturday.

NATIONAL PARKS

About 28 percent of Tasmania is protected, some of which constitutes World Heritage areas: there is an entry charge for all 14 National Parks in Tasmania. A daily pass costs $5 and a monthly pass $30.

For information on National Parks contact the Tasmanian Conservation Trust, ((002) 343-552.

Convenient to Hobart is the **Mt. Field National Park**, 80 km (50 miles) west of the capital on the Lyell Highway. Its forests contain many ancient trees — Huon Pines, gums and sassafras. Several walking tracks through the National Park are popular in summer and at higher altitudes there is good skiing in winter.

The **South-West Wilderness** is a World Heritage Area and featuring rugged terrain and a remote, untouched coastline. While **Federation Peak** is a modest 1,425 m (4,675 ft), scaling it challenges the best climbers; the last section is up a steep rock face. Watch out for the weather which can change suddenly on the mountains!

FESTIVALS AND SPORTING EVENTS

FEBRUARY During the last weekend of the month vintage bike enthusiasts gather for the **Village Fair and Pennyfarthing Championships** at Evandale, 20 km (12 miles) south of Launceston. The festivities also include market and craft stalls, side-shows and street entertainment.

FEBRUARY/MARCH Despite its hilly terrain Tasmania is a favorite place for touring cyclists. About 1,000 of them tour the island during the **Great Tasmanian Bike Ride** from Hobart to Devonport, a trip lasting ten days. Bookings can be made through Bicycle Victoria (GPO Box 1961R, Melbourne, 3001).

MARCH Learn everything you need to know about that important ingredient they add to beer during the **New Norfolk Hop Festival** held in the Derwent Valley, 38 km (24 miles) from Hobart.

SEPTEMBER The **Tasmanian Tulip Festival** is held in the Royal Tasmanian Botanical Gardens and the theme of festivities is Dutch with dancing and, of course, thousands upon thousands of those beautiful flowers.

ABOVE: Russell Falls, one of several cascades in Mount Field National Park. OPPOSITE: Wallaby and little wallaby.

me for a Carlton.

Victoria

a Place Fit for a Queen

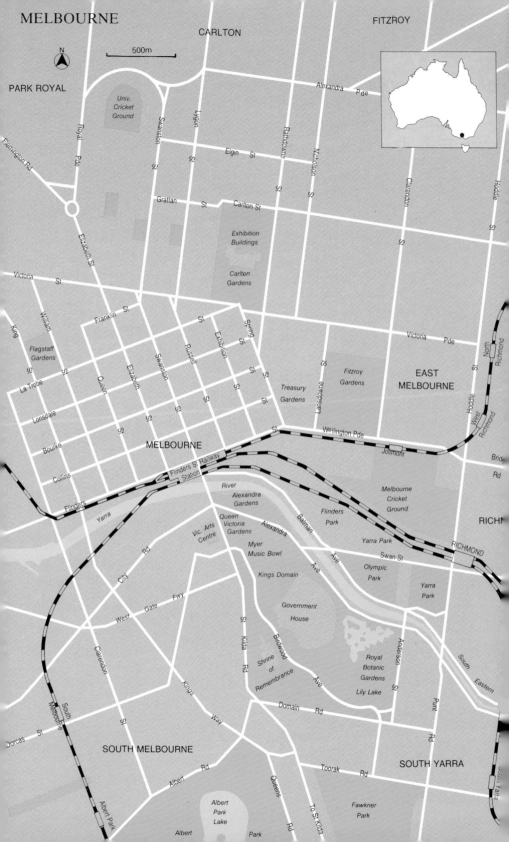

MELBOURNE

Queen Victoria never visited Australia but had she done so, I'm sure that she would have gravitated towards Melbourne where many of its public buildings and houses would have looked so familiar, built as they were during her glorious reign.

As Melbourne went through cycles of boom and bust, the city's skyline and suburban streetscapes were shaped by architectural styles of the Victorian period — neo-Gothic, Italianate and Classical.

Writing about the Melbourne of 1856, a contemporary admired "its wide and spacious thoroughfares, fringed with edifices worthy of the wealth of its citizens, and corresponding in architectural pretensions of their occupants." Fortunately much of Melbourne's architectural heritage remains intact, and though skyscrapers line the streets of the central city many fine buildings have not been sacrificed to the developers' passion for high rise boxes of steel and glass.

Walking around Melbourne and its suburbs it is still possible to see lavishly embellished buildings from the mid-1850s, a taste which became more outrageous during the boom years of the 1880s and 1890s. All of this, I'm sure, would please the fickle Queen Victoria who was notoriously difficult to "amuse."

GENERAL INFORMATION

Tourist information and accommodation booking services are available from the **RACV Touring and Travel Centre** at 422 Little Collins Street, ((03) 790-2121 or (008) 337-743.

The City of Melbourne publishes the monthly *Melbourne Events*, available free of charge from most hotels. There is also a phone information service on (0055-30-000. Calls to this service are time-charged.

For information on Melbourne's public transport call the **Met Information Centre** on (131-638 or visit its shop in the city at 103 Elizabeth Street. For information on country trains phone **V/Line** on (132-232.

BACKGROUND

Melbourne was "bought" by John Batman in 1834 from the Aboriginal landowners. After handing over what he thought was a fair price, namely 20 blankets, 30 knifes, 12 red shirts, four flannel jackets and the like, he was able to boast that "I am the greatest landowner in the world." What the local tribal people thought of this bargain, involving 600,000 acres (243,000 hectares) of prime real estate, is not recorded.

If they had had any regrets they could have put the 50 handkerchiefs Batman provided as part of the price to use and wiped their eyes.

The colonial government, unimpressed with Batman's business acumen, did not recognize his land claim.

The outline of Melbourne was devised by Robert Hoddle in 1836. His vision for what was then only a village of a few makeshift houses and muddy streets, was of a city with wide avenues laid out in a neat grid.

ABOVE: The monumental architecture of Melbourne's Exhibition Hall.

Melbourne grew slowly at first, but when gold was discovered in Bendigo in 1851 the city boomed and Hoddle's vision became a reality. Within a few years the population quadrupled to 80,000 and the government embarked on a civic building program which established Melbourne as a great nineteenth century Victorian city. In 1853 alone 1,000 buildings were erected in the city area, and this growth continued in fits and starts until early into the twentieth century. At the height of this activity the city was justifiably known as Marvelous Melbourne.

WHAT TO SEE AND DO

The central city area has much to offer during the day, although at night and at the weekend it quietens considerably. After sunset, activity focuses on the theater area of Bourke Street, between Swanston and Exhibition Streets, in Chinatown along Little Bourke Street, and Southgate on the Yarra River.

At night and weekends the main action moves to the inner suburbs, each of which has its own character and is worth visiting. Melbourne has an extensive tram system making the suburbs easily accessible.

City Strolls

The city's architectural character was set in the mid to late nineteenth century. Unfortunately, over the last thirty years Melbourne has lost some fine buildings to developers. Many beautiful old buildings, however, remain.

The city is set out in a grid, making it easy to move around. Start at the corner of Flin-

ders and Swanston Streets at **Flinders Street Station**. Before the underground train loop was built, this was the hub of Melbourne. When the railway management threatened to remove the clocks over the entrance that announced the arrival of trains, the city blew its collective stack because meeting "under the clocks" had become an institution.

Walk north along Swanston Walk, now a pedestrian mall. The plan has failed and at the time of writing remains a street without cars. Beware of trams and bikes: they are still allowed along the mall. At the corner of Collins Street is the **City Square** with water cascading around its boundary. During lunchtime and at the weekend free entertainment is often provided in the Square.

Turn left into Collins Street and walk two blocks to Queen Street where you are surrounded by the buildings which once housed Melbourne's financial institutions, built during the land boom of the 1880s and early 1890s when each building society tried to outdo its neighbor in ostentatiousness. Many have spires and turrets more suited to a Bohemian castle, and interiors resplendent with ceiling paintings and gold trim. Buildings at the corner of Collins and Queen Streets are worth looking at; at 388 Collins Street griffins guard the entrance of what was once the **E.S.& A. Bank**, built in 1883. Its embellishments pushed it to the limits of outrageousness, even for a neo-Gothic building.

In the block past Williams Street, between 471 and 483 Collins Street, are four buildings that give some idea what Melbourne's streetscape looked like a hundred years ago.

Take a tram back along Collins Street to Spring Street, facetiously known as the Paris end of the street, shaded by plane trees and at night lit up with fairy lights. Ahead of you is the **Old Treasury Building** (1858), in classical Renaissance-style, which the government plans to turn into an outdoor restaurant.

Turn left at Spring Street and walk a block to Bourke Street: to your right is the State **Parliament House**, built in stages between 1856 and 1930. The original design included plans for a dome on top of the building, which unfortunately failed to materialise.

The interior is richly adorned, the highlight being the Legislative Council Chamber with its ornate, painted vaulted ceiling. There are guided tours on weekdays but bookings are necessary, ((03) 651-8568. For the very hardy it is possible, when the House is sitting, to endure the public gallery when Parliament is in action.

Opposite Parliament is the **Windsor Hotel**, one of Melbourne's institutions with a colorful history. In 1886 it was bought by the Honorable James Munro, president of the Temperance Party who ceremoniously

in the company of Melbourne's Establishment.

Nearby is the **Princess Theatre**, at which such blockbusters as *Phantom of the Opera* and *Les Miserables* were shown recently. Built in 1887, this is a thoroughly vulgar piece of Victoriana with ludicrous decoration: its facade includes figures of the Muses, urns, lions and a golden angel tooting a trumpet.

Catch a tram down Bourke Street and alight at Swanston Walk. This is the beginning of the **Bourke Street Mall**, usually

burnt his liquor license and renamed the hotel the Grand Coffee Palace. Under the guidance of the temperance philosophy the Grand went into a decline until 1921, when a new owner obtained a new liquor license. Today the Windsor has several bars but it has not turned its back on more sober beverages. In the Lounge between 3 pm and 5:30 pm, afternoon tea is served on a full silver tea service, cucumber sandwiches (with the crusts trimmed off), cakes and fresh tea or coffee. This Melbourne institution is popular with wealthy farmers and their wives down to the city "for a spot of business." It also has the Grand Dining Room with a stained glass dome. Ease back into the leather chairs and relax

crawling with buskers who will importune you. Make payment conditional upon their guarantee never to darken your doorstep again.

Melbourne's Art Complex

Just outside the central city area as you head south along Swanston Street over the Yarra River is the **Victorian Arts Centre**, ((03) 684-8484, consisting of three buildings. There is always a full program of plays, dance and ballet, details of which are listed in the daily newspapers. The **Theatres Building** is topped with a 115 m (377 ft)

ABOVE: The mogul facade of a theater (LEFT) and St. Paul's Cathedral and Civic Square (RIGHT). OPPOSITE: Art in the park.

spire-frame, illuminated at night. Along the wall of the stalls' Foyer are 800 tiles, called **"Paradise Gardens,"** commissioned from the late Sidney Nolan, which you must see. The building also contains the **Westpac Gallery**, almost opposite the entrance. Entry is free and exhibitions varied but always interesting. There are guided tours of the Victorian Arts Centre, ((03) 684-8151, which start at 12 noon and 2:30 pm weekdays. Backstage tours are conducted on Sunday at 12:15 pm and 2:15 pm, and last about an hour and a half.

Next to the Centre is the **Concert Hall**, a

very plain building with a functional interior where the main auditorium has excellent acoustics. Within the building is the **Performing Arts Museum**, ((03) 684-8263, with eclectic exhibitions dealing with all aspects of entertainment, past and present.

On the other side is the **National Gallery of Victoria**, ((03) 685-0222, which has a permanent exhibition of Australian works as well as regular exhibitions from overseas. Open daily from 10am to 5pm, and an entrance fee is charged. There is also an excellent collection of Chinese robes and ceramics.

ABOVE: Flinders Street Railway Station, on the Yarra River side of the business district, serves the suburban areas — a good place for buskers to attract passers-by. OPPOSITE: Melbourne's Arts Centre.

Just below the complex beside the Yarra River is **Southbank**, with its outdoor cafes and shops. This development is relatively new but already popular, with its restaurants and bars well patronised.

Queen Victoria Market

At the edge of the city at the corner of Elizabeth and Victoria Streets is the Queen Victoria Market, ((03) 658-9600, which started in 1878 and has the largest stock of fresh produce in Melbourne. Over 1,000 stalls spread over 7 hectares (17 acres). A few similar markets remain around Melbourne, and are popular despite the proliferation of dreary multi-storey shopping complexes, supermarkets and malls in the suburbs.

The market is divided into four sections — meat and fish, fruit and vegetables, delicatessen and a diverse section containing clothing, souvenirs, footwear, toys, kitchenware and hardware products.

The first customers arrive as early as 6 am to pick out the best of the fresh produce, followed by a coffee (and if the stomach is up to it, a *bratwurst* from shop 99/100 in the Deli section where Irene and Nino Greco have been catering to this early morning craving for over 25 years). **Le Croissant des Hades** (corner of Elizabeth and Thierry Streets) offers a more civilized choice for breakfast — a croissant, fresh out of the oven, and fresh coffee. The market provides an ideal source of inexpensive food for a picnic on the Yarra River or in one of the many parks that ring the city. **Tina's Deli** (shop 33–35) is a wonderful source of Australian cheeses, while bread baked in woodfired ovens can be bought from **Andrew's Bread Shop** (shop 29–30).

On Saturday at midday the pace becomes frenetic as shoppers rush for bargains before closing time at 1 pm. Stallholders stand in the aisle shouting out special deals. Bags of beans or trays of glistening trout are offered for a few dollars, and a box of fruit can be bought for under $5.

On Sunday no fresh food is sold and the Victoria Market is given over to serving tourists looking for a sheep-skin coat, a cheap cuddly koala for their children or a tee-shirt with a local design. The regulars, with a keen eye for a bargain, are also out in droves.

St. Patrick's Cathedral and District

Behind Parliament House is St. Patrick's Cathedral, built between 1858 and 1897. Gargoyles guard its bluestone exterior, and it is possible to visit the inside of the Church during the day.

Other denominations built their places of worship nearby. The sturdy **Lutheran Church** (24 Parliament Place) was built in 1853, **Baptist Church House** (486 Albert Street) was built between 1859 and 1863 and **East Melbourne Synagogue** (488 Albert Street) was finished in 1877. It is worth wandering around the streets behind Parliament where there remain lovely examples of late nineteenth century houses and public buildings.

Melbourne's Stately Houses

The National Trust owns a number of stately homes in the suburbs, open to the public and providing an insight into a more gracious era in the history of Melbourne.

Built between 1869 and 1887, **Rippon Lea** at 192 Hotham Street, ((03) 523-9150, is a grand house located in suburban Elsternwick. The Romanesque building is surrounded by 5.6 hectares (14 acres) of garden, considered the best surviving nineteenth century example in Australia. On a fine day, picnickers flock to its grounds.

Como in Como Avenue, South Yarra, ((03) 827-2500, was built in the 1840s and retains its original furnishings. This beautiful house overlooking the Yarra River, contains a ballroom and has a delicacy, an elegance and lightness quite out of place in Australian society.

Just a 30-minute drive from Melbourne, **Werribee Park**, ((03) 741-2444, is an imposing 60-room Italianate mansion built in 1877 with 12 hectares (30 acres) of gardens including an ornamental lake.

Carlton

Carlton is adjacent to the city and can be reached by tram (N°1 or 15) along Swanston Street, but it is close enough to to be able to walk.

The south end of Drummond Street which intersects Latrobe Street in the city has many wonderful terrace houses, dating back to 1864. Most of the nineteenth century streetscape is intact. Other streets in Carlton con-

tain many more examples, shaming boring modern suburbs with their mediocrity, sameness and lack of inspiration. Through the center of Carlton runs Lygon Street which has acquired an Italian character. Many post-war immigrants settled here, and Melbournians should be grateful to them for introducing cappuccino, decent pasta and outdoor cafes into their complacent city.

Although many Italian families have moved out of Carlton to more affluent suburbs, their children return to promenade along Lygon Street on warm summer evenings and dine in its numerous cafes.

Brunswick Street

Brunswick Street starts at Victoria Parade in Fitzroy, and can be reached by taking any tram

east along Collins Street. The start takes in Melbourne's first suburb — Newtown — established in the 1840s and later absorbed into the municipality of Fitzroy. The oldest houses in the street are at N°21, built in 1851, and N°9, which is now a nurses' home. The **Eastern Hill Hotel**, at the corner of Gertrude Street, was built in 1855. Once the headquarters for the Eight Hour Day movement it it it was a spawning-ground of early union radicalism.

At the city end of the street is **Roar 2 Gallery** (N°115A), which has become a Melbourne institution among avant-garde artists. Started in 1981 by recent art school graduates, it provided them with a place to show works rejected by mainstream galleries. Droll. Many artists from Roar 2 have gained recognition and moved on, but a new

generation has taken their place. Two other galleries are worth a visit: **Pigtail** (N°382) exhibits brightly colored contemporary ceramics. Anne Rittan and Gillian Welch design and make endearing piglets, which are for sale. Across the road is the **Woman's Gallery** (N°375) which devotes its space to showing prints and paintings by women. Just over Johnston Street is the **Brunswick Street Bookshop** (N°305), which stays open until late. They have a good selection of novels and art books: arm chairs are provided for serious browsers. On fine evenings buskers interpose themselves into this

Like many big cities, Melbourne's skyline has been dramatically elevated with glossy skyscrapers, however some fine buildings remain from its 19th century growth period.

part of the street, which is always crowded at weekends.

For a little piece of heaven, try an admirable ice cream from **Charmain's** (N°370). Three scoops cost $4.20, and a banana smoothie $3.20.

Down by the Beach

St. Kilda is a bayside suburb 8 km (5 miles) from the city. Its fortunes have fluctuated, starting as an affluent suburb in the mid-nineteenth century with white mansions lining its Esplanade, where families "took the sea air" at weekends.

The twentieth century has not been kind to St. Kilda, and as the gentry left for Kew, Toorak and South Yarra, Art Deco apartment buildings invaded and mansions were sub-divided into boarding houses. St. Kilda is undergoing a rebirth and hopefully the sparkle will return to the seaside suburb.

The best place to survey it is from the end of the pier. From the vantage point of the historic **St. Kilda Pier Kiosk**, the skyline looks quite Moorish with domed buildings and a foreshore fringed with palm trees.

There is a walking track and bike lane running parallel to the beach. One way to view St. Kilda beach at high speed is to hire roller blades from **Rock'n'Roll'n** at 11a Fitzroy Street for $7. Val Guerra will help the inexperienced with an impromptu lesson.

South of the pier is Acland Street, the main meeting place for the Jewish community. If you want to flirt with hyperglycemia try the rich confections of **Monarch Cake Shop** at N°103 Acland Street, or you can sit down with a cake and coffee at **Acland Cakes** at N°97. Further up the road is **Linden**, at N°26, a stuccoed brick mansion built in 1870 and converted into an art gallery, where admission is free.

Luna Park, between the Esplanade and Acland Street shouldn't be missed with its gaudy 4 m (24 ft) entrance in the shape of a laughing clown. The amusement park has seen better days but plans are under way to revitalize this old fun fair.

On Sunday there is an art and craft market along the Upper Esplanade, which is popular with tourists.

From the pier it is possible to take a ferry over to **Williamstown** on the other side of the city. The ferry departs from St. Kilda every hour. Williamstown still has the feeling of a village rather than a suburb, despite its proximity to Melbourne. It started life as a port town in 1837 but as the Port of Melbourne developed, fell into disuse. Its streets are lined with Edwardian laborers' cottages, and a stroll around is well worthwhile. On the last Sunday of every month a market is held in the park opposite Nelson Place.

MELBOURNE BY NIGHT

At night the action concentrates on the strip between the Bourke Street mall and Exhibition Street, the location of theaters and cinemas.

For live music the pubs provide a choice of jazz, folk, heavy metal and good old rock 'n' roll. For most of these gigs there is no entrance fee but check beforehand. For traditional jazz try the **Fountain Inn** at the corner of Bay and Crockford Streets, Port Melbourne or the **Emerald Hotel** at 415 Clarendon Street, South Melbourne. With a name like **Molly Blooms**, at 39 Bay Street, Port Melbourne, all you are likely to hear in this pub is Irish folk music. For something a little noisier try rock and roll at the ultra chic **Wooden Parrot Bar** at 175 Clarendon Street, South Melbourne. **The Lounge** at 243 Swanston Walk in the city offers an eclectic selection of music on most nights. In Carlton, Brunswick and Fitzroy there are quite a few establishments where aspiring bands perform.

New Australian plays often play at **La Mama** at 205 Faraday Street, Carlton. This theater has acquired renown for launching some of Australia's better-known play-

WHERE TO SHOP

Melbourne Central is Melbourne's newest shopping complex, dominated by the **Daimaru** department store and containing over 150 specialty shops. Entertainment is often provided at lunchtime under its conical skylight that covers a shot tower built in 1889. The old and modern have been successfully integrated and this area is always crowded with lunchtime shoppers.

wrights and actors. The audience seldom exceeds fifty people and in winter a fire blazes in one corner. The actors and the playwright usually stay around afterwards to chat and sip coffee. There are also several up-market theaters in the Arts Centre on Swanston Street.

The free newspapers *In Press* and *Beat* are available in most entertainment venues and provide an excellent guide to music, films and bands. They cater mainly for younger people but on Fridays the daily newspaper *The Age* has a lift-out section, *Entertainment Guide*, which is the most comprehensive source of information on what will happen in Melbourne the following week.

Several galleries sell Aboriginal paintings. **Gallery Gabrielle Pizzi** at 141 Flinders Lane sells works from major Aboriginal artists and has taken many of its exhibitions on overseas tours. A wide range of paintings and artifacts from central Australia can be purchased from **Aboriginal Desert Art** at 13 Bourke Street; overseas shipment can be arranged.

A good selection of stores sell souvenirs and are usually clustered around the larger hotels. For something special try the **Maker's Mark** at 85 Collins Street. Every month exhibitions of Australia's foremost

Taking in the panoramic view of the city skyline from St. Kilda's pier.

craftsmen are held and everything is for sale. You are given an opportunity to buy jewelry or a gift of the best natural materials available in Australia, such as Broome pearls, Argyle champagne diamonds and native woods.

The **Meat Market** craftshop at 42 Courtney Street, North Melbourne is just a short walk from Victoria Market. Its name is hardly mellifluous for a craftshop, but as it was indeed a meat market this eccentricity may be forgiven. It offers pottery, hand-painted fabric, woodcrafts and leatherwork by contemporary artists and has regular exhibitions of other crafts, also for sale.

Toorak Road and Chapel Street in South Yarra are lined with trendy boutiques stocked with the latest fashions.

SPORT

Melbourne has some of the best sporting facilities in the country.

During winter there are league football games on Friday nights and Saturday afternoons. The best stadiums to see a game and soak up the atmosphere are the MCG in Brunton Avenue and Jolimont and Waverley Park in Wellington Road, Mulgrave. Special trains and buses are put in service for these games.

In spring you have the choice of two horse races every weekend, Caulfield and Flemington Racecourses. The highlights of the season are the Caulfield and Melbourne Cups in which everyone seems to take an interest, even if they may not during the rest of the year. The newspapers devote more space to women's fashions than to horse flesh, so occasional punters get no further than enjoying chicken and champagne in the car park, a sensible diversion.

WHERE TO STAY

Luxury

At the top end of the market there has been an encouraging growth in boutique hotels in Melbourne, combining luxury with intimacy. These being small, it makes sense to book well ahead.

An easy walk from the city, **Magnolia Court** at 101 Powlett Street, East Melbourne, ((03) 419-4222, fax: (03) 416-0841, has an old world charm. Ask for a room in the older Victorian buildings dating back to 1858 and 1862, rather than in the extension added in the 1960s.

Located in the ritzy suburb of South Yarra is another small gem of a hotel. **The Tilba** at the corner of Toorak Road West and Domain Street, ((03) 867-8844, fax: (03) 867-6567, is an old Victorian house filled with light from its leadlight windows and skylight.

The **Beaumont** at 7 Studley Park Road, ((03) 853-2722, (008) 338-578, fax: (03) 853-3773, is in Kew, one of the Melbourne's leafier suburbs, 5 km (2 miles) from the city. The building is modern with a good restaurant, **Sequins**, attached to the hotel. Guests can also hire a golf buggy and clubs and tackle the 18-hole golf course at nearby Yarra Bend.

Another place a little way out from the city is the **Novotel Bayside** at 16 The Esplanade, St. Kilda, ((03) 525-552, fax: (03) 525-5678. This hotel is just above the beach and its rooms provide excellent views of Port Phillip Bay on one side and the city skyline on the other. This 244-room hotel is quite new: its modern design raised a few eyebrows when it was first built but now the architecture is compatible with the beach environs.

In the city are several luxury hotels with some character. **Le Meridien** at 495 Collins Street, ((03) 620-9111, (008) 331-330, fax: (03) 614-1219, is in a renovated late-Victorian building brilliantly converted into a top hotel. Downstairs there bars, restaurants and coffee lounges. **The Windsor** is at the corner of Spring and Bourke Streets, ((03) 653-0653, (008) 033-100, fax: (03) 654-5183, and the hotel has been classified by the National Trust.

If you prefer modern surroundings, there is the very new **Grand Hyatt** at 123 Collins Street, ((03) 657-1234, (008) 222-188, fax: (03) 650-3491, with potted palms and pseudo-antique statuary in the lobby, or the **Central** at the corner of Flinders and Spencer Streets, ((03) 629-5111, (008) 222-446, fax: (03) 629-5624, overlooking the Yarra River.

Moderate

The Victoria at 215 Little Collins Street, ((03) 653-0441, (008) 331-147, fax: (03) 650-9678, is an unpretentious hotel in the center of the city which is more interested in providing comfortable, affordable accommodation than covering its lobby with oceans of marble and over-dressed bellhops.

Outside the city are good motels which are not too pricey. The **Ramada Inn** at 539 Royal Parade, ((03) 380-8131, (008) 805-813, fax: (03) 388-0519, is quite reasonable, while a little further up the road is the **Princes Park Motor Inn**, ((03) 388-1000, (008) 335-787, fax: (03) 387-3749.

Inexpensive

One of the most remarkable budget hotels in Melbourne is **The Nunnery** at 116 Nicholson Street, Fitzroy, ((03) 419-8637, fax: (03) 417-7736, located in a beautiful terrace building. Rooms vary from six-bed dormitories, to single rooms which once were the cells of nuns. TV is discouraged in the communal lounge because it stifles conversation, and this friendly bed and breakfast is a great place to meet other travelers and swap traveling tips. In St. Kilda there is **Olembia Private Hotel** at 96 Barkly Street, ((03) 537-1412 or (008) 032-635, which is a bed a breakfast place, while **Enfield House** at 2 Enfield Street, ((03) 534-8159, fax: (03) 534-5579, caters to backpackers.

There are also quite a few backpacker hostels in St. Kilda, in and around Fitzroy and Barkly Streets.

WHERE TO EAT

Melbournians love to eat out, and the number and variety of restaurants is mind-boggling. The choices range from inexpensive foreign places which reflect the numerous nationalities who have chosen to make their home in Melbourne to the more refined restaurants of the Establishment. Between these extremes are sidewalk cafes and informal bistros.

Restaurants tend to congregate in each area, offering a scale from one end of the price range to the other. Some included in this section are away from these precincts but are included because they offer an exceptional setting or offer outstanding cooking.

Richmond has become the home of the Vietnamese community which is served by unpretentious establishments congregated along Victoria Street, just ten minutes from the city. Although you may have to queue, which is a good sign in itself, try the **Thy Thy** at 116 Victoria Street, ((03) 428-5914, or for the best *pho* (beef or chicken soup) in Melbourne go to the **Dzung Tan Dinh** at 196 Victoria Street, ((03) 427-0292.

For an inexpensive feed in the city try

Ong International Food Court at 265 Little Bourke Street, which is in the basement of the Welcome Hotel. The food of eight different Asian cuisines can be ordered from stalls, and no dish costs more than $8. Little Bourke Street and the lanes leading off it between Swanston and Spring Streets, comprise **Chinatown**, with its many good restaurants. Inexpensive meals are available from the **Supper Inn**, upstairs at 15 Celestial Avenue, ((03) 663-4759, where the adventurous can try duck's tongues (recommended) or congee, a Chinese rice gruel (not recommended). You decide! In the higher price bracket is the **Flower Drum** at

A city center haven in Collins Place.

17 Market Lane, ℂ (03) 662-3655, rated as one of the best Chinese restaurants in Australia.

Brunswick Street in Fitzroy started as the place for poseurs and the avant-garde. There are still a few restaurants which reflect its early days, like the **Black Cat** (Nº252, ℂ (03) 419-6230). This inexpensive cafe in decked out with 1950s memorabilia. Try its Widgie spider, a scoop of ice cream in crimson lemonade, which I have never encountered elsewhere.

There are some superb moderately priced Thai restaurants in Melbourne, and if you don't mind sitting cross-legged at a low table, there is the **Thai E'san** at 223 Brunswick Street, ℂ (03) 419-2095.

The **Cafe Provincial** at 299 Brunswick Street, ℂ (03) 417-2228, boasts a wood-fired oven and makes the best pizza in Melbourne. I strongly recommend the **Calazone di Prosciutto**, which is a pizza pastry filled with Parma ham, eggplant, spinach, onions and cheese.

In St. Kilda the **Tolarno Bar and Bistro** at 42 Fitzroy Street, ℂ (03) 525-5477, offers excellent French food and Iain Hewitson's menu is always changing to reflect the availability of ingredients according to season, is elegant, and the task of eating his Blue Swimmer Crabs with dignity is beyond me.

Overlooking St. Kilda beach is the **Stokehouse** at 30 Jacka Boulevard, ℂ (03) 525-5555. Its downstairs area offers moderately priced meals and snacks: you can have pizza made in their wood fired oven, and then enjoy one of Kim Lever's delicious cakes. Upstairs is more formal and therefore more expensive. Just before sunset is the best time to enjoy its panoramic view of the southern end of Port Phillip Bay.

If you generally prefer good Italian food then Lygon Street in Carlton is the best place to go.

Trotter's at Nº400, ℂ (03) 347-5657 is a small friendly restaurant with most dishes under $10. It also does breakfast from 8 am, and has the best poached eggs and hash browns in Melbourne. Across the road is **Tiamo** at Nº303, ℂ (03) 347-5759, which is small, smoky, and a favorite place for generations of students looking for an inexpensive meal and really good coffee.

Established in 1952 the **Universita Bar and Ristorante** at Nº257, ℂ (03) 347-2142, is also a place frequented by students in search of good Italian food, as well as Italians who enjoy the buzz given by students in the cafe. It has maintained its reputation and excellent value, and there is no main dish over $15.

Chalky's Bar and Restaurant at Nº242, ℂ (03) 663-6100, located in a renovated Victorian terrace has chairs and tables outside for dining under the stars. Open 24 hours a day it provides a wide choice of Italian dishes, good Victorian wine from its large cellar. After 10 pm a supper menu is provided, offering moderately priced snacks.

Donnini at 312 Drummond Street, Carlton, ℂ (03) 347-3128, is moderately priced. It specializes in northern Italian cuisine, but its flag-bearer is Donini's pasta, reputed to be the best in Melbourne.

The **Great Australian Bite** at 18 Molesworth Street, North Melbourne, ℂ (03) 329-9068, has a reputation for experimenting with indigenous foods and unusual combinations. While the menu changes to reflect seasonal produce, one thing is constant: the chef, Karl Ferrern's, speciality that was placed in the Gourmet Olympics a few years back — rack of salt and sugar cured lamb, smoked over gum leaves.

For a meal either before or after a concert or performance at the Arts Centre, the **Treble Clef**, ℂ (03) 684- 8264, provides simply prepared food which is moderately priced.

The **Colonial Tramcar Restaurant**, ℂ (03) 676-4000, is a converted 1927 tram that allows diners to watch Melbourne pass by, while enjoying their repast. The cost of the five course meal and drinks on Friday and Saturday night is $85, justified more by a pleasant experience than the standard of food. The Tramcar is booked well ahead, so a reservation is essential.

Borsalino's at 57 Cape Street, Heidelberg, ℂ (03) 459-0434, serves a combination of Italian and French food, and is moderately priced. The restaurant is located in a two storey house built in 1898, with many of its original fixtures. The menu changes frequently and the chef always ensures a good selection of vegetarian on the menu.

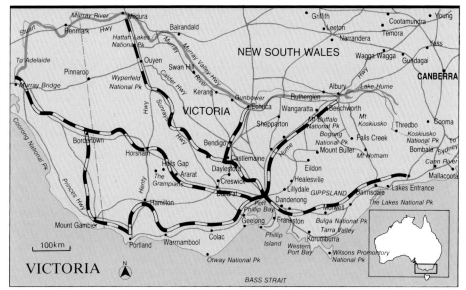

VICTORIA

Expensive restaurants in Melbourne often have a club atmosphere, as behooves the home of the Establishment. Fortunately Melbourne's upper crust have discerning palates and demand the best food and service from their preferred restaurants.

The chefs at **Chinois** at 176 Toorak Road, South Yarra, ((03) 826-3388, have successfully married the flavors of western and eastern cuisines to produce memorable dishes.

Mietta's at 7 Alfred Place, ((03) 654-2366, is run by Mietta O'Donnell. This restaurant is a Melbourne institution, loved equally for its fine food and elegant surroundings. They have regular soirees where good food can be enjoyed to the music of a string quartet, or afternoon tea followed by a book reading.

Tansy's, upstairs at 159 Spring Street, ((03) 639-0705, has established its reputation in a relatively short time as one of Melbourne's foremost restaurants. There is no pretentiousness here, unlike some of Melbourne's nouveau riche establishments. It's the place for people who enjoy fine food a little out of the ordinary, and unobtrusive service.

HOW TO GET THERE

Tullamarine is an unimaginatively conceived but major international airport, and certainly better than Sydney's. Regular flights

arrive from Asia, Europe and the Americas. Melbourne is also a major stop on bus routes along the south-eastern seaboard.

By car, the trip from Sydney takes about 12 hours and 10 hours from Adelaide.

DAY TRIPS FROM MELBOURNE

THE DANDENONGS

Taking the family for a drive to the Dandenongs is a favorite day trip for Melbournians. They hardly justify the grand name of "Ranges," at their highest point 630 m (2,060 ft) above sea level. In its hamlets and villages European trees have been introduced, providing colorful displays in autumn and away from built-up areas large tracts of native forest remain.

General information

As you enter the foot of the Dandenongs, at the entrance of the **Ferntree Gully National Park** is the **Dandenong Ranges Tourist Information Service**, ((03) 752-5455, which provides walking maps free of charge.

What to see and do

Before white settlers established themselves in the Dandenongs, it was an important area for Aborigines. The Yarra Yarra tribe hunted here in summer. Monbulk, corrupted from the Aboriginal word *Monbolloc* and meaning "hiding place in the hills," was reputed to have naturally healing springs.

In 1935, sculptor William Ricketts obtained 1.8 hectares (4.5 acres) of bushland, where he retired to live as a hermit. On his allotment he carved native animals and Aboriginal figures from clay. Ricketts' property was acquired by the Victorian Government in 1964, extended it to six hectares and opened to the public. The **William Ricketts Sanctuary** is at 92 Mt. Dandenong Tourist Highway, ((03) 751-1300, just past Kalorama, an enchanted place where sculptures have been molded into rocks or set into fern-lined nooks and grottos where water trickles over carved possums and kangaroos. Ricketts' vision was of harmony between man and the universe: he believed that no one understood this relationship better than the Aborigines.

Dotted among the hills are a number of Bavarian and Swiss-style restaurants, such as the **Cuckoo**, ((03) 751-1463, in Olinda, moderately priced. For something special, dine in the nearby **Kenmore Manor**, ((03) 751-1008.

There are also numerous tearooms in the Dandenongs. Just outside **Sassafrass** there is **Henry the Eighth**, ((03) 755-1008, with its open fires in winter, and in town is the **Miss Marple's Tearoom**, ((03) 755-1610, with its tweed English interior. Devonshire tea consisting of scones, fresh cream and jam is best enjoyed on a clear autumn or winter's day in front of an open fire. Such an indulgence can only be justified after a brisk walk in the nearby **Sherbrooke Forest Reserve**. In its shady glades the very lucky may be rewarded by the sight of a lyre-bird, always retiring and shy. The lyre-bird is flightless and the male displays its large tail (resembling a lyre, surprise, surprise!) during the mating dance.

There are also many small galleries in the villages in the Dandenongs where the artists have a fixation on gum trees.

At Belgrave you can catch **Puffing Billy**, ((03) 754-6800, a narrow gauge railway running 13 km (8 miles) to **Emerald Lake Park** through beautiful fern glades, over old wooden bridges and across farmland. The line closed in 1954, but was restored by steam-enthusiasts. It's a hit with children, who sit on the carriage window sills, dangling their feet outside the train.

How to get there
Trains leave Flinders Street for Belgrave Station every hour or so, where the train connects with buses which visit all the main attractions.

PHILLIP ISLAND

Phillip Island has long been a favorite summer vacation spot for Melbournians. It has the advantage of being close by, with beaches less dreary than the sluggish waters of Port Phillip Bay. Phillip Island has, more recently, gained an international reputation for its **penguins**.

General information
The **Phillip Island Tourist Information Centre** is in Newhaven, ((059) 567-447, and is open daily, providing visitors with maps of the island and taking bookings for the penguin parade. Most of the coach companies and hotels have information on tours to see the penguins.

What to see and do
As night falls over **Summerland Beach**, fairy penguins make their way to the burrows further up the beach, watched by hundreds of tourists on terraces built along the foreshore. Photographers are asked not to use flash cameras because these upset the penguins whose number varies from a handful to a few hundred, depending on the season. There may be better places to see penguins in Australia, but none more convenient.

Fortunately, there are other things to do on Phillip Island while waiting for the penguins. For some great walks try **Churchill Island** which is connected by a walkway to the main island. Explore its historic buildings and gardens established in the 1860s. Just south of the Newhaven is **Cape Woolamai State Fauna Reserve**, which has good walking tracks and is an important nesting ground for mutton birds. Care should be taken not to disturb them; their migratory pattern may have taken them some 30,000 km (19,000 miles), in a round trip to and from the northern hemisphere.

SPA COUNTRY

Just an hour-and-a-half's drive from Melbourne are the spa towns of **Daylesford** and **Hepburn Springs**, where for years people came to "take the waters." Therapeutic treatment provided included taking baths in spring water claimed to provide relief for a variety of complaints. Today the town has added to its natural asset, providing visitors with a chance to heal the body with spa baths (complete with aro-

What to See and Do

The main decision when visiting spa country is whether to have a massage and spa on arrival or on departure. The **Hepburn Spa Complex**, ((053) 482-034, offers a public heated indoor swimming pool or private spa baths (with air jets and aromatic oils) for one or two people. I recommend a spa first, then the massage. The Spa Complex is very popular and you should book well ahead. Smaller places in Daylesford provide a more personal service: I recommend the **Rose of Daylesford**, ((053) 481-482, at 58 Raglan

matic oils), massages and walking tracks. Afterwards the digestion is challenged by tantalizing restaurants and the rest cure completed in a guesthouse that caters to every need.

While the Spa Country is an easy day trip from Melbourne, a longer stay is strongly recommended. This will allow sufficient time to feel the full benefit of the restorative power of this restful region, and allow its therapeutic treatments time to work.

General Information

Information is available from the **Spa Centre Tourist Centre** at 49 Vincent Street, ((053) 481-387, which is the main thoroughfare in Daylesford and is open seven days a week.

Street, where the prices are the same as the Spa Complex but the welcome from Annette Canterbury much more friendly and the service more personal.

On Wombat Hill in Daly Street is a Catholic Convent which has been imaginatively converted to a restaurant/gallery. The **Convent Gallery** exhibits pottery, paintings and jewelry from top Victorian artists and craftspeople.

There are two artificial lakes in Daylesford — **Jubilee Lake** and **Lake Daylesford**, and it takes about an hour to walk around both. An alternative way to take your exer-

Private bathing huts, quaintly reminiscent of Edwardian times (graffiti apart), at a bayside resort.

cise is to hire a boat or canoe from the **Boathouse Cafe**, ((053) 481-387.

If the weather lets you down drop into the **Bookbarn** next to Lake Daylesford, which has a wide selection of books: its owner, Kerry Bolton, invites browsers to sit around the pot-bellied stove and dip into any books they are thinking of purchasing.

Where to Eat and Stay

There are several excellent restaurants in Daylesford, of which the most stylish is the **Lakehouse** in King Street, ((053) 483-329, where bookings are essential. It also offers accommodation overlooking Lake Daylesford. For an inexpensive meal try **Argus Terrace** at 83 Vincent Street, ((053) 483-200 or **Sweet Decadence** at 57 Vincent Street, ((053) 483-202, named after the chocolate made on the premises.

Luxury accommodation is available at Hepburn Springs in the **Bellinzona Country House** in Main Street, ((053) 482-271, while the comfortable **Liberty House** at 20 Mineral Springs Road, ((053) 482-809, is moderately priced.

How to Get There

Daylesford is 109 km (68 miles) north-west of Melbourne, off the Midland Highway. Hepburn Springs is a further four kilometers (two miles) north.

GOLD FIELDS

Marvelous Melbourne was founded on the wealth of the gold fields which sprang to life in the rush in 1851, centering around Ballarat and Bendigo. In the following decade 1,000 tons of gold were extracted, worth 110 million pounds and accounting for 40 per cent of the world's total production. The find attracted miners who had tried their luck on the Californian fields and adventurers hoping to get rich quickly. Some did, but most didn't.

To help the successful miners spend their hard earned money townships like Ballarat, Bendigo, Castlemaine and Maldon sprouted

The gold-rush days live on at Sovereign Hill, a reconstructed mining town at Ballarat.

like toadstools, satisfying the needs of the miners with banks, stores and brothels. To sate their thirst bars and grog shops did a roaring trade everywhere.

Many of the gold-mining towns continued to prosper after the gold ran out, although their populations today are a fraction of what they were during the rush.

GENERAL INFORMATION

There are tourist information centers in all the major towns. They are:

Castlemaine Tourist Information Centre, Duke Street, ((054) 722-480, open weekends, school and public holidays 10 am to 4:30 pm.

Bendigo Tourist Information Centre, Charring Cross, ((054) 415-244, open daily 10 am to 4 pm.

Ballarat Visitors' Information Centre, 39 Sturt Street, ((053) 322-694, open weekdays 9 am to 5 pm and weekends and public holidays 10 am to 4 pm.

Maldon Visitors' Centre, High Street, ((054) 752-569, open weekdays 11 am to 3 pm and weekends and public holidays 10 am to 4 pm.

WHAT TO SEE AND DO

Ballarat

The State's largest inland city, with a population of 63,800 Ballarat lies 112 km (70 miles) from Melbourne. It has matured from a rough tent city during the gold rush into a provincial center with pretensions to style and graciousness with its mid-to-late nineteenth century architecture. The National Trust strives to justify its existence in Ballarat where over 60 buildings have been classified for their historical importance. Wherever you go you can see decorative cast iron verandah friezes and balustrades common to all British colonial architecture from Calcutta to Cape Town. Take a look in the shops at the north end of Lydiard Street typical examples of lace embellishments.

Sovereign Hill Gold Mining Township, at the corner of Main Road and Bradshaw Street, ((053) 311-944, is a re-creation of a gold rush township. The main drag represents the Main Street of Ballarat as it was 150 years ago. It is a living museum, with over

40 buildings housing a forge, bakery, confectioner and hotel — all operational and open for business. At Red Hill Gully in the township you can pan for gold or inspect the underground mine nearby. In the evening there is a sound and light show *Blood and the Southern Cross* which relates the melodrama of the rumpus at the Eureka Stockade. Sovereign Hill is great fun for adults and children alike, and has won national awards for its living history museum.

If the prospect does not make you weep or sink into a coma and you insist on

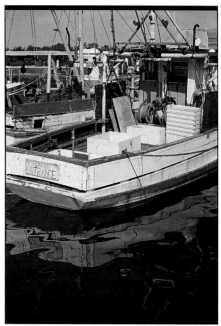

seeing where a rebellious rabble at the **Eureka Stockade** was dealt with, a replica of the "fortification" stands at the corner of Stawell and Eureka Streets. There is also a memorial in the park to the 22 trouble-makers and five soldiers who died during the rebellion.

Bendigo

North of Ballarat is Bendigo, queen city of the goldfields. The former wealth of the city is obvious when you arrive at the center of town where the magnificent **Alexandra Fountain** stands at the crossroads. Nearby is the elegant **Shamrock Hotel**, at the corner of Pall Mall and Williamson Street which once served hooch to the many Irish miners of Bendigo. It was said that the hotelier would earn himself another £4 by cleaning the floor and collecting gold dust brought in on their boots. On a warm night there is still no nicer place to be than on the balcony of this fine hotel enjoying a cold ale.

Chinese indentured labor also left its mark on Bendigo. The **Chinese Joss House** in Finn Street, Emu Point, ((054) 421-685, is a temple built in the 1860s by the lonely men of See Yup to honor their ancestors in the China of their youth. The best way to get to there is on the vintage **Talking Tram**, ((054) 438-070, which starts in the center of town.

The tram, by the way, visits the **Central Deborah Mine** in Violet Street, ((054) 438-070, which operated in the 1940s and 1950s and is linked to shafts sunk a century earlier. The gold mine is 422 m (1,385 ft) deep with 17 levels: tours are conducted daily and the conditions of mining may be viewed and pondered.

Maldon

Gold was mined at Maldon from 1854 until the 1930s and the town retains much of its goldrush streetscape, protected by the National Trust. Visitors to the **Blacksmith and Wainwright Shop** in High Street will see a blacksmith working at restoring nineteenth century wagons.

To experience what the miners must have seen when they were underground, there is a candle-lit tour of **Carmans Tunnel**, a 570 m (1,870 ft)-long horizontal shaft 2 km (1 mile) from town, off Parkin's Reef Road. This only operates at weekends and on public holidays.

At Hornsby Street is the Maldon Station where you can sample the delights of a **steam train to Castlemaine** on weekends and during school holidays.

Castlemaine

The rush at Castlemaine started about a year after the first diggings at Ballarat.

Castlemaine today is a leisurely country town, justifiably proud of its gardens and galleries. The **Art Gallery and Museum** at 14 Lyttleton Road has a good collection of art dating from the late nineteenth century until the middle of this one: it is open from 10 am to 5 pm. In Mostyn Street you will find

the **Market Museum**, built in 1861, which has exhibitions and audio-visual displays telling the story of the Castlemaine gold rush. Daily opening hours are from 10 am to 5 pm. There are also good private galleries showing contemporary arts and crafts, such as the **Wallace Bros Gallery** at 50 Hargraves Street and **Federation Fine Art Gallery** at 8 Parker Street.

The **Buna Historic Home and Garden** at the corner of Hunter and Urquhart Streets is open for inspection daily. The house was built in 1861 and on two hectares (five acres)

of beautiful gardens it has been furnished to re-create the nineteenth century colonial style; on display is silverware by Hungarian silversmith Ernest Leviny, who once owned Buna.

WHERE TO STAY

The best places to stay on the gold fields are in historic hotels and cottages which provide bed and breakfast. **Heritage Cottages of Maldon,** ((054) 751-094, offers a choice of historic cottage accommodation at moderate prices. In Castlemaine the **Midland Private Hotel** at 2 Templeton Street, ((054) 721-805, retains much of its late nineteenth century interior.

For a bit of luxury and a lot of history stay at the **Shamrock** at the corner of Pall Mall and Williamston Street in Bendigo, ((054) 430-333, which also serves excellent meals in its dining rooms. In Ballarat **Craigs Royal Hotel** at 10 Lydiard Street South,

ABOVE: The worn coastline near Port Campbell.
OPPOSITE: Fishing boats at Lakes Entrance.

℃ (053) 311-377, was built in 1867 and is classified by the National Trust. The more expensive rooms have spa baths.

There are also a number of moderately priced motels along the highways out of Ballarat and Bendigo.

HOW TO GET THERE

The gold fields are about two hours from Melbourne, and driving around them provides an opportunity to take in a good deal in a relatively short time. There are regular bus and train services to Bendigo and Ballarat and on weekdays bus services between the main towns in this area.

GREAT OCEAN ROAD

The **Great Ocean Road** stretches about 300 km (186 miles) from just beyond Geelong, an hour's drive south-west of Melbourne, to Warrnambool along spectacular coastline. Built to create employment in the depression, the Great Ocean Road hugs the coastline, overlooking sheer cliffs. The road plunges down to empty bays and passes through the small holiday towns which dot the coastline. Occasionally the road takes a turn inland, passing through virtually untouched remnants of rain forest providing contrast to the sea views.

GENERAL INFORMATION

There are information centers in most of the towns along the Great Ocean Road. They are:

Torquay Information Centre, The Esplanade, ℃ (052) 613-310.

Apollo Bay Information Centre, 155 Great Ocean Road, ℃ (052) 376-529.

Lorne Tourist Information Centre, 144 Mountjoy Road, ℃ (052) 891-152, is open Monday to Wednesday 9:30 am to 4 pm, Thursday and Friday 9 am to 5 pm and weekends 10 am to 3 pm.

Warrnambool Information Centre, 600 Raglan Parade, ℃ (055) 647-837, is open weekdays, school and public holidays 9 am to 5 pm and weekends 10 am to 12 pm and 1 pm to 4 pm.

Port Fairy Information Centre in Bank Street, ℃ (055) 682-682, is open weekdays 10 am to 4 pm and weekends 10 am to 12:30 pm and 1:30 pm to 4 pm.

WHAT TO SEE AND DO

The Great Ocean Road starts at **Torquay** and heads south-west through **Anglesea, Aireys Inlet, Lorne** and **Apollo Bay**, all of which are popular seaside resorts. There are good surf beaches along this stretch of coastline and the national surfing championships are

often held in the region. Just after Apollo Bay the road turns inland, climbing the Otway Ranges and providing memorable views of the sea and rugged cliffs.

Lorne is a good base for exploring the **Otway National Park**. Walk through a rain forest of towering mountain ash and gullies of myrtle, beech, mosses and ferns while you take in the beauty of waterfalls tumbling down the mountain sides.

After cutting the corner at Cape Otway the road returns to the coast at **Princetown** and leads to the eastern end of **Port Campbell**

OPPOSITE: The whorls of the plough stretch across a corner of the vast wheatlands of Victoria's Wimmera. ABOVE: Dunes at Croajingolong, which stretches 38 km (60 miles) of wild ocean.

National Park, star attraction of the coastline. In the shallows sandstone pillars stand, carved by wind and waves into unique formations like the **Twelve Apostles** and **London Bridge**, which collapsed in 1990 leaving the two sandstone uprights.

The Great Ocean Road ends at **Peterborough** but you can continue westward for another 53 km (33 miles) to **Warrnambool**, a modest city of 25,000 people which guards one of Australia's most intriguing mysteries — the **Mahogany Ship**. Argument has raged whether the shipwreck seen in the sand dunes in 1880 was a Portuguese vessel which had made its way to the east coast in 1522 only to founder on this treacherous coastline. The sand dunes here are constantly shifting and the boat has been buried again. If the theory is confirmed the wreck would re-write the history of the discovery of the east coast. As incentive to resolve this mystery the Victorian Government has offered a reward for the discovery of Mahogany Ship, which remains unclaimed.

Past Warrnambool is **Port Fairy** which was inhabited by whalers and sealers as far back as the 1820s, today a sleepy fishing village which only comes to life in early March for Australia's largest folk festival, which takes over the town.

WHERE TO STAY

The holiday towns along the Great Ocean Road have a good range of moderately priced accommodation, from motels to self-contained flats and holiday houses rented by the week. Bookings are essential during school holidays, and over summer most places are filled with holiday-making families.

The **Surf City Motel** is off the Highway at Torquay opposite Zeally Bay, ((052) 613-492, fax: (052) 614-032, while **Banyandah** at 7 Zeally Bay Road, ((052) 612-419, is a pleasant bed and breakfast joint.

On the Great Ocean Road at Lorne there are the **Kalimna**, ((052) 891-407, and **Anchorage**, ((052) 891-891.

Princetown is a perfect place to stay to be near the most spectacular attractions of the Great Ocean Road. **Apostle's View** in Booringa Road, ((055) 988-277, and **Mackas** on Simpson Road, ((055) 988-261, are moderately priced.

At the end of the Great Ocean Highway, 15 km (9 miles) from Warnambool is the historic village of **Koroit**. At the center of this charming little dairy town is **Bourke's Koroit Hotel**, ((055) 658-201, a classical bush pub lovingly restored by Mick Bourke and filled with nineteenth century furnishings.

HOW TO GET THERE

Take the Princes Highway out of Melbourne to Geelong and then turn off to Torquay on the Coast Highway, eventually intersecting with the Great Ocean Road. There are also package coach tours along the Great Ocean Road.

MURRAY RIVER PORTS

The golden days of the riverboats, between 1850 and 1880 is a chapter often forgotten in Australia's history but the romance of those adventurous and colorful times lingers on.

Just over a century ago before railways and macadamised roads, the Murray was the nation's trading highway with hundreds of riverboats plying its 2,590 km (1,610 mile) length. With its tributary, the Darling, it formed a commercial artery for the entire south-east of the continent.

GENERAL INFORMATION

There are tourist information centers in most of the main towns along the Murray. The **Swan Hill Regional Tourist Information Centre** at 306 Campbell Street, Swan Hill, ((050) 323-033, **Golden Rivers Tourist Information Centre** in Murray Street, Barham NSW, ((054) 533-100, and the **Echuca Tourist Information Center** at 2 Leslie Street, Echuca, ((054) 807-555, provide information on the Murray River and local attractions.

WHAT TO SEE AND DO

The Murray River is often little more than a muddy trench these days because its waters are manipulated by the Snowy Mountain scheme to provide hydro-electric power and irrigation for south-eastern Australia. It only meanders slowly westward towards South Australia, running parallel to the Murray Highway on its southern side.

Echuca, an hour's drive north of Bendigo, is the patriarch of the great Murray River ports. Flourishing, strutting Echuca was once the greatest inland port and second only to Melbourne in Victoria. The wooden wharf, preserved in the Port of Echuca area, has three tiers to allow for the 10 m (30 ft) variation in river heights which once plagued this stretch of river.

At the turn of the century the town had 80 bars, and photographs of those days are on display at the **Echuca Wharf Museum** at 45 Murray Esplanade, ((054) 824-248, the entrance to which is the **Star Hotel**, which boast an underground tunnel once used by those patrons wishing to avoid the attention of the local constabulary. At the museum it is possible to book a cruise on the **Pevensey**, a steam-driven cargo boat built at the turn of the century, for a one hour journey down the river. Another company offers cruises aboard the **M.V. Mary Ann**, ((054) 826-000, which boasts a fully licensed restaurant.

Half an hour drive from Echuca the road passes **Gunblower Island**, a 50 km (31 miles) long rookery, 53 km (33 miles) later reaching **Kerang**, an agricultural town at the end of a chain of lakes with the largest breeding grounds in the world for ibis and certain other species of waterfowl.

Swan Hill was the other great river port of last century. On three hectares (seven acres) at Horseshoe Bend is the **Pioneer Settlement**, ((050) 321-093, centered around the *Gem*, in its day the biggest and most powerful vessel on the river. The streets are lined with shops, a forge, a bakery and coach offices which recall a lost era.

Another 250 km (155 miles) downstream is **Mildura**, garden city of the river and center of the Sunraysia fruit-growing district.

WHERE TO STAY

A novel place to stay is on a houseboat: these are self-contained units of accommodation *Victoria*

and a great way to tour the Murray River. Bookings can be made through **Sun Centre Houseboats**, ((054) 542-333.

There are some fine bed and breakfast and cottage accommodation in Echuca. The **River Gallery Inn** at 578 High Street, ((054) 806-902, has an old world charm where guests are invited to breakfast in its sunny courtyard. **Murray House** at 55 Francis Street, ((054) 824-944, fax: (054) 806-432, offers bed and a cooked breakfast.

In Swan Hill two motels in the moderate price range are the **Swan Hill Motor Inn** at

405 Campbell Street, ((050) 322-726, and **Paruna Motel** at 386 Campbell Street, ((050) 324-455.

WHERE TO EAT

The paddle-steamer, the Gem in Swan Hill has a restaurant aboard, where local yabbies and fish are offered with wine. For a sense of history enjoy a light lunch or afternoon tea at the **Murray Downs Homestead**, 1.5 km (one mile) from Swan Hill, and afterwards take a walk around this 1866 mansion.

Carriages at the Pioneer Motor Inn, 421 Campbell Street, Swan Hill, ((050) 322-017, has a good varied menu. **Silver Slipper** at the Swan Hill Motor Inn, ((050) 322-726, specializes in fresh river fish.

HOW TO GET THERE

V/Line trains run from Melbourne to Swan Hill and a rail/coach service provides access

Mildura Post Office.

to Echuca. The Vinelander MotoRail runs to Mildura.

Coach tours to Echuca itself are operated by Australia Pacific and Australian Colonial Tours. Tour operators offer extended tours of the Murray region. Greyhound buses bound for Broken Hill pass through Echuca and Swan Hill, and Pioneer buses to Deniliquin stop at Echuca.

NATIONAL PARKS

Details of national parks can also be obtained from **Information Victoria** at 318 Little Bourke Street, Melbourne, ((03) 651-4100 or from local tourist bureaux.

The **Victorian National Parks Association**, ((03) 654-8296, fax: (03) 654-6843, organizes walks every weekend around Victoria's parks. Non-members pay $4 and transport to the park can usually be arranged. Bookings, however, need to made two to four weeks ahead.

The **Organ Pipes**, 25 km (15 miles) north of Melbourne, is off the Calder Highway. This National Park features dramatic 20m (60ft) high basalt columns recalling — wait for it — organ pipes. Contact the ranger, ((03) 390-1082, for further details.

The **Point Nepean National Park** stretches along 40 km (25 miles) of scenic coastline and contains several rare plants and animals; between November and March dolphins can be seen cavorting in the waters off the coast. Approach via the Mornington Peninsula, 100 km (62 miles) south of Melbourne. Contact the local ranger, ((059) 844-276, for further details.

Its numerous walking tracks make the **Little Desert**, 375 km (230 miles) north-west of Melbourne, ideal for hikers. The park supports a wide range of ecosystems and is the home of mound-building Mallee fowl. In spring the wildflowers color the landscape. The park can be reached from the Western Highway, near Dimboola. Contact the local ranger, ((053) 911-275, for further details.

A walking holiday of Victoria would not be complete unless **Wilson Promontory**, 250 km (155 miles) south-east of Melbourne were part of the itinerary. It is a mixture of picturesque beaches and a wide range of

natural vegetation including heaths, forest, coastal areas and wetlands. This national park is one of the most popular in Victoria and bookings for accommodation are essential during holiday periods. Contact the local ranger, ((056) 808-538 for further details.

FESTIVALS AND SPORTING EVENTS

1 JANUARY Provided your hangover from New Year's Eve is not too unspeakable,

make a trip to Hanging Rock, 78 km (49 miles) north-west of Melbourne for the **annual picnic races** and at least one brawl.

EARLY JANUARY The **Australian Open Tennis Championship** is played at the new Tennis Centre in Batman Avenue where the world's top seeds compete in this Grand Slam event.

FEBRUARY/MARCH The **Food and Wine Festival** allows Melbourne's best restaurateurs to show off. Tastings are arranged at advertised venues around Melbourne.

MARCH Ballarat celebrates its favorite bloom during the **Begonia Festival**. The highlight of the weekend is the floral carpet made out of begonias woven into designs, the best of which are at the Botanic Gardens. The festival also embraces theater, a carnival and crafts.

MID-MARCH Chinese **Dragon Boat Festival** sees teams of paddlers competing in a race along the Yarra River starting at the bridge over Swanston Street, in celebration of a Chinese holiday.

APRIL Starting appropriately on April 1, the **Comedy Festival** in Melbourne lasts two weeks and generates good theater.

EASTER **International Bell's Beach Surf Classic** attracts the world's greatest boar-

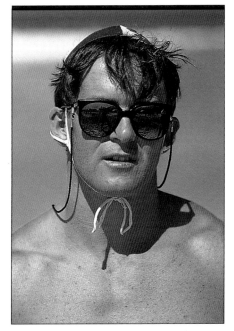

driders. Bell's Beach itself can be reached from the Great Ocean Road.

JUNE See new local and foreign films at the **Melbourne Film Festival**.

AUGUST/SEPTEMBER Prepare to have your senses assaulted in the **Fringe Arts Festival**, with performance art, avant-garde theater, music and dancing at various venues around Melbourne.

EARLY SEPTEMBER Melbourne's **Writer's Festival** features Australian and foreign writers reading their own works.

MID-SEPTEMBER The **International Festival of the Arts** brings to Melbourne performances by local and overseas artists.

LATE SEPTEMBER The **Royal Melbourne Show** at the Royal Melbourne Show-

grounds provides farmers with an opportunity to show off animals and agricultural produce to city folk. The **Australian Rules Football Grand Final** is played at the Melbourne Cricket Ground, although this can change if two different state teams are in the play-off. To obtain tickets it is necessary to book early, ℂ (03) 654-1244.

OCTOBER Wycheproof, 140 km (87 miles) from Bendigo, is where real men come from: to prove it competitors undertake a foot-race up Mt. Wycheproof during the **King of the Mountain Festival**. The climb is only 43 m (140 ft), so to make the race interesting each competitor is required to carry a sack of wheat on his back.

EARLY NOVEMBER The **Melbourne Cup** is held on the first Tuesday of November when the best nags in Australia and New Zealand race over two miles for the coveted cup. The day is a public holiday, and mind your pocket!

MID-NOVEMBER Lygon Street is turned over to its annual **Festa** when the Italian community creates the opportunity for some fun together: the highlights are a contest to climb a greasy pole and an Italian Waiter's Race.

DECEMBER On Christmas Eve people gather at the Myer Music Bowl in Melbourne for **Carols by Candlelight**.

DECEMBER/JANUARY Take yourself off to the Melbourne Cricket Ground where Australia is challenged by the world's best cricketers in test matches and exciting one day matches.

OPPOSITE: Soldiers and spectators relax on Melbourne Cup day which is a public holiday in early November. ABOVE: Australian man.

Western Australia

the Irrepressible State

WESTERN AUSTRALIA has always been a bit different from the rest of Australia. Even though it is not much younger than the other States it has a feeling of "newness." Its citizens have a nationalism that is parochial — more Western Australian than Australian.

Its geographical isolation forced Western Australia to be self-reliant, a task made easier by its healthy mining industry. More than any other place in Australia Western Australia sees its future in Asia, hardly surprising when you consider that Sydney is further than Singapore from Perth.

Perth is the fastest-growing city in Australia. Over the past few years its skyline has shot up, reflecting the State's confidence. Unfortunately many new developments were promoted by home-grown entrepreneurs, who in the 1980s used borrowed money to take over companies. The bubble finally burst in the early 1990s and thousands of small investors lost their savings.

There have been other booms and busts in its history. Each time the irrepressible Western Australians bounce back to new heights.

The State covers a third of the continent, most of it desert which comes alive in spring with a carpet of wildflowers. The northern part of the State is watered by monsoons, receiving between 500 and 1,000 mm (20 to 40 inches) of rain between December and April.

PERTH

Perth exudes confidence and lauds success. While sections of "old Perth" remain, it is its newness that strikes the visitor, the skyscrapers which dominate the skyline.

Just as the people of Perth are willing to work hard, they play hard. The temperate climate makes Perth an outdoor city: at night its streets are alive while at the weekend Perth's beaches, tennis courts and sidewalk cafes are crowded.

Western Australians enjoy their spare time to the full, eschewing formality and insisting on the best when they go out.

BACKGROUND

The Swan River Colony was founded in 1829 by Captain James Stirling; its growth was retarded by its natural disadvantages of remoteness from the other colonies on the eastern seaboard, and the virtual un-navigability of the Port of Fremantle for seagoing vessels.

It began as a free settlement but grew slowly because of a labor shortage. In 1850 the colonial government requested convict labor to boost its flagging economy.

Western Australia's next growth spurt occurred when gold was discovered in Coolgardie and Kalgoorlie in the early 1890s. After Federation locals were able to boast that their State was the "Golden Gate of Australia."

There were other finds of mineral wealth, with iron ore in the Pilbara and enormous reserves of natural gas off the north-west coast.

The state's relationship with the rest of Australia has not always been harmonious. On 8 April 1933, Western Australian held a referendum on whether to secede from the rest of the country. There was overwhelm-

OPPOSITE: Sand patterns at Eucla. ABOVE: View across the Swan from the Royal Perth Yacht Club.

ing support for the proposal, with 138,653 voting "yes" and just 70,706 voting "no." Western Australians objected to the federal government's high tariff policy which disadvantaged their State's exports. In particular the high price of sugar to protect Queensland's growers raised their ire. To dramatize their point the Fremantle Sugar Party was held to emulate the famous Boston Tea Party, threatening to dump sugar into Fremantle Harbour. This not very original act of defiance never took place and the west soon lost its enthusiasm for secession.

travels between the city and Northbridge. Buses in the central city are also free.

For information on public transport phone **Transperth Service Information** at (13-22-13. For information on country and interstate trains phone ((09) 326-2222.

WHAT TO SEE AND DO

Perth
Perth is situated on a broad stretch of the Swan River of almost lake-like proportions, which gives a feeling of spacious-

GENERAL INFORMATION

The **Tourist Information Centre**, at the corner of Forrest Place and Wellington Streets, ((09) 483-1111, has a good selection of brochures and can arrange accommodation and tours.

In Fremantle the **Tourist Information Centre** is located in King Square, ((09) 430-2346, and is open seven days a week.

Getting around the city is easy as a free *City Clipper* bus service operates in the centre. Each line is color coded. The red service runs between the city and East Perth, yellow takes in the inner city circuit, green is for west Perth and the blue bus

ness; sailing boats provide an attractive backdrop to the city.

Overlooking the Swan River is **King's Park and the Botanic Gardens**, 400 hectares (1,000 acres) of gardens and bushlands on the western edge of the central business district. The park was reserved by explorer/politician John Forrest in 1872 for children "a thousand years hence to see what the bush was like when Stirling arrived." In spring the park is a mass of beautiful wildflowers, a living example of the wisdom of Forrest's bequest. The best way to see it is on a bicycle hired from **Koala Bicycle Hire**, ((09) 321-3061, located near the rear of Garden Restaurant.

The park overlooks Narrows Bridge and the colony's first flour mill. The **Old Mill**, ((09) 382-4144, is a Perth landmark. Built in 1835 it is open to the public Sunday, Wednesday and Thursday between 1 pm and 5 pm, and on Saturday it closes at 4 pm.

Take the green *City Clipper* from the park back to the city and Perth's main thoroughfare, **St. George's Terrace**. Strolling along "the Terrace," you pass a mixture of the city's oldest buildings and the glittering glass towers erected during the last boom. At your feet are 150 bronze plaques which

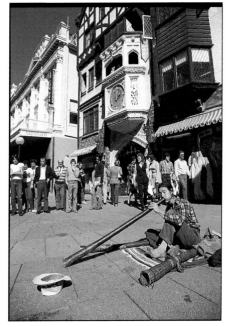

have been embedded into the sidewalk. Each one honors a Western Australian who made an outstanding contribution to the life of the State's first 150 years.

At the corner of Hay and Barrack Streets is Perth's **Town Hall**, built by convicts in the 1860s in the fashion of an English Jacobean market hall.

Running along the southern side of the Terrace is **Stirling Gardens**, which stretches east from Barrack Street, stopping just short of Victoria Street. These are a popular venue for concerts and art shows. Facing them and opposite Pier Street is **Government House**, the official residence of the Governor built between 1859 and 1864. Across the road is **The Deanery**, built in the late 1850s. Walk

west up the Terrace and near King Street is the **Old Perth Boys' School** built in 1854, Western Australia's first and Australia's second oldest school. If you wish to inspect it you can enter the fine limestone building, which contains a cafe and souvenir shop.

Exhibitions relating to different aspects of the State are on show at the **Western Australian Museum** in Francis Street, Northbridge, ((09) 328-4411, reached by catching the blue *City Clipper* from the city. The pride of its collection is the 11-ton Mundrabilla meteorite; opening hours on weekdays are between 10:30 am and 5 pm and on weekends between 1 pm and 5 pm.

One of the best ways to see Perth and its environs is from a river cruiser; there is a good selection of trips to choose from, most of which start at the Barrack Street Jetty. Bookings are essential. The **Transperth Ferry**, ((09) 425-2651, departs daily (except Saturday) at 2 pm for a half day tour of the Swan River.

Fremantle
Fremantle, 19 km (12 miles) downstream from Perth, is at the mouth of the Swan River. It was once a humble work-a-day seaport.

For years locals valued Fremantle's old world charm and leisurely pace, which contrasted with Perth. The suburb retains many buildings dating back to the first half of the nineteenth century, an unpretentious seaside town which was the place to go for an inexpensive meal, a walk along the foreshore or a visit to an art gallery.

"Freo," as it is known to the locals, was thrust into the international limelight when in 1987 the America's Cup defence was held in the waters off Fremantle. A powerful lot of money was spent doing up the town, and some of the eye-sores along the foreshore were tastefully renovated. The development included a broadwalk which was built where waterfront restaurants cluster. Several hotels were built to accommodate the yachting crowd and fortunately do not spoil the feel of Freo.

Showing how it's done with a didgeridoo ABOVE in Perth's pedestrian-only shopping center, ABOVE and OPPOSITE.

During the day or night, Fremantle is full of people enjoying the sidewalk cafes and pubs or just promenading. There is always something to do.

At the south end, near the river's mouth, is the **Round House,** ((09) 335-9283, built in 1831. This 12-sided building, the oldest in Western Australia, was first used to jail minor offenders: when convicts first arrived in 1850 it accepted more serious offenders. There are daily tours.

Further up High Street, towards the center of town, is the **Town Hall**. In 1884 the municipal council put itself in hock for fifteen years to pay for this building, with its ornate facade and elaborately decorated balconies and balustrades. Opened on 22 June 1887, the celebration was spoilt for one councillor when he was shot dead by a gatecrasher.

It is well worth the effort to visit the **Western Australian Maritime Museum** on Cliff Street, ((09) 335-8211, where admission is by donation. Pride of place is taken by the restored hull of the Dutch treasure ship, *Batavia*, wrecked off the Western Australian coast near Geraldton, 330 km (206 miles) north of Perth in 1629.

One of the nicest places in Fremantle is the **Fremantle Arts Centre**, at 1 Finnerty Street, ((09) 335-8244. This has three downstairs galleries showing works mainly by Western Australian artists. Exhibitions change every four weeks and works are for sale. Upstairs is a permanent collection of the best from local artists and craftspeople, though during winter this venue is used for Sunday afternoon poetry readings and music is played in the downstairs courtyard in summer. Daily opening hours are between 10 am and 5 pm.

The Swan Valley

Vineyards were established in the Swan Valley over a hundred years ago; not as well known as its counterparts in South Australia, this region produces award-winning Shiraz, Cabernet and Chenin Verdelho wines.

An enjoyable way to tour the Swan Valley is to take a cruise along the Swan River. The **Boat Torque Cruises**, ((09) 325-6033, depart daily for a tour of the wineries — **Houghtons** on Wednesday, Friday and Sunday, while on the remaining days it visits **Sandalford** where you may meet the vintner, Bill Krapsley, who knows a great deal about Western Australian wines.

PERTH BY NIGHT

The Swan River is at its prettiest at night, surrounded by the lights of Perth. See it on an evening cruise offered by **Boat Torque Cruises,** ((09) 325-6033, aboard the *Star Flyte* where you can eye the sights over a meal and then spend the rest of the evening dancing. The dinner cruises depart Wednesday, Friday and Saturday evenings at 7:45 pm.

On the Great Eastern Highway is the $300 million **Burswood Resort Casino**, ((09) 362-7777, which incorporates a top-

class hotel and 14,000-seat entertainment center. The casino is open until 3 am, and if you aren't successful at one of its 109 gaming tables and the roulette wheel has been uncharitable, at least enjoy the cabaret provided for patrons.

After dark the city is fairly quiet, except for a few clubs such as **Pinocchio's** at 393 Murray Street and **Gobbles Nightclub** at 613 Wellington Street.

The main action is in **Northbridge**, just north of the city, and Fremantle. These suburbs are full of people looking for a good time.

In Northbridge, party until 3 am at **D.V.8** at 78 James Street or **James Street Nightclub** at 139 James Street. For some lively jazz drop into the **Hyde Park Hotel** at 331 Bulwer Street.

The younger crowd looking for hot music goes to **Metropolis** at 58 South Terrace in Fremantle, and the **Havana**, at 69 Lake Street in Perth, has discoing until 5 am.

The **Concert Hall** in St. George Terrace features anything from grand opera to folk concerts, and there are also a concert hall and theater at the University of Western Australia campus in Nedlands.

WHERE TO SHOP

The main shopping areas in Perth are **Hay** and **Murray Street Malls**, linked by multi-level arcades. These provide shoppers with

Perth has grown rapidly in the past two decades adding ever taller buildings to its skyline.

a wide range of choices, concentrated in a small area. Of the arcades, **London Court** is brimming with character with its mock-Tudor alley of carved woodwork, lattice windows and wrought iron trim.

Perth has good selections of Aboriginal art galleries from which to buy a unique souvenir of Australia. The **Aboriginal Art Gallery** at 32 King Street, ((09) 322-3398 has a wide selection of authentic items, from bark paintings to modern works by prominent Aboriginal painters. In Fremantle Aboriginal art, craft and artefacts are for sale from **Birukmarri Gallery** at 47 High Street ((09) 335-4741.

Opals are a specialty in several shops. At **Opal Exploration Company** at 616 Hay Street, ((09) 325-2907, you can watch gemstones being cut and polished. Argyle diamonds from West Australia's Kimberley region come in a variety of colors including the rare pink or "champagne" diamonds. Jewellery, incorporating Argyle diamonds, can be bought from **Charles Edwards Jewellers** at 704 Hay Street, ((09) 321-5111.

SPORT

With such good weather, it is no mystery that so many of Perth's attractions are sports or outdoors related.

Its climate is perfect for golf and more than 20 courses are close to the city. Five minutes away is the **Collier Park Golf Course** in Hayman Road, Como, ((09) 450-6488, where you can play 18-holes on a course bounded by a pine plantation and with a couple of lakes to keep the game interesting. For details about other courses contact the **Western Australian Golf Association** on ((09) 367-2490.

Few places in the world still have grass tennis courts. At **Point Walter Grass Courts** at the corner of Honor and Point Walter Road, ((09) 330-3262, ten grass courts are available for hire between 6:30 am and 5:30 pm weekdays, and between 6 am and 5:30 pm weekends.

Perth's suburban surf beaches are some of the best in the country. On a fine day those between North Fremantle and Scarborough are crowded with sun-seekers.

In the sheltered waters of the Swan River hundred of yachts and sailboards catch the Fremantle Doctor, a cool breeze that blows most afternoons. You can hire a sailboard from the **Pelican Point Windsurfing Hire** in Hackett Drive, Crawley, ((018) 915-136 or **Funcat Hire** in Coode Street, South Perth, ((018) 926-003.

The waters around Perth are also popular with scuba divers. About 25 km (16 miles) from Perth is the **Marmion Marine Park** that features limestone reefs and the wealth of sealife living off them. For more information contact the park management at ((09) 448-5800. Off Rottnest Island are eighteenth century wrecks to explore and some spectacular underwater caves. The **Perth Diving Academy** at 283 Wanneroo Road, Nollamara, ((09) 344-1562, organizes charter trips to reefs near Perth and run courses for beginners.

Western Australia has recently joined the Australian Football League, and nothing elates them more than beating a Victorian side. In 1992 their team, the West Coast Eagles, won the Australian Football League's Grand Final, much to the chagrin of Victorians. They don't play in Perth every week but when they do it is at Subiaco Ground or the WACA in Nelson Crescent, a cricket venue in summer.

WHERE TO STAY

In Perth hotels are judged good if they are "new" and "large" and few boutique hotels or quaint guesthouses survive. Some of the latter can be found in Fremantle. Being close to the city, Fremantle is a good place to be based.

Luxury

In Fremantle, the **Esplanade Hotel** at the corner of Marine Terrace and Essex Street, ((09) 430-4000, (008) 998-201, fax: (09) 430-4539, is a grand old hotel that was refurbished in 1988 without losing its character; most rooms open out onto a verandah where breakfast can be served in summer.

Overlooking the Indian Ocean and about 20 minutes from the city in Scarborough is the **Radisson Observation City Resort Hotel** on the Esplanade, ((09) 245-1000, (008)

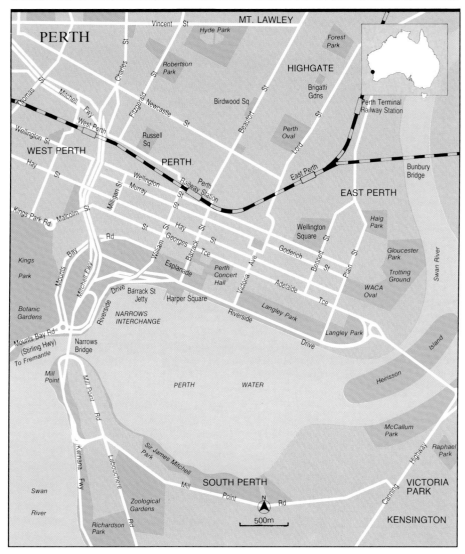

PERTH

333-333, fax: (09) 245-2345. The hotel has several bars and two discos.

The **Perth Parmelia Hilton** in Mill Street, ((09) 322-3622, (008) 222-255, fax: (09) 481-0857, has views of the Swan River. In the center of town is the **Hyatt Regency**, ((09) 225-1234, (008) 222-188, fax: (09) 325-8785.

Moderate

In North Perth, just five minutes from the city is **Federation Homestay** at 11 Knutsford Street, ((09) 444-8850, which is a restored homestead mansion. **Tradeswinds Hotel**, ((09) 339-8188, (008) 999-274, fax: (09) 339-2266 is near the Swan River.

A selection of bed and breakfast accommodation is offered in the suburbs by **Inn Homes**, ((09) 249-1230.

Inexpensive

The **"Beauforts" Lone Star Hotel** at the corner of Beaufort and Newcastle Streets, ((09) 328-7566, fax: (09) 227-7937, is a refurbished pub near the center of town.

Bed and breakfast accommodation has only recently gained in popularity and **Homestays of Western Australia**, ((09) 293-5347, fax: (09) 316-2840, and **Perth Bed & Breakfast**, ((09) 364-4498, offer a range of inexpensive to moderately priced places to stay.

WHERE TO EAT

Dining in Perth is often out of doors, and even the best restaurants are casual. The emphasis is on having a good time rather than peering through candle-lit gloom or being patronized by pompous waiters.

At night, the place to be is Northbridge and Fremantle, where the choice is mind-boggling.

There are quite a few moderately priced restaurants within a few blocks of one another in Northbridge. The **Brass Monkey** at 209 William Street, ((09) 227-9596, is an old pub specializing in trendy beers. Try one from the Matilda Bay Brewery before adjourning to its restaurant upstairs. **Toledos** at 35 Lake Street, ((09) 227-5282, is a Spanish *tapas* type restaurant with an outside dinning area popular in summer. There are tables outside the **Fishy Affair** at 132 James Street, ((09) 328-3939, whereas the atmosphere inside is intimate.

Good seafood restaurants abound in Fremantle, where locals have been buying seafood from Kailis since 1928; **Kailis' Cafe** on the harbor, ((09) 335-7755, serves great fish and chips. Two establishments in the more expensive price bracket are **Bridges** at 22 Tydeman Road, ((09) 430-4433, and **William's** at 82 Stirling Highway, ((09) 335-2775.

There always seems to be a queue outside **The Sicilian** at 47 Mews Road, ((09) 430-7024, unavoidable because this popular inexpensive restaurant will not take bookings.

HOW TO GET THERE

Perth is a terminus for one of the world's great train journeys — the transcontinental *Indian-Pacific*. Starting at Sydney the journey takes 64 hours including 482 km (300 miles) of absolutely straight track through the Nullarbor Plain.

There are daily direct flights into Perth from Melbourne, Sydney, Adelaide and occasional flights from Darwin and Brisbane. The time to Melbourne is about four hours.

By road it is a long way from anywhere: the drive from Adelaide takes about 32 hours, and from Darwin 46 hours. Care should be exercised if undertaking a car journey through the Outback.

DAY TRIPS FROM PERTH

ROTTNEST ISLAND

Rottnest Island, 19 km (12 miles) from Fremantle, provides a range of holiday attractions and is best known for its abundant wildlife. The island is 11 km long and 5 km wide (7 by 3 miles) and easily warrants a couple of days' sightseeing.

Background

In the seventeenth century the Dutch explorer, Willem de Vlamingh, landed on a small island off the west coast of Australia. Believing it to be infested with rats, he named it Rottenest ('rats' nest') Island, quite rightly in a manner of speaking, because the island is the home of perhaps the least known but most endearing marsupial — the quaintly named Quokka. Quokkas, a species of short tailed wallaby, once roamed the south-west tip of Australia but are now mainly confined to Rottnest and Bald Islands.

General Information

There is a **Visitor's Centre** opposite the ferry terminal, ((09) 372-9729, and accommodation can be booked by the **Rottnest Island Authority**, ((09) 372-9727.

What To See And Do

There are no private cars on Rottnest Island, so the choices for traveling around are by foot, bike or mini-bus. A great way to see the island is on a bicycle which can be rented from **Rottnest Bike Hire**, ((09) 372-9722, located behind the **Rottnest Hotel** (also known as the **Quokka Arms**). Most of the terrain is flat but there are a few low hills to ensure that you keep in trim. I give you my personal guarantee that you will come across friendly Quokkas after just a few kilometers on the road, who are always more than willing to share a meal with you if invited politely.

Rottnest also has a grim secret. Between 1838 and 1903 the island was used to imprison Aboriginal offenders often under brutal conditions. The prison, known as the **Quad**, is an octagonal limestone building now transformed into the **Rottnest Lodge**, with cells converted into tourist units. In the center of the Quad stood the gallows, since removed, perhaps in consideration of the sensibilities of guests who stay there.

The rest of the island provides a variety of activities from fishing along its coastline to swimming, scuba diving among ship wrecks and surfing. The island also has numerous lakes reflecting a mosaic of colors at sunset and attracting a huge variety of birds.

you can enjoy a 45-minute trip down the Swan River. The island can also be reached by plane (Rottnest Airbus, ((09) 478-1322), which takes 15 minutes from Perth Airport.

THE GOLDEN MILE

Gold found at Coolgardie in 1892 triggered the Western Australian gold rush. Eleven months later, nearly 100 ounces of gold were found at Mt. Charlotte near Kalgoorlie-

Where to Stay

Accommodation is available at the **Rottnest Hotel**, ((09) 292-5011, fax: (09) 292-5188, which was built in 1864 as the summer residence of the Governor of Western Australia, and at **Rottnest Lodge**, ((09) 272-5171. Camping, ((09) 292-5112, and cabin hire, ((09) 372-9737, provide inexpensive alternatives

How to Get There

Rottnest Island can be reached by a ferry service that runs every day from either Barrack Street Jetty in Perth, ((09) 211-5844, Hillarys Marinas, ((09) 246-1039, or off Northport Rous Head, Fremantle, ((09) 430-5844. Taking the ferry from Perth means that

Boulder by Paddy Hannan, Tom Flanagan and Daniel Shea. They uncovered the richest square mile in the world, hence the area being known as the Golden Mile.

It is dry and supplies of fresh water had to be trucked in. In 1903 a pipeline was opened supplying water to the gold fields from a dam at Mundaring, 565 km (350 miles) away, pumping across 27,300 cubic meters (35,800 cubic yards) of water every day. It did not, however, fully quench the thirst of everyone: that was left to the 93 pubs and eight breweries which opened in Kalgoorlie for its 30,000 thirsty miners.

Fremantle's Round House, originally a jail and the West's oldest (1831) building.

Coolgardie boasted 23 hotels and three breweries.

To date a staggering 1,800 tons of gold have been extracted from the area but the days of people picking up gold nuggets off the ground are long gone. Still, there are small-time prospectors in Kalgoorlie, combing the ground with metal detectors and hoping to find another rich lode. These men who spend a lot of time in the bush can be found in town propping up the bar ready to tell a tall story, if only someone asks.

WHAT TO SEE AND DO

Coolgardie

At its peak, there were about 16,000 people in Coolgardie. Today the population has dropped to less than 1,000, making it almost a ghost town. **The Goldfields Exhibition,** ((090) 266-090, in the original Warden Courts building, tells of the rise and fall of Coolgardie. A 35-minute video Gold Fever complements the exhibition, open daily from 9 am to 5 pm; an admission fee is charged.

GENERAL INFORMATION

The **Coolgardie Tourist Bureau** at 62 Bayley Street, ((090) 266-090, is open daily between 9 am to 5 pm.

The **Kalgoorlie-Boulder Tourist Centre** at 250 Hannan Street, ((090) 211-966, provides information on Kalgoorlie and will arrange travel booking in the area; it is open Monday to Friday 8:30 am to 5 pm and weekends and on public holidays between 9 am and 5 pm.

The **Tourist Bureau** is in Irish Mulga Drive, Kambalda, ((090) 271-446, and is open on weekdays between 9 am and 5 pm.

Another way to appreciate Coolgardie's history is to walk around town and the surrounding area where traces of workings can still be seen. 150 markers, illustrated with old photographs, help visitors identify the main landmarks. Much of the early transport was provided by camels, and these contrary beasts are available for one and two day safaris from the **Camel Farm**, three kilometers (two miles) west of Coolgardie on the Western Highway, ((090) 266-159.

Kalgoorlie-Boulder

One of the most famous visitors to Kalgoorlie was Herbert Hoover, who worked there as a mining engineer in 1898 before going on to become the thirty-first President of the United States. He found the place too rough for his taste, such that he described Kalgoorlie as being only "three yards inside civilization."

The streets in the twin towns of Kalgoorlie and Boulder still have that rough and ready look they had 100 years ago when Hoover worked there. Kalgoorlie is still a man's town. The pubs are filled with hard drinking men and the entertainment runs to satellite TV and topless barmaids. The best known street in Kalgoorlie is **Hay Street**

The **Golden Mile Loopline**, ℂ (090) 933-055, starts at the Boulder City Station from which visitors can take an hour's journey on a rail-car around the Golden Mile on a guided tour. Departure is at 11 am Monday to Saturday and 1:30 pm and 3 pm on Sunday.

On the Eastern By-Pass Road, 5 km (3 miles) north of Kalgoorlie is **Hannans North Tourist Gold Mine**, ℂ (090) 914-074, which has various displays and demonstrations relating to gold mining and extraction. Visitors can go underground to

where prostitutes stand outside shacks waiting for customers. The police turn a blind eye to this illegal trade, quietly acknowledging that the street's activity serves a purpose.

The **Palace Hotel** is worth a visit. From the outside it exudes an Edwardian atmosphere, with its wooden verandahs and wrought iron balconies. Inside there is serious drinking going on and the **Shaft Bar** disco is filled with young people ready to rage until dawn.

Seven kilometers (four miles) north of Kalgoorlie is a legalized **Two Up School**, ℂ (090) 211-413, which allows visitors to gamble on the fall on two coins; it stays open from 1:30 pm until dark.

seethe work in progress. There is also a daily bus tour to the "Super Open Pit," which takes about an hour.

Kambalda

There was a short-lived gold rush in Kambalda in 1906 after which the town lay dormant until nickel was discovered there in 1966.

The town is located on Lake Leroy, and the surrounding countryside can best be viewed from **Red Hill Look-out** on Gordon Adams Road.

Kalgoorlie: gold mine OPPOSITE and historic main street ABOVE.

WHERE TO STAY

Kalgoorlie-Boulder has a good choice of accommodation and is the best place to base yourself for a tour of the goldfields. **Quality Plaza Hotel** at 45 Egan Street, ((090) 214-544, (008) 090-600, fax: (090) 912-195, and **Sandalwood** in Hannan Street, ((090) 214-455, (008) 095-530, fax: (090) 213- 744, provide luxury accommodation.

There are moderately priced motels in town but for a bit of character try the **Exchange Hotel** at 135 Hannan Street, ((090) 212-833, **Cornwell Hotel** at 25 Hopkins Street, Boulder, ((090) 932-510, or the **Palace Hotel** at the corner of Hannan and Maritana Streets, ((090) 212-788, fax: (090) 211-813.

Kambalda Motor in Blue Bush Road, ((090) 271-333, is moderately priced, as is the **Coolgardie Motor Inn** on the Great Eastern Highway, ((090) 266-002, fax: (090) 266-310.

Inexpensive accommodation can be obtained at **Railway Lodge** at 75 Baley Street, Coolgardie, ((090) 266-166.

All three towns have caravan parks and vans can be hired quite cheaply.

HOW TO GET THERE

There are Ansett flights to Kalgoorlie-Boulder from Perth, Adelaide, Melbourne and Sydney.

There are trains from East Perth every day; the *Prospector* and the *Indian Pacific* run between Adelaide and Perth, with a twice weekly stop at Kalgoorlie.

Australian Coaches and Westliner Coaches run a bus service from Perth twice a week. The Adelaide–Perth Pioneer and Greyhound bus services run daily through Kalgoorlie, Coolgardie and Kambalda.

THE WEST COAST

Heading north along the Western Australian coast there are vast distances between towns. This stretch of coast, however, has

Statue boldly echoes Kalgoorlie's dominant activity.

some real tourist gems and the effort will be rewarded with unparalleled experiences and sights.

GENERAL INFORMATION

Information about tours to Monkey Mia can be obtained from the **Shark Bay Tourist Centre** at 83 Knight Terrace, Denham, ((099) 481-253. At Monkey Mia there is a dolphin information center where rangers are available to help tourists.

Information on the **Ningaloo Marine**

Park is available from the park ranger, ((099) 491-676.

The **Wittenoom Tourist Information Centre** on Sixth Avenue, ((091) 897-096, is open daily from 8 am to 5 pm.

WHAT TO SEE AND DO

Monkey Mia

If you want to meet a dolphin face to face (or more precisely face to beak) then Monkey Mia provides a unique opportunity to see these highly intelligent mammals at close range.

There are few places that can offer just one attraction to justify a visit but seeing the dolphins in the shallows at Monkey Mia is more than sufficient. A family of them comes

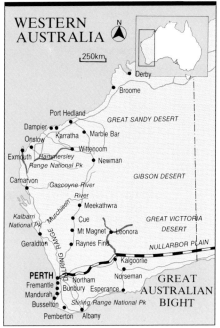

WESTERN
AUSTRALIA

in most days, weather and other conditions permitting. They speed into the shore and rear out of the water to welcome tourists. They love being patted and their skin feels a little like wet velvet. The best time to see them is between early morning and late afternoon when you can watch them being fed.

Denham

Besides being the access town for Monkey Mia, Denham is popular for both boating and fishing and the bay provides sheltered beaches.

Ningaloo Reef

Because of its remoteness, Ningaloo Reef, running 260 km (160 miles) along the Western Australian coast from Exmouth to Amherst Point is not nearly as well known as the Great Barrier Reef. This is in pristine water and the small number of visitors has ensured that the destructive development along the Great Barrier Reef be avoided at Ningaloo. Access from the coast is easy.

Wittenoom

Wittenoom is situated on the northern slopes of the Hamersley Ranges, an area rich in minerals. The town is a convenient place to stay while exploring the stunning gorges nearby.

There are five major examples within a short distance with pools in which you can swim in the shadow of rugged rock faces.

There is nothing to beat local knowledge, and I recommend that visitors take one of the organized tours offered out of Wittenoom. These include one to six day tours offered by **Design-a-Tour**, ((091) 897-059, and **Dave's Gorge Tours**, ((091) 897-026, which can be for either one or two days. The best time to visit the Hamersley Ranges is from April to September. Further information can be obtained from the local ranger, ((091) 898-157.

WHERE TO STAY

The best place to stay is the **Monkey Mia Dolphin Resort**, ((099) 481-320, which provides a range of accommodation from on-site caravans and cabins to serviced apartments costing $110 for a double. In Denham there is the moderately priced **Hartog Holiday Villas**, ((099) 481-323, and the **Shark Bay**, ((099) 481-203.

The accommodation offered in Wittenoom is limited, and mostly inexpensive to moderately priced. The **Wittenoom Holiday Homes** on Fifth Avenue, ((091) 897-026, has cottages. At the **Auski Tourist Village Roadhouse**, ((091) 766-988, there are 40 powered sites and on-site cabins. There are also camping sites available in the **Karijini National Park**, ((091) 898-157, about 60 km (37 miles) from Wittenoom and good value provided you don't mind pit toilets.

The **Ningaloo Reef Resort** in Coral Bay, ((09) 362-6188 or fax: (09) 362-6616, is moderately priced.

HOW TO GET THERE

Pioneer coach service from Perth to Darwin stops at Wittenoom. Greyhound has an overnight service to Monkey Mia, leaving Darwin on Sunday, Thursday and Tuesday, and Perth on Tuesday, Thursday and Saturday. A Greyhound service to Ningaloo Reef leaves Perth on Sunday, Tuesday and Thursday.

To reach Ningaloo Reef by air fly into Exmouth on Ansett Australian and organize connecting transport locally.

The west coast can be explored by car along the North West Coastal Highway which is surfaced all the way.

THE KIMBERLEY RANGES

The Kimberley Ranges are a group of mountains and plateaux in the sparsely populated north-west corner of Australia. Rivers which run fast during the Wet season have cut deep gorges into the landscape: the coastline is lined with steep cliffs, some 250 m (16 ft) high, making its rugged beauty well worth the trip to this remote part of the continent.

William Dampier visited the Kimberleys in 1688 and made unflattering observations about the infertile land he found. The first European expedition into the Kimberleys was led by Lieutenant George Grey in 1837. On his first day ashore Grey almost came to grief when he tried to swim Prince Regent River, and while he just failed to lose his life he did succeed in losing his trousers in the attempt.

In the 1890s there was effectively a guerrilla war waged by the Bunuba Aborigines under the leadership of Jundumurra, known by the whites as Pigeon because he was shorter than other Bunuba males and fast-footed. He started by spearing the sheep and cattle of the invaders but was captured and taken in chains to Derby. Pigeon's reputation among his people grew after he escaped from custody. When he killed Constable William Richardson in 1894 and freed Bunuba prisoners he became the indisputable leader of the local resistance around Fitzroy River. Capturing a cache of guns he began training his warriors and conducting successful ambushes. Weakened through loss of blood from an earlier wound and hunger, Jundumurra was finally hunted down in 1897 at Tunnel Creek.

Touring the Kimberley it is possible to see how a skilled bushman could evade superior forces for such a long time. Unfortunately, few tourists make the effort to get off the beaten track to explore this area, rich in wildlife and the natural land forms that give the Kimberleys' wide open spaces their majesty.

GENERAL INFORMATION

Broome Tourist Bureau is located at the corner of Broome Road and Bagot Street, ☎ (091) 922-222.

The **Tourist Information Centre** at 1 Clarendon Street in Derby, ☎ (091) 911-426, is open Monday to Saturday.

WHAT TO SEE AND DO

Broome
One of the most interesting towns in Australia is Broome which at the turn of the century was the center of a lucrative pearling industry attracting divers and adventurers from many countries. In its heyday a fleet of 300

pearling boats was headquartered here. While the rest of Australia was inward turning and hiding behind the White Australia Policy this boom town was developing a face as much Asian as European. Faces in the street reflect the high level of intermarriage in the area.

Today Broome still has a wild feel to it, and the usual heavy-drinking male stereotypes can still be found propping up the bar in the town's pubs.

Pearls are available for sale in a number of shops along **Dampier Terrace**. The dark blue, almost black Harvest pearls are highly prized.

In the **Japanese Cemetery** many pearl divers from Japan lie buried where some 900 headstones mark their graves.

For drive-in buffs, trade in your car seats for deck chairs and enjoy true open air viewing. **Sun Pictures** is reputed to be the oldest operating picture garden in the world, having operated since 1916. Movies start at 7.55 pm.

A dinosaur footprint thought to be 130 million years old can be seen on the rocks at the beach at low tide at **Gantheaume Point**.

Cable Beach is clean, white, and near Broome, as well as one of the last opportunities, if you're traveling north, of safely swimming in the sea. Salt-water crocodiles infest coastal waters beyond.

Sculpted by the wind over thousands of years these limestone pillars, some 5 m (16 ft) tall, stand in the Pinnacles Desert ABOVE.

Broome is a good base for visiting the **Bungle Bungle National Park**, stripped beehive-shaped sandstone domes. Walking in the park is for the dedicated, and the effort is amply repaid by the scenery. **Broome Aviation**, ℂ (091) 922-222, has scenic flights on weekdays out of Broome which provide an opportunity to take in the scale of the rock formations from the air. There are also tours to the **Argyle Diamond Mine**, a major producer and home of the rare pink diamond.

Wyndham

At the north-east edge of the Kimberleys is Wyndham, which has a model of an 18 m (16 ft) crocodile at the entrance to the town. There is a crocodile look-out in town: while the table manners of these primitive beasts at feeding time are deplorable no one seems to have the courage to reprimand them.

WHERE TO STAY

In Broome accommodation is provided by the luxury **Cable Beach Club**, ℂ (091)

Derby

The local authorities in Derby once made an unusual use of the area's distinctive baobab tree, the trunk of which is shaped a little like a fat skittle. A thousand-year-old specimen, seven kilometers (four miles) from town, was used as a cell for prisoners and is reputed to have housed up to twenty Aborigines overnight on one occasion. Directions on how to find the tree can be obtained from Derby Tourist Information Centre.

The area is rich is Aboriginal rock art galleries, and it was Wandjina representations of heads with large eyes and "halos" that lead Erick Von Däniken, in *Chariots of the Gods*, to suggest that they were drawings of extraterrestrial beings.

920-400, (008) 095-508, fax: (091) 922-249. The resort's bungalows reflect the Chinese and Malaysian heritage of Broome with latticework and verandahs modeled after old pearl masters' homes. They are scattered in lush gardens and the grounds are intersected by canals. The **Quality Tropicana Inn** at the corner of Saville and Robinson Streets, ℂ (091) 921-204, fax: (091) 922-583, provides motel type accommodation at moderate prices. For a friendly guesthouse atmosphere there is the inexpensive **Forrest House** at 59 Forrest Street, ℂ (091) 935-067, fax: (091) 922-429.

To the north there is moderately priced accommodation at the **Derby Boab Inn** in

Loch Street, ((091) 911-044, and at **Wyndham Town Hotel** at 19 O'Donnell Street, ((091) 611-003, fax: (091) 911-568.

HOW TO GET THERE

The Pioneer daily service from Perth to Darwin stops at Broome and Derby, and the Greyhound service stops at Broome, Derby and Wyndham.

There are daily Ansett Australia flights to Broome and Derby from Perth.

By road, Broome, Derby and Wyndham

can be reached from the Great Northern Highway. Check with the Royal Automobile Club of Western Australia, ((09) 421-4444, about local hazards when crossing from Broome to Wyndham during the Wet season.

NATIONAL PARKS

GENERAL INFORMATION

For details of National Parks contact the **WA Department of Conservation and Land Management**, ((09) 367-0333 or the **Conservation Council of Western Australia**, ((09) 321-4507.

WHAT TO SEE AND DO

Yanchep, 51 km (32 miles) north of Perth, features limestone caves, heath and after rain a profusion of wildflowers. Contact the local ranger, ((09) 561-1661, for further details.

The Pinnacles haunt the landscape of the **Nambung National Park**, 250 km (160 miles) north of Perth off the Geraldton Highway. Thousands of limestone pillars, some 5 m (16 ft) tall, stand in the **Pinnacles**

Desert. These ancient totems have been sculpted by the wind over thousands of years. Contact the local ranger, ((096) 527-043, for further details.

Kalbarri, 590 km (366 miles) north of Perth, can best be reached from Geraldton. The National Park features spectacular river gorges, mallee and wonderful coastal scenery. The best time to visit is from May to October. Contact the local ranger, ((099) 371-178, for further details.

In spring the **Stirling Ranges**, 322 km (200 miles) south of Perth, comes alive

Gorge country. OPPOSITE: Red Bluff LEFT and old mine RIGHT in Wittenoom Gorge. ABOVE: Dales Gorge LEFT in HamersleyRange National Park and Windjana Gorge RIGHT.

with a richly colored carpet of wildflowers. The Ranges can best be reached from Albany and feature rugged mountains with both woodland and heathlands. Contact the local ranger, ((098) 279-278, for further details.

Walpole/Nornalup, 111 km (69 miles) west of Albany has extensive karri and tingle high forest, and secluded inlets. Contact the local ranger, ((098) 279-278, for further details.

Cape Range, 1,700 km (1,000 miles) north-west of Perth, can best be reached

from Exmouth. The National Park features rugged limestone ridges, scrub and heathland. The best time to visit is from April to September. Contact the local ranger, ((099) 491-676, for further details.

FESTIVALS AND SPORTING EVENTS

JANUARY See in the New Year in real Australian style at the annual **bush dance** in Perth organized by the WA Folk Federation, ((09) 370-1145.

FEBRUARY/MARCH The **Festival of Perth** provides an extensive program of music, theater and dance at a variety of venues around the city.

MARCH/APRIL For surfers there is the **Margaret River Masters**, where towering waves challenge the world's best. The event draws a crowd of approximately 20,000 people to the venue, 227 km (141 miles) south of Perth.

JUNE There is good fishing around Carnarvon, and the annual **Carnarfin** fishing tournament is a highlight among local anglers.

AUGUST/SEPTEMBER The **Festival of Pearl** (or Shinju Matsuri) is a nine day festival in which the conclusion coincides with a full moon. A Chinese dragon leads the main street parade and the program includes a pearling lugger race, the Ball of the Full Moon, crowning of the Pearl Queen and the Sayonara Ball. Various groups put on displays, there are fish-bakes and also a beach carnival.

OCTOBER The **York Fair** was held regularly in the last century and was revived in 1971. York lies 97 km (60 miles) east of Perth.

NOVEMBER In Broome during the **Mango Festival**, this delightful fruit is served in every conceivable way by the "great chefs of Broome" in the annual cook-off, which is happily followed by wine tastings.

The **Fremantle Festival** turns the port city over to ten days of culture, ending in a parade and party.

ABOVE: The Byzantine-style St. Francis Xavier Cathedral at Geraldton. OPPOSITE: TOP Weathered tree in the Pilbara outback; BOTTOM aeriel view of the Fitzroy River, Geikie Gorge National Park.

Travelers' Tips

INTERNATIONAL FLIGHTS

More than twenty international airlines fly into Australia. Most enter through Sydney and Melbourne, although others arrive, albeit less frequently, at Hobart, Darwin, Perth, Brisbane and some provincial centers. Airports are generally close to their respective cities and distances are given below:

Adelaide   6 km (4 miles)
Brisbane   13 km (8 miles)
Canberra   8 km (5 miles)
Darwin   15 km (9 miles)
Hobart   22 km (14 miles)
Melbourne   19 km (12 miles)
Perth   12 km (7 miles)
Sydney   7 km (4 miles)

In each State capital there are shuttle buses from the airport to the city, and often also to major hotels and the suburbs.

On leaving Australia, don't forget to keep at least $A25 in your pocket for the departure tax.

The major international carriers can be contacted on:

Air New Zealand
All States   13-24-76.
British Airways
Adelaide   (08) 238-2138; Brisbane   (07) 223-3123; Hobart   (002) 347-433; Melbourne   (03) 603-1133; Perth   (09) 483-7711; Sydney   (02) 258-3300; Other places (008) 222-432.
Canadian Pacific
Sydney   (02) 299-7843; Other places   (008) 251-321.
Cathay Pacific
All places   13-17-47.
Japan Airlines
Adelaide   (08) 212-2555; Gold Coast   (075) 920-443; Melbourne   (03) 654-2733; Perth   (09) 481-1666; Sydney   (02) 233-4500;
KLM Royal Dutch Airlines
Sydney   (02) 231-6333; Other places   (008) 222-747.
Lufthansa German Airlines
Brisbane   (07) 229-2666; Adelaide   (08) 212-6444; Melbourne   (03) 602-1155; Country Victoria   (008) 136-106; Sydney   (02) 367-3888

Malaysian Airline System
Sydney   (02) 232-5066; Other places   13-26-27.
Northwest Airlines
Sydney   (02) 290-4455; Other places   (008) 221-714.
Qantas Australian
All States   13-13-13.
Singapore Airlines
All States   13-10-11.
United Airlines
Sydney   (02) 237-8888; Other places   (008) 230-322.

INTERNAL FLIGHTS

There are two major internal airlines — Ansett Australia and Qantas Australian — which provide services to over 100 destinations.

There are about 20 small regional airlines providing services off the main routes as well as linking major provincial cities and popular tourist destinations. All these are associated with either of the two major carriers, and bookings can be made through Qantas Australian or Ansett Australia.

For reservations or inquires, both airlines provide single numbers that connect the caller anywhere in Australia with the closest office for the cost of a local call. The numbers are:

Qantas Australian   13-13-13
Ansett Australia   13-13-00

OPPOSITE, Waiting for a bite on the Norman River, which flows into the Gulf of Carpentaria. ABOVE: A local carrier drops off passengers in Darwin.

Both airlines offer a number of discount fares and both have frequent flier clubs, which provide free travel and other benefits for travelers who accumulate points based on kilometers traveled.

Ansett Australia provides a 25 percent discount fare called "See Australia" which is only available to tourists and must be booked from overseas or within 30 days of arrival. The "Kangaroo Pass" provides discounted travel and is $1,499 for 10,000 km (6,200 miles). Restrictions apply.

Qantas Australian has an "Ultrasaver" fare which offers significant savings on journeys which include visits to more than one place. Restrictions apply.

There are also special deals, from time to time, details of which can be obtained from a travel agent or by contacting the airline directly.

VISAS

All visitors require a passport and visa to enter Australia, except for New Zealanders who do not require a visa. Application should be made before entering the country at the nearest Australian consulate or embassy. The visa will state the permitted length of stay, usually a maximum of six months. Applications for extensions are made through the Department of Immigration and Ethnic Affairs, whose offices are in most States.

CUSTOM ALLOWANCES

Visitors over 18 years of age may bring into Australia 200 cigarettes or 250 g (9 oz) of cigars or tobacco and one liter (1.75 pints) of alcohol.

Strict prohibitions apply on guns and drugs.

Prescription drugs should be accompanied by a doctor's certificate and should not exceed one month's supply.

Australia is extremely strict about protecting local wildlife from imported pests. It is prudent to declare any foodstuffs, plants and seeds that you have in your luggage. Even products made out of plant material, such as bamboo hats, should be shown to the custom officials.

To prevent importation of pests all incoming planes are sprayed. The spray used is not harmful to human beings but people with respiratory problems should cover their mouths and noses during this operation.

CURRENCY

Australia uses a decimal system of currency, expressed in dollars and cents. There are silver-colored coins, increasing in size — five, ten, twenty and fifty cent denominations. There are two gold-colored coins — one and two dollars — that are smaller than the twenty cent piece, a fact which can be confusing.

Notes come in different colors and are available in denominations of $5, $10, $20, $50 and $100. The five dollar note differs from the others in that it is made of plastic.

Travelers' checks present no problems and can easily be cashed at international airports, hotels and motels, money changers, or *bureaux de change,* and banks. Banks are open from 9:30 am to 4 pm on Monday to Thursday and until 5 pm on Friday.

A range of International credit cards are accepted in most places; Mastercard and Visa cards are most widely accepted, followed by American Express, Diners Club and Carte Blanche.

WEIGHTS AND MEASURES

All weights are metric. If you come from a country that is not metric, then here are a few approximate equivalents:

1 kilogram   two pounds
8 km   5 miles
20°C   68°F;   25°C   77°F;   30°C   85°F
one meter   three feet
one hectare   two and half acres
one liter   quarter US gallon

For a bird's eye view of the Dutch mansions around Medan Merdeka ride the lift to the top of the National Monument.

GETTING AROUND

BY RAIL

In a country with large distances between destinations, trains provide a less expensive alternative to air travel. A long train journey can be an enjoyable experience in itself, and an opportunity to see the countryside at a leisurely pace in comfort.

There are interstate trains connecting all the State capital cities except Hobart. Each

(100 mph). This service is offered between Sydney, Melbourne, Brisbane and some provincial cities in New South Wales. On MotoRail services it is possible to take your car with you.

Interstate trains are comfortable, the carriages are air conditioned and overnight trains have sleeping berths. Not all have dining cars, in which case meals are served from a buffet counter.

On the more popular routes, train fares are competitive with long distance coaches, and are faster and more comfortable. Watch

state has its own suburban and country rail network linking its major provincial cities and tourist destinations. Details can be obtained from State rail authorities:

New South Wales ℓ(02) 224-4513; (008) 043-126; Fax: (02) 240-289

Victoria ℓ(03) 619-5000; (008) 136-109; Fax: (03) 619-2728.

South Australia ℓ(08) 231-7699; Fax: (08) 217-4682.

Queensland ℓ(07) 235-1323; Fax: (07) 235-2940.

Western Australia ℓ(09) 326-2222; Fax: (09) 326-2619.

Trains usually have first and economy class carriages, and some interstate routes use XPT trains which can travel at 160 km/h

out for special deals offered from time to time.

Overseas visitors can take advantage of rail passes (Austrailpass and Austrail Flexipass), rail and road passes (Kangaroo Road'n Rail Pass), sector fares and advance purchase fares.

Austrailpass and Budget Austrailpass, which are available for 14, 21, 30, 60 and 90 days, allow unlimited travel on long distance, inter-capital, provincial and city trains.

Austrail Flexipass allows any eight days' travel within a period of 60 days, or 15 days

Houseboating on Myall Lakes, near Newcastle, New South Wales.

travel within 90 days, giving the flexibility of long stopovers between rail trips. Note that the eight day pass is not available for travel to Perth or Alice Springs.

All passes must be purchased before arrival in Australia by contacting:

Canada ((416) 322-1034; Fax: (416) 322-1109.

Denmark ((31) 358-844; Fax: (31) 358-022.

France ((1) 45-535839; Fax: (1) 47-559593.

Germany ((69) 920-4912; Fax: (69) 920-4914.

Hong Kong (369-5051; Fax: 311-8166.

Japan ((3) 3820-8011; Fax: (3) 3820-8014

Korea ((2) 753-8585; Fax: (2) 753-9076

Malaysia ((3) 242-5184; Fax: (3) 242-6652

Sweden ((31) 774-0025; Fax: (31) 774-0228.

Singapore (336-6816; Fax: 338-1071.

United Kingdom ((0733) 51-780; Fax: (0733) 89-2601.

United States ((818) 841-1030; Fax: (818) 841-0345.

The main line runs down the eastern seaboard from Cairns to Sydney. It then continues, via either Melbourne or Broken Hill to Adelaide and across the Nullarbor Plain to Perth. There is also a rail link between Adelaide and Alice Springs.

There are country rail services in the states but some of these are being closed down and it is necessary to contact the local representative for more information on routes and timetables.

There are several great train journeys in Australia which are an experience in themselves.

The *Ghan* links Adelaide and Alice Springs. The *Ghan* takes its name from the Ghan camel drivers who opened up the Red Center of the country in the late nineteenth century. See the rugged scenery of the Outback from air conditioned comfort on a journey that takes 20 hours and covers 1,555 km (960 miles).

The *Indian Pacific* traverses the continent twice weekly from Perth, on the Indian Ocean, to Sydney, on the Pacific Ocean — a distance of 4,348 km (2,695 miles). From Sydney the train climbs through the Blue Mountains and then into Outback New South Wales to Adelaide. From Adelaide the Nullarbor Plain presents the longest stretch of straight line in the world. Passing through the goldfields of Western Australia, the *Indian Pacific* arrives in Perth three days after leaving Sydney.

By Bus

Bus travel around Australia is fast, relatively comfortable, and a low-cost alternative to train or air travel.

Long distance coaches are air conditioned with wash rooms and adjustable seats. Some are introducing videos to keep passengers entertained on long distance journeys, such as the sixty hour trip from Perth to Darwin.

There are three main companies which provide regular scheduled bus services throughout the continent. They are:

Pioneer   13-20-30

Greyhound   13-12-38

Bus Australia   13-23-23

All three companies offer the Aussie Pass which allows you to travel on any of their buses, and is based on the number of days traveled. Passes, from 21 to 90 days, can be purchased directly from the bus companies or booked through a travel agent. Road and Rail Passes and Tassie Passes are other packages offered.

McCafferty's services run everywhere except Tasmania and Western Australia, and can be contacted through their regional terminals. They are at:

Adelaide ((08) 212-5066

Brisbane ((07) 212-3033

Cairns ((070) 515-899

Coolangatta ((075) 361-700

Melbourne ((03) 670-2533

Rockhampton ((079) 272-844

Surfers' Paradise ((075) 279-076

Sydney ((02) 361-5125

Townsville ((077) 725-100

There are two major coach companies that organize package tours to specific destinations:

AAT King

Melbourne ((03) 274-7422

Other places ((008) 334-009

Australia Pacific

Melbourne ((03) 689-7999

Country Victoria ((008) 335-003

Tasmania ((008) 335-003

Sydney ((02) 669-1769

Country NSW ((008) 425-353
Adelaide ((08) 212-5233
Brisbane ((07) 236-1017
Cairns ((070) 519-299
Country Queensland ((008) 177-658
Perth ((09) 221-1163

There are also a number of regional bus tour companies, and details about their packages can be obtained from tourist bureaus or travel agents.

Meals are usually included in package tours and accommodation can be in motels or tents, depending how the tour is organized.

Hertz Melbourne ((03) 698-2555; other places, (008) 333-377.

Thrifty Sydney, ((02) 380-5399; Melbourne, ((03) 663-5200; Adelaide, ((08) 211-8788; Brisbane, ((07) 252-5994; Canberra, ((06) 247-7422; Hobart, ((002) 485-678; Perth, ((09) 481-1999; Darwin ((089) 818-555.

Budget All States, (13-28-48.

Four and six cylinder cars are available on request, and some outlets hire out four-wheel drive vehicles and caravans.

A deposit must be left when picking up the vehicle. Compulsory third-party insur-

Tour buses don't just keep to the main highways. Getting off the beaten track is possible with packages that use four-wheel drive mini buses. This form of transport allows tourists to experience the remote Outback and tours may also include interesting diversions such as a balloon flight or camel rides.

BY CAR

Avis, Thrifty, Budget and Hertz are the four leading car rental companies, with outlets at major airports and in the capital cities. Each region also has at least one local car rental company in competition.

Avis Sydney ((02) 902-9292; other places, ((008) 225-533.

ance is included in the rental price, and comprehensive insurance is available for an additional cost. Drivers are requested to show their licenses at the time of renting cars, and if an international license, domestic licenses should also be available for inspection.

The cars do not necessarily need to be returned to where they were hired, and arrangements can be made to leave them at your destination.

Traffic in Australia travels on the left hand side of the road, and right turning cars must give way to cars turning left. Seat-belts must be worn at all times by everyone in the car,

Cruising up the Hawksbury River, less than an hour's drive north from downtown Sydney.

and hefty fines for contraventions apply. The police are particularly hard on drivers who drive under the influence of alcohol.

Pictorial road warnings follow international standards. In additional, yellow diamond-shaped signs with a drawing of kangaroo or wombat warn that local wildlife could be crossing the road. These signs should be heeded because a kangaroo may "freeze" in the middle of the road at night mesmerized, by the headlights. A collision with one can damage the car severely and is usually fatal for the 'roo.

Speed limits are in kilometers per hour, and speed cameras and radar traps are employed to trap and fine speeding cars.

Petrol (gasoline) is sold in liters and most outlets are self-service. Competition exists between petrol stations and large signs displayed outside the outlet allow consumers to shop around for the best deal. Prices tend to be higher in remote areas.

Each state and territory has its own motoring organization, which may have reciprocal arrangements with overseas equivalents. Check before leaving. These organizations provide emergency roadside assistance and will help you with information on road conditions. Some also provide general tourist information. The headquarters of these organizations are in the capitals, and lists of local outlets can be obtained from their head offices. They are:

Adelaide Royal Automobile Association of South Australia at 41 Hindmarsh Square, ℂ (08) 202-4500, fax: (08) 232-0904.

Brisbane Royal Automobile Club of Queensland at 300 St. Paul's Terrace, Fortitude Valley, ℂ (07) 361-2444, fax: (07) 849-0610.

Canberra National Road and Motorists' Association at 153 Gallery Level Mall, ℂ (06) 243-8944.

Darwin Automobile Association of Northern Territory at MLC Building, 79–81 Smith Street, ℂ (089) 813-837, fax: (089) 412-965.

Hobart Royal Automobile Club of Tasmania at corner of Murray and Patrick Streets, ℂ (002) 382-200, fax: (002) 348-784.

Melbourne Royal Automobile Club of Victoria at 422 Little Collins Street, ℂ (03) 607-2137, fax: (03) 790-2844.

Perth Royal Automobile Association of Western Australia at 228 Adelaide Terrace, ℂ (09) 421-4444, fax: (09) 221-2380.

Sydney National Road and Motorists' Association at 151 Clarence Street, ℂ (02) 260-9222, fax: (02) 260-8472.

Driving from one place to another in Australia can involve substantial distances and every care should be taken to ensure that you remain attentive, particularly in the Outback at night. There are rest areas at the side of the road, and some local community organizations provide free tea and coffee from vans set up on the side of the road to encourage drivers to take a break.

TAXIS

Cabs cruising for hire display a lighted "Vacant" sign or light on the roof. Cabs can also be hired from ranks located outside major hotels, and bus, train and airline terminals. There is a set amount for flag fall and then a charge for every kilometer. A higher tariff may apply at night and at weekends. There is a surcharge for cabs booked by telephone, and for luggage stored in the boot. In some States it is possible to share cabs with people going in the same direction at a lower charge, but this is at the discretion of the first person in the queue.

BICYCLES

Most of the capital cities have bike tracks. Alternatively, cyclists can use roads, provided they obey all the rules for cars. Bikes are banned on some highways and there are signs at access points indicating whether cycling is permitted.

Helmets are compulsory in most states and territories.

Bicycles can be taken on suburban trains, but usually not at peak hours, and there may be additional charges. On country trains accompanied bikes are stowed in the guard's van and prior notice is usually required. Bikes can also taken on planes as normal luggage but they must be put into bike boxes, the pedals removed and tires deflated. Buses will not take them.

ACCOMMODATION

Australia provides a full range of accommodation choices, from the most exclusive five star resort to a humble country pub or camping ground. Luxury hotels provide service and facilities at an international standard. At the lower end of the market, such inconveniences as having to share bathrooms can be more than compensated for by an opportunity to meet the locals.

Local tourist bureaux have brochures

is worth joining either club just to use this service.

HOTELS

All the capital cities have top-class international hotels, with Hilton and Sheraton Pacific found in most capital cities. Most of the top hotels have toll free 008 numbers through which reservations can be made anywhere in Australia. Most offer special weekend packages, and enquiries should be made when placing your reservation.

on hotels on display. Only a few states provide comprehensive lists of accommodation available and up-to-date rates. This void has been filled by the Australian motoring organizations which have produced *A-Z Australian Accommodation Guide*, which sells for $10. The Guide covers almost every corner of Australia with comprehensive listings and tariffs. A free accommodation booking service is provided by the Royal Automobile Club of Victoria for its members, by phoning ((03) 607-2213, or if outside Melbourne by calling the toll free number ((008) 337-743. The Royal Automobile Association of South Australia, ((08) 202-4540, provides the same service. For visitors who intend to move around the country a lot, it

Many top quality private hotels are not part of a chain. These combine the luxury and character that the larger hotels cannot match. Smaller ones are often referred to as "boutique" hotels combining luxury with intimacy; it makes sense to book well ahead. Some of those recommended in the text are also of historic interest.

Two services take bookings for independent hotels around the country. They are:

Small Luxury Hotels Sydney (02) 267-2988; other places, (008) 800-896.
Historic Hotels of Australia Sydney, (02) 369-4155; other places (008) 021-802

Goldrush ostentation of a Kalgoorlie hotel.

There was once a requirement, as part of their liquor license, for pubs to provide accommodation. Alas, few do so now, but those that have inexpensive no-frills rooms are full of character and surprises.

MOTELS

Considering Australia's dependence on the car, it is not surprising that the backbone of the accommodation business is the motel. These are dotted along most highways, particularly on the roads into and out of town.

Average motel prices are in the range $40 to $70 for a double, while a top one should cost no more than $140. Special deals can be made if you intend to stay for more than a few days.

An average motel is clean and comfortable, with air conditioning, a television, an electric jug and everything else you need to make a cup of tea or coffee. Breakfast is usually not included in the tariff, but can be ordered the night before: the menus include juice, toast, cereal and eggs and bacon. Some have a restaurant but these are not necessarily the best places in town to eat. Some, particularly those further north, have a swimming pool. Spas for guests are becoming increasingly popular.

Reservations with the three largest motel chains can be made by calling the following numbers:

Flag   13-24-00.

Best Western   (008) 222-166.

Golden Chain Motor Inns   (008) 023-966.

The Budget Motel Chain does not have a central booking number, but a booklet with contact numbers for its motels can be obtained by phoning (051) 431-077.

BED AND BREAKFAST AND FARM STAYS

The tradition of Bed and Breakfast accommodation is new to Australia, but sprouting up as increasing numbers of tourists are looking for inexpensive places to stay, are intimate and provide an opportunity to meet the locals and fellow travelers. This industry is not well organized and while the occasional book listing Bed and Breakfast places has been published, a second edition seldom appears. One association still promoting this type of accommodation is **Bed & Breakfast Australia**, ((02) 498-5344, fax: (02) 498-6438. Tasmania is strong on colonial accommodation, and the Tasmanian Tourist Bureau can furnish you with an up-to-date list.

Bed and Breakfast accommodation is also offered on farms, which helps the farmer make ends meet and provides him with an opportunity for some company in what otherwise can be an isolated lifestyle. Accommodation ranges from self-contained cottages on the property to a room in the main homestead. Lists of farm stays can be obtained from State tourist organizations.

YOUTH HOSTELS AND BACKPACKERS - HOTELS

More than 140 youth hostels are spread across the country, providing inexpensive accommodation and friendly company. These are not restricted to the young and people of any age are welcome.

Costs are kept to a minimum by requiring hostlers to share jobs, like cleaning the place every morning. Kitchen facilities are shared. Hostlers are expected to have a slip sheet, but blankets and pillows are provided. The Australian YHA is affiliated with the International YHA and you can join overseas or in Australia.

Lists of hostels can be obtained from the State offices, which can be found at:

New South Wales   422 Kent Street, Sydney, ((02) 261-1111.

Victoria205 King Street, Melbourne, ((03) 670-7991.

Queensland   1st Floor, Westpac Building, corner George and Herschal Streets, Brisbane, ((07) 236-1680.

South Australia   Recreation and Sports Centre, 38 Sturt Street, Adelaide, ((08) 231-5583.

Tasmania   1st floor, 28 Criterion Street, Hobart, ((002) 349-617.

Western Australia 65 Francis Street, Northbridge, ((09) 227-5350.

Northern Territory Darwin Hostel Complex, Beaton Road, Berrimah, ((089) 843-902.

There is an increasing demand by backpackers for inexpensive accommodation. To cater for this need private hostels are cropping up in the capital cities and towns. Backpackers share rooms, where bunks are provided for a charge of about $8 to $14 a night. Some hostels have a cheap cafe attached or kitchens where meals can be cooked.

TIPPING

There is no obligation to tip in Australia. Wages are generally good, and tipping should only be done if the standard of service is exceptional.

In restaurants and hotels there are no service charges, and tips up to about 10 percent are customary but not expected. When buying drinks in pubs it is acceptable to leave the change behind for the barman and rounding the fare to the nearest dollar in taxis is common.

TOURIST INFORMATION

There are tourist bureaux in major cities and many towns. Most States also have tourist bureaux in other state capitals where tourist can make inquiries.

The range of services provided by tourist bureaux varies from state to state, but they usually have a good range of brochures, information on local attractions and addresses of local sporting events and venues. Many bureaux provide a booking service for accommodation, package holidays and organized tours.

When coming into a small town look for a big white "i" sign on a blue background, indicating a tourist bureau nearby. Other good sources of information are local councils, branch offices of the State automobile clubs, and of course the locals.

NATIONAL PARKS

Australian national parks are areas of conservation, not always beautiful in a conventional sense but invariably unique in their own way; frequently of great scientific interest, they reflect a sense of responsibility on the part of the authorities to ensure the survival of untouched, primeval antiquity.

The Royal National Park in Sydney was declared in 1879, making it the second such institution, after Yellowstone, to be established in the world. This precedent was followed by the declaration of the Belair Recreational Park, South Australia in 1891, Kuring-gai Chase National Park, New South Wales in 1892 and Wilson's Promontory, Victoria in 1898.

As Australians began to appreciate the wild beauty and variety of their country's landscape, more areas were being declared reserves.

Today national parks cover over 40 million hectares (100 million acres) or about 5.3 per cent of Australia's land area. About 38 million hectares (95 million acres) has been reserved as Marine and Estuarine Protected Areas, including three on the World Heritage List of natural and cultural significance. They are Kakadu, Willandra and Western Tasmania.

Most parks provide camping facilities, usually near the main access road, and huts. The main camping site usually includes fireplaces, wood, fresh water and toilets. Camping away from the main camping sites may need permission from the park ranger.

Weathered rocks in the Pilbara, Western Australia.

Often there is an information booth in the main camping area which will provide maps, details of walking tracks (and their grading) and fact sheets on what to see and do. Some parks provide number pegs which indicate natural features, unique habitats and points of interest that can be cross-referenced with the fact sheets. To cover the cost of maintaining services to visitors there is a modest charge for entering some national parks.

Touring them can be done by coach, self-drive in a four-wheel drive or walking. Parks generally have few access roads, and seeing them from a car or bus is extremely limited. Only walking provides the opportunity for (literally) getting off the beaten track, but long treks should not be attempted by inexperienced hikers as the Australian bush can be dangerous. Organized walking tours are available in several parks and details obtained from the park ranger or local tourist bureau. It is standard procedure, when walking into a national park, to leave details with the ranger of your route and when you expect to complete the walk.

Another thing to remember when traveling around the bush is that Australia is dangerously susceptible to bush fires, and every care should be used. I recall traveling with a bushman once who would stub his cigarette out in the palm of his hand before throwing it away to ensure that it was out.

Sufficient water should be taken for the trip and all rubbish should be removed from the park. Park rangers frown on hikers who pick native flowers or plants.

There may seem to be a lot of "don'ts" on entering a national park, but these rules are usually designed for the safety of visitors and to ensure that the park can be enjoyed in its natural state by all.

WOMEN ALONE

Australia was once a very male society, and parties usually divided into the men around the barbecue and women in the kitchen preparing the salads or fussing over the children. In pubs it was unheard of for women to enter the public bar, and there were Ladies' Lounges where the fe-

male sex could enjoy a gin and tonic or shandy (beer and lemonade).

These attitudes are changing, although in the Outback women are still likely to suffer some discrimination such as not being served quickly in a public bar.

Hitchhikers have been known to disappear, and women should certainly not travel alone on the road.

HEALTH

It is wise to arrange health and accident insurance before departing for Australia. If you sign up after arrival, there is likely to be a qualifying period of three months; it may be worth including dental insurance in the policy.

Public hospitals are well equipped and the medical staff highly qualified.

A twenty minute consultation with a doctor will cost about $35. General practitioners are listed in the phone book, and ask, when making your appointment, whether the doctor charges the basic fee for a consultation.

Drug stores, called chemists or pharmacies in Australia, are staffed by qualified pharmacists and all cities have an all-night roster for emergencies.

DANGEROUS ANIMALS

On land most of Australia's dangerous creatures are small, with the singular exception of crocodiles. There are several venomous snakes slithering around the bush and its spiders are among the most poisonous in the world.

Estuarine or salt-water **crocodiles**, which can grow to 7 m (23 ft) long, have been known to attack people. The freshwater crocodile is not dangerous unless provoked.

Of the 110 varieties of **snakes** in Australia eight can inflict a fatal bite.

In unprotected, open waters around Australia **sharks** have been known to attack people. However, the chances of being attacked are remote, and most city beaches have mesh barriers erected off-shore to keep sharks out, or at least the acquatic variety!

The **blue-ringed octopus** has a fatal bite if handled. Don't. This species is widespread and can be recognized by its irregular blue markings.

There are now antivenins for the deadly **funnel-web spider**, found within about 160 km (100 miles) of Sydney, and the **redback spider** which is much more widespread.

The **box jellyfish** lives and stings in tropical northern waters. Other acquatic hazards are the **stonefish** and **cone shell** which live in waters between Brisbane and Geraldton. **Stingrays** and **Puffer fish** are widely distributed around the coastline.

It is best to ask locals what hazards to watch out for. Despite this seemingly alarming list, few deaths are caused in Australia by any of these creatures.

CLOTHING

With a wide range of climates in the country at any given time, it is advisable to bring warm and cold weather clothing. Even if you come in the middle of summer there are occasional days in the south-east states when the temperature can drop. In the Outback, scorchingly hot days can be followed by freezing nights. A light jacket or pullover will never go amiss. In winter in the south-east corner of Australia the temperatures can get quite low, but never much below 0°C (32°F), and a light overcoat or raincoat and warm clothing are strongly advised.

Australians generally dress fairly casually by overseas standards, and a jacket and tie are usually expressly mentioned if required for a dinner or theater engagement. Otherwise smart casual dress is expected. Even when the weather is hot men wear a good pair of trousers with long socks and women a light frock.

Australia has one of the highest rates of skin cancer in the world and the sun's rays can be very strong, even on cloudy days. It is essential, when out in the sun, to use 15+ sun screen which should be re-applied after a swim. Being well tanned is no longer fashionable, and many people are covering up to protect themselves from the sun.

SHOPPING

Foreign visitors are allowed duty-free concessions on a variety of goods, including cameras, electrical equipment and jewelry. A number of shops at the airports, popular tourist destinations and capital cities specialize in duty-free goods. It is worth shopping around for the best deals, which are seldom at shops at the airport. A list of duty-free shops is listed in the *Yellow Pages* phone book under "Duty Free."

To make a purchase you will require your passport and airline ticket. Retain all the paperwork, which may be required at your destination to meet local customs requirements.

Opals, "champagne" diamonds and jewelry made from Australian gemstones are widely admired. There are also high quality crafts and handmade woolen goods which make good presents.

Aboriginal art is just being discovered by visitors, and many galleries will arrange for purchases to be posted safely back to your home. These are better bought at reputable galleries than shops catering for tourists.

COMMUNICATIONS

POST

Post Offices are open between 9 am and 5 pm on weekdays, and they will hold mail *poste restante* for visitors. Outside of these hours, the capital cities have Post Office shops open on Saturday morning and some newsagents also sell stamps.

Mail posted anywhere in Australia costs $0.45 for a standard letter while aerogrammes cost $0.60. The rate for postcards is less than air-mailed letters, and these vary depending on their destination.

TELEPHONES

Local calls cost $0.30 from pay-phones and $0.25 from home telephones and are not timed. Some hotels charge an additional fee for outgoing calls.

Pay-phones are found in most hotels and motel rooms, and public call boxes are spread around populated areas. Public phones take 10, 20, 50 cent and one dollar coins. It is possible to prepay for calls by purchasing a Phone Card from newsagents in $2, $5, $10, $20 and $50 units. Many public phones have been converted to take them: when inserted, the display on the telephone shows the residual value on the card. They are particularly useful for making long distance calls.

It is possible to make long-distance (STD) calls in Australia and overseas calls (ISD) from most public phones. The rate varies according to the time of day and distance. Rates are cheaper after 6 pm and yet cheaper after 10 pm, Monday to Saturday, and on Sunday. For example, a three minute call to Brisbane from Melbourne will cost $1.62 during a weekday, but just $0.75 after 10 pm or on Sunday.

The prefix for telephone numbers listed in the *Guide* in brackets is the STD district code, and omitted for local calls. If the prefix is 008, the call is free anywhere in Australia. Such numbers may not be used for local calls, and a second number may be listed for use in that district. Long distance calls made on six digit phone numbers beginning with 13, are charged at a local call rate.

Few telephone boxes have phone books so if you need assistance dial 013 for a local number, 0175 for an STD number and 0103 for international inquiries. There is no charge but the operator will only give you the telephone number and not the address. For Operator-connected calls within Australia dial 0176, and for an overseas number dial 0107.

To telephone overseas on ISD dial 0011, the country code, city code and then the number.

There is also a service that allows you to dial an overseas operator who will make the connection for credit card or reverse charge (collect) calls in order to overcome language problems with local operators. Popular destinations are listed below. For a full list consult the telephone directory or ring 0103. The numbers are:

Canada 0014-881-150
France 0014-881-330
Germany 0014-881-490
Hong Kong 0014-881-852
Italy 0014-881-390
Japan 0014-881-810
Malaysia 0014-881-600
Netherlands 0014-881-310
Singapore 0014-881-650
Sweden 0014-881-460
UK 0014-881-440
USA Direct (AT&T) 0014-881-011
USA (MCI) 0014-881-100

USA (SPRINT) 0014-881-877

For life threatening emergencies, the police, fire brigade and ambulance service can be contacted on 000, a free call.

NEWSPAPERS

Australia has three national newspapers. *The Australian* and *Australian Financial Review* appear Monday to Friday, and *The Australian* has a bumper issue on Saturday. *The Independent Monthly*, which provides news analysis of allegedly high quality is available on the first Wednesday of each month.

Each state and territory has at least one daily newspaper, many of which contain an

---

Chrismas shopping in Perth.

entertainment guide on Thursday or Friday and run a lift-out magazine on Saturday and Sunday. On other days there are sections on dining out and TV guides.

Certain foreign journals like *Time* and *Newsweek* are freely available from newsstands, and a variety of others in foreign languages at major hotels and in the central districts of larger cities. Some higher circulation foreign newspapers are available in the larger news agencies.

TELEVISION

Five channels are screened in the major cities — two of which are financed, fully or partially, by the government. The government stations are the Australian Broadcasting Commission (ABC) which serves locally produced shows, good quality British and American programs and documentaries. The Special Broadcasting Service (SBS) shows subtitled foreign language programs, films and sporting events from abroad.

The three commercial networks are much of a sameness, with insipid American serials, telemovies and some awful homegrown soaps. Program details are available in the daily newspapers.

EMBASSIES AND CONSULATES

The telephone numbers for the major foreign embassies and consulates in Canberra are:

Canada   (06) 273-3844
Denmark   (06) 273-2195
Finland   (06) 273-3800
France   (06) 270-5111
Germany   (06) 270-1911
Great Britain   (06) 270-6666
India   (06) 273-3999
Indonesia   (06) 286-2555
Israel   (06) 273-1309
Italy   (06) 273-3333
Japan   (06) 273-3244
Malaysia   (06) 273-1543
Netherlands   (06) 273-3111
Norway   (06) 273-3444
Singapore   (06) 273-3944
South Africa   (06) 273-2424
Spain   (06) 273-3555

Sweden   (06) 273-3033
Thailand   (06) 273-1149
United States   (06) 270-5000

A number of countries also maintain consulates in other State capital cities. They are:

Canada Sydney, ((02) 364-3000.

China Melbourne, ((03) 822-0604; Sydney ((02) 698-7929.

Denmark Perth, ((09) 335-5122; Adelaide, (08) 212-4903; Hobart, (002) 349-966

France Sydney, ((02) 261-5779; Melbourne, ((03) 820-0921; Perth, ((09) 321-1940; Adelaide, ((08) 231-8633; Darwin, ((089) 815-351.

Germany Sydney ((02) 328-7733; Melbourne, ((03) 828-6888; Perth ((09) 325-8851; Adelaide, ((08) 231-6320; Hobart, ((002) 231-814; Darwin, ((089) 843-770.

Great Britain Sydney ((02) 247-7521; Melbourne, ((03) 650-4155; Perth, ((09) 221-5400.

Greece Sydney ((02) 247-4593; Melbourne, ((03) 866-4524; Perth,((09) 325-6608; Adelaide,((08) 211-8066; Hobart,((002) 252-825; Darwin, ((089) 817-979.

Indonesia Sydney, ((02) 344-9933, Melbourne, ((03) 690-7811; Adelaide, ((08) 364-0233.

Israel Sydney ((02) 264-7933.

Italy Sydney (02) 247-8442; Melbourne, ((03) 867-5744; Perth, ((09) 367-8922; Adelaide,((08) 337-0777; Hobart,((002) 345-458.

Japan Sydney,((02) 231-3455; Melbourne, ((03) 867-3244; Perth, ((09) 321-7816; Adelaide, ((08) 372-0598; Hobart, (002) 380-200; Darwin, ((089) 818-722.

Malaysia Sydney, ((02) 327-7565; Melbourne, ((03) 867-5339; Brisbane, ((07) 268-7837; Perth, ((09) 325-9146; Adelaide, ((08) 211-2236.

Netherlands Sydney, ((02) 387-6644; Melbourne, ((03) 867-7933; Adelaide, ((08) 31-2111; Hobart, ((002) 44-3449.

New Zealand Sydney,((02) 233-8388; Melbourne, ((03) 696-0399; Brisbane, ((07) 221-9933.

Norway Sydney, ((02) 251-2388; Melbourne, ((03) 654-8020; Brisbane, ((07) 854-1855; Adelaide, ((08) 231-8711; Hobart, ((002) 380-200; Darwin ((089) 843-677.

Spain Sydney,((02) 261-2433; Melbourne, ((03) 347-1966; Brisbane, ((07) 221-8571;

Perth, ℓ (09) 322-4522; Adelaide, ℓ (08) 253-1469.
Sweden Sydney, ℓ (02) 299-1951; Melbourne, ℓ (03) 301-1888; Brisbane, ℓ (07) 221-0405; Perth, ℓ (09) 244-3699; Adelaide, ℓ (08) 267-4977; Hobart, ℓ (002) 34-2477; Darwin ℓ (089) 81-2971
United States Sydney (02)261-9200;Melbourne, ℓ (03) 526-5900; Brisbane, ℓ (07) 405-5555; Perth, ℓ (09) 231-9400.

RELIGION

The main Christian religions are well represented in Australia, with Roman Catholicism and Anglicanism making up the majority, and there is usually a Church for your denomination nearby. There are sizable Jewish and Moslem communities in the capital cities, and mosques and synagogues are located where the communities are concentrated.

Details of services for Christian denominations can be found in Saturday newspapers across the country, including the local Press. *The Australian Jewish Times* and *Moslem Times* have several pages on services for their respective religions.

EASY STRINE: AUSTRALIAN SLANG AND WORDS

arvo afternoon
the Alice Alice Springs
back o' Bourke in the remote Outback
bang on precise or correct
Banana-bender Queenslander
barbie barbecue
bathroom a bathroom is not used as a euphemism for toilet
beaut excellent
belt up keep quiet
bikkie a biscuit or cookie
billy can for boiling water for tea over an open fire
bloke man
bloody universal oath; the great Australian adjective
bludger scrounger
blue fight
bookie bookmaker

Bugs short for Moreton Bay Bugs which are a native crab-like crustacean found off the coast of Queensland.
bush anywhere which isn't in the cities or towns
Captain Cook rhyming slang for "take a look"
cackle berries eggs
chemist pharmacist or druggist
chips French fries
chook chicken
crook unwell
Crow-eater South Australian
Damper bush bread cooked on coals of an open fire
deli delicatessen
dingo wild native dog; also serves as an insult
dinkum the truth
dinky di genuine
dunny toilet
fag cigarette
fair go plea to be reasonable
flog sell
footy football
g'day good day or hello
galah idiot
grog alcohol
heart starter first drink for the day
icy poles popsicles
jackaroo cowboy
jam jelly
jelly jello
jillaroo cowgirl
jumper sweater or pullover
Kiwi New Zealander
knocker a critic
knuckle sandwich a punch
lurk a racket
mate a friend or acquaintance
Milk Bars corner stores that sell milk, bread, newspapers and foodstuffs
mozzie mosquito
mug fool; a person who has been tricked
nappy diaper
ocker hick Australian
O/S overseas
one-armed bandits slot machines
Oz Australia
parka ski jacket
plonk cheap wine
pokie slot machine
Pom Englishman

ratbag   an idiot, eccentric or loud-mouthed political agitator
ripper   terrific
roo   kangaroo
Sandgroper   West Australian
she's sweet   everything is fine
sheila   young woman
shoot through   leave in a hurry
silvertail   rich establishment figure
stockman   cowboy
stubby   small bottle of beer
supper   late evening snack or light meal
ta   thank you
TAB   legal betting shop
tea   evening meal, dinner
togs   swim suit or bathers
tube   can of beer
tucker   food
two-pot screamer   someone who gets drunk easily
up the creek   in trouble
ute   pick-up truck
wowser   killjoy
Yabbie   a native freshwater lobster, about 15 cm (6 in).

Photo Credits

Adina Amsel, 51, 121R, 207, 208, 225. **Globe Press**, 19. **David Austens**, 121T, 111. **Douglas Baglin**, 13, 110, 124, 125, 190. **Bob Davis**, 63, 84, 89, 166, 167, 223. **Terry Duckham**, 54. **Alain Evrard**, 24, 44, 52, 83, 133, 151, 152, 153, 157, 163, 164, 172, 174, 175, 177, 201, **Robert Gale**, 59, 101. **S.T. Gill**, 21. **Manfred Gottschalk** (Globe Press), 11, 15, 18, 118, 123, 215. **Dallas & John Heaton**, (Globe Press) 12, 17, 31, 103T, 119. **Dallas & John Heaton**, 34, 55, 61, 98, 113, 117, 170, 183, 198, 230. **Geoff Higgins**, 26, 29, 32T, 32B, 33, 35, 46, 47, 49, 50, 56, 57, 60, 65L, 65R, 68-69, 72-73, 76, 77, 78, 79, 80, 86, 87, 90L, 90R, 92, 93, 95B, 95T, 103B, 107L, 107R, 108, 109, 115L, 115R, 126, 127, 130, 131, 135, 138, 139, 141, 143T, 143B, 144, 145, 146, 147, 148, 154, 161, 162, 165, 169, 171L, 171R, 173, 179, 185-5, 186, 187, 188, 189, 191, 194, 196, 197, 206, 212L, 212R, 213L, 213R, 214, 215T, 216, 217, 218, 221, 227. **Denis Lane** (Globe Press), 193. **P. J. Mackay**, 88, 155. **Tony Nolan** (Globe Press), 37. **David Ryan** (Globe Press), 219. **Paul Steel** (Globe Press), 16, 23, 45, 97, 205, 211 and back cover Top. **R. Talmont** (Globe Press), 192. **Penny Tweedle**, 27. **Robert Wilson**, 121L, 160. **Carl Wolinsky**, 41, 195, 199.

Recommended Reading

ASTLEY, THEA. *It's Raining in Mango*. Penguin, Melbourne 1989.

AUSTRALIAN INFO INTERNATIONAL. *Australian Aboriginal Culture*. Australian Government Publishing Service, Canberra 1993

BAIL, MURRAY. *Contemporary Short Stories*. Faber and Faber, London 1988.

BERNDT, RONALD and CATHERINE. *The Speaking Land*. Penguin, Melbourne 1988.

BLAINEY, GEOFFERY. *The Tyranny of Distance: How Distance shaped Australia's History*. Melbourne 1966.

CHATWIN, BRUCE. *The Songlines*. Picador, London 1987.

FIGGIS, PENNY (ED.) *Rainforests of Australia*. Ure Smith, Sydney 1985.

HUGHES, ROBERT. *The Fatal Shore: The Epic of Australia's Founding*. Pan Books, London 1988.

JACOBSON, HOWARD. *In the Land of Oz*. Penguin Books, London 1987.

JOLLY, ELIZABETH. *Mr Scobie's Riddle*. Penguin, Melbourne 1983.

KNIGHT, STEPHEN. *The Selling of the Australian Mind: From the First Fleet to Third Mercedes*. William Heinemann, Australia 1990.

LAWSON, HENRY. *Best Stories of Henry Lawson*. Australian Literary Heritage Series, Sydney 1990.

LOW, TIM. *Bush Tucker*. Angus & Robertson, Sydney 1992.

LUCK, PETER. *This Fabulous Century*. Landsdowne Press, Sydney 1980.

MORCIMBE, MICHAEL and IRENE. *Discover Australia's National Parks and Naturelands*. Ure Smith, Sydney.

RANKIN, ROBERT. *Classic Wild Walks of Australia*. Rankin Publishers, Brisbane 1989.

RAYMOND, ROBERT. *Discover Australia's National Parks*. Ure Smith, Sydney 1985

STEWART, DAVID. *Burnum Burnum's Aboriginal Australia: A Traveller's Guide*. Angus & Robertson, Sydney 1988.

WHITE, PATRICK. *The Tree of Man*. Penguin, Melbourne 1961.

WINTON, TIM. *Cloudstreet*. McPhee Gribble, Melbourne 1991.

Quick Reference A–Z Guide
to Places and Topics of Interest with Listed Accommodation, Restaurants and Useful Telephone Numbers

GENERAL LISTING

NEW SOUTH WALES   (pages 47 to 85)

NORTHERN TERRITORY   (page 109 to 123)

QUEENSLAND (pages 87 to 107)

SOUTH AUSTRALIA   (pages 125 to 145)

V Victor Harbour 137
access
Southern Encounter steam train
((08) 231-1707 137
accommodation
Warringa Guest House ((085) 525-970 137

general information
tourist information center ((085) 524-255 136
W Wilpena Pound See Flinders Ranges
wineries See Barossa Valley See McLaren Vale
Y Yourambulla Caves See Flinders Ranges

TASMANIA	(pages 147 to 165)

* Star ratings for accommodation indicate price
relationships only. Refer to the text for rates,
facilities and recommendations

B Bicheno 164
access 165
accommodation
**Diamond Island Resort ((003) 751-161 165
*Wintersun Lodge Motel ((003) 751-225 165
Gaol House Cottages ((003) 751-430,
fax: (003) 751-368 164
attractions
Douglas-Apsley National Park 164
Bothwell 162
access 162
accommodation
**Bothwell Grange ((002) 595-556 162
**Mrs Woods Farmhouse ((002) 595-612 162
Bruny Island 155–156
access 156
attractions
Big Hummock 156
Bruny Island Venture Tours ((002) 732-886,
fax: (002) 730-269 156
lighthouse 156
restaurants
Lyndenne Restaurant ((002) 606-264 156
Penguin ((002) 723-170 156
C Central Highland 161
access 162
attractions
Land of Three Thousand Lakes 161
Poatina Power Station ((003) 978-254 161
Coles Bay 164
accommodation
**Freycinet Lodge ((003) 570-101 165
*Coles Bay Caravan Park ((003) 570-100 165
attractions
Feycinet Peninsula National Park 164
Cradle Mountain 158
access 159
accommodation
***Cradle Mountain Lodge ((004) 921-303,
(008) 030-377 159
*Cradle Mountain Campgrounds
((004) 921-395 159
attractions
Overland Track 158
E East Coast 164–165
access 165
accommodation 164–165
attractions
Bicheno (see also under Bicheno) 164
Coles Bay (see also under Coles Bay) 164
Swansea (see also under Swansea) 164
Wineglass Bay (see also under Wineglass
Bay) 164

Evandale 160
attractions
Clarendon House ((003) 986-220 160
F festivals and sporting events
FEB: Village Fair and Pennyfarthing
Championships, at Evandale (near
Launceston) 165
FEB/MAR: Great Tasmanian Bike Ride, from
Hobart to Devonport 165
MAR: New Norfolk Hop Festival, at Derwent
Valley (near Hobart) 165
SEP: Tasmanian Tulip Festival, at the Royal
Tasmanian Botanical Gardens 165
G Great Lake 162
access 162
accommodation
**Compleat Angler Lodge, at Haddens Bay
((002) 598-179, fax: (002) 598-147 162
attractions
fishing 162
H Hobart 149–154
access 154
accommodation
***Innkeepers Leena ((002) 323-900,
fax: (002) 240-112 153
***Sherridan Hotel ((002) 354-535,
fax: (002) 238-175 153
***Tantallon Lodge, fax/((002) 241-724 153
***Wrest Point Casino ((002) 250-112
fax: (002) 253-909 153
**Barton Cottage ((002) 241-606,
fax: (002) 241-724 153
**Colville Cottage ((002) 236-968,
fax: (002) 240-500 153
**Cromwell Cottage ((002) 236-734 153
*Black Prince Hotel ((002) 343-501 153
*Waratah Motor Hotel ((002) 343-685 153
hotel booking service:
Central Booking Office ((003) 317-900 153
Heritage Accommodation ((002) 241-612,
fax: (002) 240-472 153
attractions 150–151
Anglesea Barracks 150
Arthur Circus 150
Battery Point 150
Brake Out Cycling Tours ((002) 782-966,
fax: (002) 781-056 151
Cascade Brewery ((002) 241-144 151
Constitutional Dock 150
Essalisa ferry trips ((002) 235-893 150
Franklin Wharf 150
Maritime Museum ((002) 235-082 150
Mt. Wellington 151
National Trust ((002) 236-236 150
Parliament House 150
Risdon Cove ((002) 308-399 151
Salamanca Place 150

VICTORIA (pages 167 to 193)

WESTERN AUSTRALIA   **(pages 195 to 215)**

Illustrated Blueprints to Travel Enjoyment

INSIDER'S
GUIDES

The Guides That Lead